MISSION:
A PRACTICAL
APPROACH

D— 4

MISSION:
A PRACTICAL APPROACH
to church sponsored mission work

Daniel C. Hardin

William Carey Library

533 HERMOSA STREET • SOUTH PASADENA, CALIF. 91030

Published by the William Carey Library
533 Hermosa Street
South Pasadena, Calif. 91030

In accord with some of the most recent thinking in the academic press, the William Carey Library is pleased to present
this scholarly book which has been prepared from an author-
edited and author-prepared camera-ready manuscript.

Library of Congress Cataloging in Publication Data

Hardin, Daniel C., 1932-
  Mission : a practical approach to church-spon-
sored mission work.

  Bibliography: p.
  Includes index.
  1. Missions. I. Title.
BV2061.H35   266'.023   77-27424
ISBN 0-87808-427-4

Contents

Figures

Foreword

With the increase in evangelistic zeal has come the need for instruction in how to effectively carry the gospel to peoples of other races and cultures. It is one thing to have a zeal to do it, and quite another thing to possess the acumen required to do an effective job.

"Missionary work" is not new. Many religious organizations have been doing it for hundreds of years. And for the most part have been doing it in the same way, making the same mistakes, and repeating the same procedural patterns. Times have drastically changed, but missionary methods have changed but little in centuries.

Churches of Christ have blazed some new trails since World War II, and have met with rather phenomenal success. Because of the unique structure of Churches of Christ, and an unwillingness to follow human patterns of any kind, they have followed a path somewhat parallel to, but not in the same rut with, other religious orders. Their mistakes have been peculiarly their own. Their successes have been peculiarly their own.

Increasing from a very small force of workers on foreign soil to an army of many hundred men and women, active in approximately one hundred and eighty nations of the world since World War II, Churches of Christ have demonstrated 'some new approaches to the old problems that have evidently worked.

In an attempt to share with others who have a desire to reach the world with the gospel, some of the more experienced mission-

aries have drawn upon their years in the field to provide information and guidelines. They do not claim to have all the answers. There is no pat formula that will fit all situations
and all occasions. But experience is a good teacher, and men
who have spent many years at trial and error on the field can
provide valuable guidance to those who are preparing to go.

This work draws upon that experience. At the same time it
is written in layman's language, yet preserves the research
abilities of a true scholar. This work is both a manual for
those in the field and a textbook for those who are preparing
for a lifetime of work in the field.

One element that should not be overlooked is the assistance
given church leaders at home in their efforts to work effectively with a missionary many thousands of miles away. This
has always been one of the most difficult problems to solve.
The elders of the average church know very little about how to
do mission work. They are usually totally unacquainted with
the field. Even the missionary may be a stranger to them. Trying to "sponsor" or "supervise" something they know practically
nothing about, and having had no experience at all in doing the
work, the average group of elders or church leaders desperately
need this book dedicated to the practical approach to mission
work.

Some things are absolutely essential to successful work. The
missionary must be thoroughly dedicated and thoroughly trained.
His work must be very acutely defined and the plan of operation
firmly outlined. His "sponsoring" congregation must be committed to giving him firm support, and be willing to stick with
him through thick or thin. This book will help to oil the machinery for smooth and successful operation.

Reuel Lemmons
Editor, *Firm Foundation*

Preface

As missionary work is submitted to scientific analysis, there is automatically a distinction or separation made between the spiritual and non-spiritual aspects of missionary work. It is my opinion that these two are actually inseparable; however, analytically, a separation can be made and the one discussed somewhat independent of the other. In this manner, man can analyze the social, psychological, and physiological aspects of mission work and determine the extent to which he can contribute to the success of the missionary enterprise.

The result of this approach to the study of mission should not lead to the abandonment of the spiritual aspects nor even a degrading of their importance. The very opposite should be true. Once a man sees clearly the difficulty and complexity of the missionary challenge and realizes that at best his personal contribution will fall far short of the mark, he should be impressed with the contribution that God must make to give the missionary activity any hope of success.

Man and God form a team and the confidence that man can have in that relationship with the Creator was expressed by Paul in these words, "What are we than to say to facts like these? If God is for us, who can be against us?" (Romans 9:31*). When man honestly appraises the contribution that each party makes to this awesome partnership, he must be overwhelmed by the

---

*Williams, *New Testament*. (All other scriptures taken from the *Revised Standard Version*).

grace and love of God which overshadows man to the extent that man is relegated to a position of virtual insignificance.

Though man should be absolutely humbled when confronted with the full impact of the greatness of God, he still brings a little bit of something to the man/God relationship, such things as belief, response, and obedience. However little and insignificant these might have seemed, Paul said, ". . . forgetting what lies behind and straining forward to what lies ahead, I press on toward the goal . . ." (Phil. 3:13,14).

Though man's contribution may be very small beside the contribution of God, man must strain forward and press on, doing the best that he can to use himself for God. This attempt to analyze and study the problems of missionary activity and to develop viable concepts as aids to future missionary work may be quite trivial when compared to the part that God plays in the missionary enterprise but this much is man's responsibility. Thus, holding firmly to the hand of the Creator, the participants in a missionary activity must do the very best that they can while trusting God to capably execute his will in their lives.

While thinking of man's contribution to the unfolding of God's divine mission and the small part that the following pages might contribute to that great cause, I must give credit to the many colleagues, both Korean and American who provided the encouragement, advice, and criticism that led to the undertaking of this project. Thanks must also go to Ed Mathews who critiqued the section on church growth and Ed Hedrick who offered advice on the sections dealing with missionary psychology. Special thanks are in order to those who read and criticized the entire manuscript: Wendell Broom, Dan Coker, and George Gurganus, professors of mission at Abilene Christian University and Joyce, my wife and colleague who shared the years of experience as well as the hours of writing.

My daughters, Mara and Danna, were a constant source of encouragement and Terra cooperated with Miss Ja Young Yoo to turn my scratchings into a readable first draft. Finally, Patsy Strader added the finishing touch by transforming the entire manuscript into camera ready copy.

1

Introduction

The Church of Christ movement in America was seventy five years
old before there were a dozen missionaries serving outside the
United States (Elkins 1974:6). Even with the traumatic impact
of World War II the number of missionaries jumped only to
slightly over 200 in 1953 (Elkins 1974:6). There is some confusion concerning the exact number of missionaries on the field
today but whether 1,000 or 2,000, this only represents one missionary for every 3,500 or 1,750 church members. Since this
would include husbands and wives in many cases, the ratio of
full time missionaries to church members could be even less.

If the ratio of missionaries to members is not startling
enough, the ratio of missionaries to the 2.7 billion unreached*
people in the world is. Even if the Church of Christ had 2,000
missionaries, this would represent only one missionary for every
1,350,000 people, not counting those who need to be taught the
truth more perfectly.

In the light of these statistics it becomes very distressing
when mission programs fail. Each time a sponsor becomes discouraged and withdraws support and each time a missionary re-
turns home in frustration the loss is staggering. Thus it not
only behooves us to inspire the churches to greater missionary
zeal but also to alert them to the causes of missionary failure.
For the Church of Christ the avenues leading to more satisfactory
mission programs are limited by the demand for church autonomy.

---

*This figure was reported at the Lausanne congress and repre-
sents people who do not consider themselves "Christian."

In an attempt to maintain a Biblical posture with regard to church organization, authority, and control, members of the Church of Christ have avoided any organization beyond the congregational level. This limits authority and control to individual congregations and tends to frustrate attempts of one congregation to exercise control over another. One area of church activity most obviously affected by this policy of congregational autonomy is mission work.

Since a given mission program may demand more finances than a typical congregation is willing or able to supply, it is obvious that cooperation is demanded. The establishment of a missionary society or similar organization is one method of solving this financial problem and, at the same time, offers a vehicle capable of giving guidance to the missionary enterprize. However, such an organization violates the concept of local church autonomy and therefore is not an option for the Church of Christ.

To accumulate the needed funds without compromising the autonomy of any congregation, a pattern of church sponsored missions has developed. One congregation assumes the responsibility for a particular mission work and agrees to act as an overseer. Funds then may be solicited by that sponsoring church from any churches or individuals who might be willing to contribute. Those who contribute do so voluntarily and relinquish all control over funds once they have been given. In this manner churches and individuals can cooperate financially with no violation of any church's autonomy.

Congregational or church sponsored missions solves the financial problem but throws much of the remaining responsibility for the missionary enterprise onto the single sponsoring church. Since mission is a very complicated and demanding task the questions must be asked: How can a local congregation adequately prepare itself to responsibly manage a missionary program, or how can a prospective missionary, sponsored by an inadequately prepared local congregation, help both the congregation and himself avoid missionary failure?

Education is obviously the answer to the first part of this question and in a very fundamental way is bound up in the answer to the second part. However, such an answer is much too simplistic without some concrete suggestions concerning how sponsors and prospective missionaries can get the education they need.

Obviously, the missionary would derive inestimable benefit from a complete study of missiology and today's schools of mission are a testimony to the trust that many aspiring missionaries are placing in formal mission training. Likewise,

the elders or mission committee members of most sponsoring
churches would benefit from a full course of missionary training; however, full time study is not generally considered a
viable option for most elders and mission committee members.
Such men are usually businessmen with family and community
responsibilities who feel that they cannot study missions on a
full time basis.

Of course, the missionary could get the training and then
set about to transfer it to his sponsors but this is unrealistic because one cannot, in a few brief hours, pass on the knowledge obtained during many months of intensive study.

The answer must come in the form of an educational option
brief enough to meet the time limitations of the church leader
and yet sophisticated enough to meet the critical demands of
sound missiology. It is the writer's prayer that the following
material will meet these two criterion.

This material is not intended as a substitute for all of the
training a prospective missionary should have. In fact, it
emphasizes the missionary's dependence on expertise in a number
of areas and should serve to alert the unprepared missionary to
his need for proper study and preparation. This material is
intended as an introductory guide to church leaders and should
give them sufficient insight into the missionary enterprise to
vastly improve their ability to oversee such programs. Further
study is, of course, suggested even to the church leader but it
is assumed that one does not have to have all the expertise of
a prepared missionary to satisfactorily oversee a missionary
program.

Such an educational option is not merely a watered down
survey of existing missiological concepts but a carefully considered approach to the study of missions designed to focus the
church leader's attention on those elements especially related
to his sponsorship. Though terms and concepts familiar to the
student of missiology will be found in these pages, they will
be classified, analyzed and utilized in ways unique to the
above stated purpose.

In an attempt to develop realistic generalizations and
theoretical constructs capable of guiding future research and
experimentation, confirmed facts, personal experiences, and
subjective feelings were drawn together and by a process of
induction analysed, classified, and organized. Whenever
possible, generalizations were interrelated to form theoretical
constructs and these, in turn, operationally defined in model
form with suggested means of measurement. It should be

emphasized; however, that the primary purpose of the various
models and constructs presented here is to focus the church
leader's attention on important elements of the missionary
enterprize so that he can take them into account as he sponsors
mission work. The potential for measurement is a secondary result of the study which must be viewed in the light of numerous
limitations and constraints, i.e., many measurements are highly
subjective, unweighted and untested.

To present a systematic approach to church sponsored
missions, the broad outlines of missionary activity were sur-
veyed. This included (1) the sponsor, (2) the missionary, and
(3) the mission field. Significant elements of these three
areas were isolated, classified, and interrelated, i.e.,
missionary control structure, the synergistic variable, and
mission field development levels (see figure 1). Other elements
involving one or more of the three basic areas were also identified and determined important to successful mission work.
These elements are (1) Mission Philosophy, (2) Mission Policy,
(3) Missionary Background, (4) Culture, (5) Mission Goals, and
(6) Mission Methods (see figure 1).

Since members of the Church of Christ tend to agree that
mission is God's imperative for the seeking and saving of the
lost and since this study is designed to help those already
engaged in, or planning to become engaged in, mission work; the
theological bases or *why* of mission was omitted and the study
limited to the methodology or *how* of mission. Thus, the second
chapter deals with the philosophies of mission which will
determine policy, goals, and general methods.

In chapter three, the missionary is viewed in terms of four
personal variables, i.e., marital status, economic background,
personal adaptability, and his propensity for cooperative
activity (the synergistic variable). Though these elements do
not comprize the total sum of all that an individual is, they
do provide important insights which will help fit the missionary
to the other variables under consideration.

Chapter four deals with ten aspects of culture considered
significant contributors to culture shock. These ten culture
variables have been incorporated into a scale designed to focus
the sponsor's attention on the elements involved and to measure
potential culture shock.

In chapter five an analysis is made with regard to the
development of missionary activity on mission fields. Since
virgin fields present the prospective missionary with a significantly different experience than fields with established

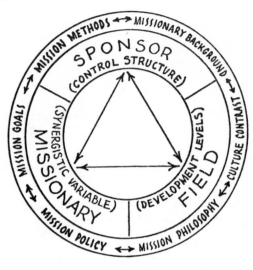

Figure 1. Relationship of Significant Elements in
         Mission Work.

mission works, this variable, though seldom considered in
mission writing, is extremely important.

Of unique significance to the church sponsored missionary
endeavor is the control which a local congregation will exercise
over a given missionary. The absence of any central controlling
organization almost precludes the possibility that any one
control structure will be used by all autonomous congregations;
therefore, in chapter six, five possible structures have been
selected and each one analyzed individually.

Chapter seven focuses on the actual application of mission
methods to specific mission goals. Emphasis is given to the
correct match between method and goal with a rather lengthy
look at institutional development as a method of evangelism.

Finally, an eighth chapter provides a platform for the
evaluation of total mission programs with a view to facilitating a clearer understanding based upon open communication
between the sponsor and the missionary.

SUMMARY

In the face of a mission challenge that demands the most
effective and efficient use of limited resources, it is

essential that every effort be made to assure success. Given
the limitations imposed by the demand for local church autonomy
this study has been designed to provide church leaders and
missionaries with an understanding of variables critical to
successful mission work.

The most significant components of the typical missionary
enterprize have been analyzed, variables identified and operationally defined, and suggestions made with regard to the
proper relationships of these variables. The study concludes
with a discussion of goals and methods with an emphasis on the
need for a clear understanding of which methods are best suited
to which goals.

Though unprepared and mismatched missionaries, with God's
help, may overcome their limitations and circumscribe all
constraints, it would certainly seem reasonable to believe that
it would be best if a sponsor with a particular philosophy of
mission would select a methodology consistent with that philosophy, choose a field where that methodology has the best chance
of working, locate a missionary compatible with both the method
and the field, prepare him for any potential culture shock,
arrange to work with him in a mutually acceptable manner, and
then carefully plan a wise mission strategy. The following
chapters have been written to provide the basis for such an
approach to mission work.

DEFINITION OF TERMS

Sponsor or Sponsoring Church

The author, a member of the Church of Christ, believes that
the Biblical pattern for church organization involves autonomous
congregations with no form of ecclesiastical hierarchy beyond
the leadership role of the elders in a local congregational
situation. Since the Churches of Christ have no missionary
societies or extra-congregational agencies of any kind, a
missionary functions under the direction of the elders of a
single congregation. There may be cooperation between congregations but formal authority rests entirely with one eldership.
This eldership is herein referred to as the *sponsor* or sometimes
the congregation is referred to as the *sponsoring church*.

Christian

Though the author teaches that a Christian is a penitent
(II Peter 3:9), immersed (Colossians 2:12), believer (He-
brews 11:6), he has made no attempt in this book to distinguish
between true, questionable, or false claims by people who consider themselves Christians. The term is used to apply to the

actual *body of Christ* (Colossians 1:18) as well as to the total movement that non-Christians would likely label *Christian*. The context itself should clearly indicate what specific group or segment is under discussion.

Mission

Though the word *mission* is not actually a Bible word it seems to be a word that has been inextricably associated with God's ultimate purpose of reconciling man to God in Christ. *Mission*, then, is actually God's mission which is singular both in concept and in structure.

Though the plural missions has been used by others to refer to (1) God's singular purpose, (2) the various means developed by man to fulfill that purpose, and even (3) the several locations of mission fulfilling activity that might be in existence at any given time, the singular form mission has generally been retained by the author with appropriate modifying words or forms to clarify specific meanings, i.e., mission stations, mission work, mission methods, etc.

Missionary

A *missionary* is any Christian who assumes the responsibility of preaching the gospel with a view toward saving souls and establishing or strengthening the church in an area where the church is relatively weak (Hardin 1974:29-36). A missionary may be self supported or church supported, at home or abroad, full time preacher or ordinary church member, male or female, young or old.

2

Philosophies of Mission

". . . I appointed you a prophet to the nations." Then
I said, "Ah, Lord God! Behold, I do not know how to
speak, for I am only a youth." But the Lord said to me,
"Do not say, 'I am only a youth'; for to all to whom I
shall send you you shall go, and whatever I command you
you shall speak. Be not afraid of them, for I am with
you to deliver you, says the Lord" (Jeremiah 1:5-8).

Some interested persons have made serious efforts to develop
theories of mission to explain the reality of mission work and
also point the way to predictable evangelistic results. They
or others have also studied the scriptures in depth to determine the *theology* of mission so that their work would be
Biblically correct as well as theoretically sound. However, it
is quite obvious that the majority of missionaries abroad as
well as the majority of church members at home have not given
much scholarly attention to either mission *theory* or mission
theology. Yet, each person who has any relationship to any
missionary enterprize, be it an active relationship or merely
a passive one, has a rationale which undergirds his thinking
with regard to mission, and this is his philosophy of mission.

   One's consciousness of mission involves attitudes, prejudices, ideas, Bible references, and a whole complex of feelings
that guide his thinking so that he can and does engage in,
support, or evaluate mission work. This complex of factors may
operate so near the level of unconsciousness that it is almost
hidden from the person himself. On the other hand this complex
of feelings and ideas may be consciously refined and developed

in such a manner that the individual is quite well aware of how he feels about mission. In both cases the persons involved have mission philosophies. One may not know that he has a philosophy while the other can articulate his clearly, but each has that guiding philosophy whether he realizes it or not.

If an individual presses on toward a well thought out theory or theology he will, undoubtedly, be guided by his philosophy. His continued search for theory and theology may refine and change his philosophy but probably never completely replace it. This present chapter is addressed to this sometimes vague, sometimes sharply focused philosophy of mission. It is hoped that vague ideas can be more accurately focused, prejudices replaced with objective reality, feelings brought into closer harmony with real understanding, and all ideas examined openly and critically.

SOCIAL REFORM

Various philosophies can be grouped under the heading of *social reform*. These might range from the most liberal social gospel concepts of the late 1920's to today's loosely defined ideas of reforming social structure through schools, aid programs, and agriculture projects. It was the feeling of those associated with the social gospel that the total message of Christ should be applied to society at large. They felt that economic life and social institutions as well as individuals should be touched by the message of salvation (Hopkins 1940:3). During the heyday of the social gospel movement, the emphasis on social reform became so great that personal salvation was almost forgotten.

Since the 1930's American and Western affluence has played a part in perpetuating a social gospel type mission philosophy. When financially secure missionaries became aware of the plight of suffering people around the world they felt compelled to help those people by helping them help themselves. So they established schools, built orphanages, opened hospitals, taught new farming methods, and gave away food in the name of Christ. The basic theme of the social reform preachers and missionaries was Christian stewardship. They emphasized that man was a steward of the physical world and had to be taught to farm, trade, and manufacture honestly and industriously.

It is obvious that doing good to all men is not only commendable from a human standpoint but is also very Biblical (Gal. 6:10; Matt. 25:31ff) and that responsible stewardship is likewise a reasonable and a scriptural concept. However, a service oriented ministry does not necessarily result in the conversion of many souls to Christ nor the establishment of

many new churches. In fact, the *giving of things* to poverty
stricken peoples may tend to alienate and drive them away. The
term *Rice Christians* is commonly used to describe those Asians
who came for a free handout but turned away when commitment to
Christ was suggested. In Christ's time, these were the people
who came for the loaves and fishes but turned away when Christ's
real message was preached (John 6:66).

Missionaries and sponsoring agencies are still strongly
influenced by this wonderful Christian desire to help people
physically as well as spiritually and the following discussion
deals with three reasons that missionaries get involved in the
area of service or benevolence. (1) Some get involved from a
simple desire to relieve pain and assuage suffering.
(2) Others get involved because they feel that physical help
will result in spiritual development. (3) Still others
minister to physical or social needs due to a series of acci-
dental circumstances.

1. In the case of those who wish to relieve pain and
suffering, the motive for service is pure and straightforward.
The Christian is interested in others, and loves them even as
he loves his own self. He helps people because of the love
motive and his interest in them may extend beyond individual
help to the correction of social injustices. The question is
not whether such motives and actions are truly Christian but
whether they are truly *mission*.

Obviously, the Church has a variety of obligations,
responsibilities, and ministries. The church must minister to
the physical needs of all men (Gal. 6:10) but does the fulfillment of this ministry void the Church's responsibility for
ministering in other ways? Although Christ did heal the sick
and raise the dead, his whole life on earth was directed toward
the cross where he sacrificed himself for mankind. Jesus'
mission was to seek and save the lost! As Christ proceeded
toward the fulfillment of this single most important priority,
he healed the sick and taught beautiful lessons dealing with
interpersonal relationships but these ministries never caused
him to swerve from his primary mission.

Matthew P. John, of the Syrian Orthodox Church, asserts that
mission and service along with perfecting, unity, etc., cannot
be separated. He contends that,

> The mission of the Church *is to be the Church of Christ
> on earth*, and in this the Godward direction in worship,
> the inward-directed quest for unity and renewal, and
> the outward-directed witness of proclamation and service,
> with a view to bringing all men into the fellowship of

the redeemed--redeeming community in obedience and faith, are integrally involved (John 1968:283).

Of course, the total response of the church to God's fatherhood and love must incorporate all of the avenues of service and ministry of which the church is capable and the challenge to the social reform philosophy of mission comes only if it de-emphasizes saving souls and over-emphasizes the all sufficiency of the service function of Christianity.

A social reform philosophy may be the unconscious product of unique missionary experiences. For example, in areas of the world where baptisms are few due to government restrictions against preaching or due to the negative reaction of the population, the missionaries may be able to do little more than demonstrate the love of Christ through service. This situation will be discussed further under the *Presence* philosophy of mission. Also, the economic disparity between Western missionaries and many of the populations to which these missionaries have gone has made service especially attractive. It makes the missionary feel good to be the agent of relief from suffering and the recipients are generally willing to receive the aid. Whether due to restrictions or just the good feeling that it gives, social reform may become increasingly popular and soul winning may become such a rare experience that it ceases to be a real motive for missionary activity.

If such reasoning influences the attitude and thinking of a large enough segment of the church it can be very dysfunctional and dangerous. Those who slide into a social reform way of thinking may become so satisfied with their service ministry and so inured to the lack of conversions that they fail to recognize and capitalize upon opportunities to save souls when such opportunities actually exist.

Populations are continually undergoing change and today's resistant population may be receptive tomorrow. However, if no one is sensitive to soul saving, yesterday's *do the best you can under the circumstances* mission method may be held to tenaciously even after a new soul saving method is indicated.

2. In the case of those who initiate a service project with the hope of reaping spiritual fruit, the service is a legitimate means to a greater end. It is suggested that if a man is cold and hungry and we say, "be warm and filled," but do nothing to relieve his suffering it is doubtful that he will pay much attention to our message. It may be true that affluent Americans will be expected to aid those who are less fortunate than themselves but it is not necessarily true that the aid will result in conversions to Christ. When James reminded his

readers that they needed to *do* their Christianity (Jas. 1:27),
he was not necessarily instructing them in mission methods.

The Christian evangelist must be and, if he is truly
Christian, will be a minister to the needs of suffering human-
ity but when he concludes that his ministry to sufferers is *the*
means of winning those sufferers to Christ, he may be assuming
more than he has any right to assume. He may also be selling
his service ministry short. Some Christians have been known
to quit ministering when they discovered that their ministry
was not bringing people to Christ. The service ministry that
is nothing more than a bribe seems inferior to a purely *love*
motivated desire to serve.

For example, in the early 60's one hundred bred heifers
(dairy cattle) were taken into one East Asian country and
distributed among dairymen who were capable of caring for them.
Each dairy man was to return the first calf to the missionaries
so that a perpetual system of help could be extended to the
dairy industry and thus improve the protein content of the diet
of the population.

If those who donated the cattle and the money for this
project did so out of humanitarian reasons they can rest
assured that the dairy industry was improved and that they had
a part in bringing better health to the people of that nation.
However, if their aim was the conversion of many souls to
Christ, they will have to admit that the project was a failure
because there is no indication that the project has resulted
in any significant increase in the Christian population of
that country.

Benevolent works are certainly legitimate works of the
Lord's Church and it would be assuming a grave responsibility
to advise a Christian to scale down his benevolence. However,
if that benevolence is only a means to an end then it is
essential that we recognize this fact, consider prayerfully
whether it should be merely a *means* to an end, and finally
determine honestly whether or not it is successful.

3. Finally, there are sponsoring agencies and missionaries
who have found themselves involved in programs of a service
nature and they are not sure how they became involved nor if
they want to be involved. Yet, they find it very difficult, if
not almost impossible, to bring the programs to a halt.

For example, consider a missionary who finds that soul
winning is slow and that he is not able to make many converts.
He begins looking to service projects as a means to soul
saving, as a means of satisfying his desire to help people or

as a means of justifying his presence on the field. On the
basis of one or more of these reasons he may become involved
in establishing any number of institutions, i.e., orphanages,
widow's homes, feeding stations, or schools.

Initial investments may be small and an uninformed sponsor
in the United States may gladly send some extra funds to meet
these new needs. Reports are now filled with human interest
stories that keep everyone excited and interested. However,
as the years go by, the projects grow, the leaders in the
sponsoring church rotate, and the missionary retires and leaves
his work to newcomers.

At this point the sponsors find themselves raising funds
for the support of long established institutions about which
they know very little. Meanwhile, the new missionary finds
himself completely enmeshed in administrative duties for which
he has little interest and no preparation. Both the missionary
and his sponsors would like to disassociate themselves from
these institutions and get back into the main stream of soul-
saving but find that institutions are difficult to dissolve
(see page 201).

To halt an ongoing project of any reasonable size may involve a large financial outlay, sophisticated legal expertise,
and even government involvement. Employees must be retired
according to local regulations, all debts must be cleared,
facilities must be sold, and clients must be relocated. It
is not uncommon to find such institutions continuing to
operate for the simple reason that no one has the finances nor
administrative ability to bring them to a halt.

PRESENCE

A second philosophy of mission is referred to as *presence*.
The philosophy of presence is not only extremely popular but
also very Biblical. As the term implies, the Christian
mission is understood to involve the Christian's presence and
the presence of his message in every nation.

Christ told his disciples to go and preach the gospel to
every nation (Matt. 28:19). Therefore, men and women have gone
and continue to go everywhere proclaiming the good news of
Jesus Christ. In some places the proclamation of the gospel
must be very indirect whereas in other places it can be proclaimed openly from any street corner.

In those areas hostile to Christianity, where public teaching or even the public offering of invitations is forbidden,
the gospel must be taught by other means than preaching. It is

here that presence has a most significant part to play. In
some countries preachers of the gospel will not be granted
visas; therefore, Christians have gone as traders, merchants,
or teachers just so they could be in the country and in small
ways show the gospel through their lives.

In such difficult circumstances these people who just maintain a presence are doing about all that can be done to communicate the gospel of Christ. But presence, as a philosophy, is
not confined to those areas where presence is all that can be
expected. It also is found in areas where people are receptive
to the gospel and where governments are friendly and generous
to missionaries.

Presence like any philosophy can become so sharply etched
in men's minds that they accept it, believe it, and teach it
without really being aware of their reasons for doing so. There
may be many reasons why this philosophy is so commonly held by
many church leaders and missionaries but two of these reasons
should suffice to illustrate how it can become one's philosophy
of mission:

1. A missionary may develop a philosophy of presence due
to the resistance to his message that he meets in certain
areas. Most missionaries go into mission work with a desire
to save souls. They have learned how to preach and teach,
studied soul saving techniques, and prayed for guidance;
however, in some areas of the world the people are very resistant to the gospel. The missionary learns the language, studies
the culture, and preaches his heart out but to little or no
avail. As the months and years pass, he spends more and more
time in personal soul searching as he feels the natural frustration and alarm at a nation or colony of people who will not
accept the truth and life that is being offered to them. He
asks himself why and then begins to search for the answers.

He notices that throughout history God has had to deal with
resistant peoples. There were times of great revival and
growth but also times of darkness and despair. He is impressed
by the theology of the *remnant*. God has always been with the
few and he tells men today that the gate to eternal life is
narrow and only a few will find it (Matt. 7:14). There is
also Paul's statement that he came not to baptize but to preach
the Gospel (I Cor. 1:17) and Ezekiel's call to be a faithful
watchman regardless of the reaction of the people to his
warnings (Ezek. 3).

With these verses and concepts in mind, whether properly
understood or not, the missionary begins to feel better. He
is preaching the gospel, sowing the seed, being an alert

watchman; and he is convinced that it is not his fault that the
people do not believe and obey. Thus a philosophy of presence
is born.*

Obviously, the way is narrow, relatively few will find it,
the seed must be sown, as watchmen our responsibility is to
warn, and all results (salvation) must come from God, i.e.,
He will give the increase (I Cor. 3:6,7). Thus in dealing with
resistant tribes or nations the missionary may feel that he is
able to do little more than present the gospel to those who are
willing to listen, reap a meager harvest of a few isolated
souls, and faithfully sow the gospel message by word and deed.
Certainly, there is no shame in doing the work of an Ezekiel
if such a work is demanded. Also, there is the understanding
that, for all of God's interest in nations and groups of people,
salvation is definitely on an individual basis (Ezek. 18:4).
Some would reason that all men deserve to hear the gospel and
they see the hand of God working on individuals in all places.
The apostle Paul, for example, was a member of a very resistant sect but God had chosen him for a very special task
(Acts 26:4,5).

There is, however, a danger that a philosophy of presence
can become so commonplace that it may guide missionaries even
when they are in situations where more than presence is
possible. When this happens, soul winning can be neglected
even in highly receptive fields because goals have been displaced and a highly specialized methodology has become an end
in itself.

God forbid that we deny salvation to eager souls just
because we know, for example, that few are chosen. Missionaries could baptize two or three times as many as they are
presently baptizing and they would still be dealing with *few*
converts. The missionary, like his savior, should not be
willing to see anyone perish but should always be seeking the
salvation of the lost (II Pet. 3:9).

Even when faced with a resistant population and the possibility of a fruitless ministry, the missionary should never
become satisfied with that fruitlessness. He should be alert
to changes in the people which might open their hearts to the
gospel in the future and he should be aware of his own limitations, constantly evaluating himself to determine if, perhaps,
the problem is in his methodology rather than in the people
themselves.

---

*For a more lengthy discussion of presence see Tippett
1973:49-63.

The presence philosophy gets considerable re-enforcement from elders, preachers, and church members in the United States where church growth is frequently slow and local congregations go for weeks and months without converting more than a few of their own member's children. Under such circumstances, there is a natural tendency for people to defend the lack of evangelistic success.

2. A missionary may develop a philosophy of presence to justify a lack of response in an area where the people are receptive. Every missionary wants to feel that he has been guided by God in his work and labor. Yet, there are cases, too numerous to mention, where well meaning missionaries have returned home prematurely due to problems and pressures beyond their ability to overcome.

There is little reason to believe that God necessarily wanted it that way. And it is a rare missionary who will place the blame for his failure on God's guidance. Generally, there is an admission that preparation was too scanty, health was too fragile, or tolerance levels were too low. Christians generally accept responsibility for failure when it is so obvious and clear.

On the other hand there are many who do not return home frustrated and discouraged but who continue to work in frustration and in discouragement. They may be among those who have gone into institutional administration (for the reasons stated on page 203), or they may be those who inherited such programs without really knowing why or how they became involved. Whatever the reason the fact is that missionaries may be involved in second or third best methods of achieving the primary goal of soul saving.

Assume that a certain population is receptive to the preaching of the gospel but an individual missionary fails to make converts because he has never taken the time to master the local language. Rather than make the necessary preparation to do that which will bring real growth, he establishes a correspondence course, preacher training school, or printing press which, in this hypothetical area does not result in many conversions. However, this second best method with almost no visible results is defended on the basis of presence. Critics are reminded that God will give the increase in His own good time and that the word is being disseminated and will not return void.

If no challenge is ever made, this philosophy can blind the church and the missionary to the need for proper preparation, improved methodology, and, most important, critical self

evaluation. All men are subject to errors in judgment, honest
mistakes, and faulty preparation. To admit the possibility
that one may be wrong is a sign of Christian humility, to
accept responsibility for one's mistakes is a sign of strong
Christian character, and to begin again with zeal and enthusiasm is a sign of great faith.

CHURCH GROWTH

For the past two decades a philosophy of mission called
church growth has made an ever increasing impact upon the
religious world. This philosophy emphasizes soul winning,
discipling, baptizing, church planting and nurturing. It
could almost be called a natural reaction to *social reform* or
presence because it so strongly re-focuses attention on soul
saving. However, the term "natural reaction" may seem entirely
too passive to those who have struggled against established
philosophies in an attempt to call attention to church growth.

Initiated by Donald McGavran, identified with the Fuller
Seminary School of World Mission and Institute of Church
Growth in Pasadena, California, offered as course work in
numerous seminaries and Christian Colleges, Church Growth is
a widely accepted philosophy of mission today.

C. Peter Wagner, in *Christianity Today* states that,

> The key book on church growth is McGavran's magnum opus,
> *Understanding Church Growth*. But the literature has now
> gone far beyond that . . . I have a shelf five feet
> long labeled "Hard Core Church Growth." . . . Church
> growth . . . has become an entire school of thought that
> is profoundly influencing missiology. . . . (Wagner 1973:
> 11-14)

Church growth is a philosophy that clearly reflects the times
in which we live. Whereas the presence philosophy emerged as
a stated philosophy long after it was in existence, the church
growth philosophy was the product of educators, anthropologists,
and sociologists working together to develop an approach to
mission. It represents the skill of the social scientist
directed toward the implementation of a Christian responsibility.

Important terms that have been popularized by church growth
writers include *resistant populations, receptive populations,
homogeneous groups, people movements, cultural overhang,* and
similar concepts influenced by social science (McGavran 1974:
174ff,74,248). One key scripture is Mark 4:1ff where the
traditional emphasis on *sowing seed* is shifted to *types of soils.*

Stated briefly, the church growth viewpoint is that mission must be concerned with seeking and *saving* the lost. The·saved must be formed into congregations or churches which will, in turn, grow and mature so that they can do their own evangelistic work of saving other souls and establishing other churches.

It is concluded that all people are not receptive at any given time, and therefore, it is important to test the soils to determine where receptivity is the greatest. It is pointed out that Christ did not tell the sower to sow seed on the pathway and on the rocky soil but merely illustrated the negative result of such sowing. So, the world is viewed through the eyes of the cultural anthropologist and broken down into homogeneous units (units of varying sizes with language, customs, caste, etc., in common). These units or populations are then tested with a few missionary workers who know the language, are prepared to enter the culture intelligently and who give full priority to saving souls.

If the population is receptive, more missionaries are encouraged to come and help reap the harvest. If a population seems resistant, a few missionaries are left there to try new methods, to keep testing in anticipation of a future positive change in the population's receptivity, or to work with other more receptive sub-cultures in the same locale. Meanwhile, the other missionaries shake the dust of the resistant population (Acts 13:51) from their feet and move on in their search for those fields which are truly white unto harvest.

Church growth has come from conservative theology and emphasizes faithfulness to the word of God and confidence in the work of the Holy Spirit. Mankind is viewed as eternally lost unless redeemed by God through Jesus Christ. The primary mission of the church is, therefore, the activity of locating, teaching, baptizing, and incorporating into active congregations those lost souls who are receptive to the gospel.

Without trying to duplicate the wealth of material that has already been written about Church Growth, it should be sufficient in this introduction to suggest some of its positive aspects, some of the misunderstandings it has created, and then some of its limitations.

Some Positive Contributions

On the positive side, church growth is a spark of light in a Christian community that has almost lost its missionary zeal. In most congregations mission work has a very low priority and in many cases missionaries, themselves, have given up hope of leading many to Christ.

People do not enjoy criticism and missionaries and their sponsors are not exceptions. However, if there is never a call to evaluate or re-evaluate methodology and philosophy, people can go on indefinitely doing a second or third rate job without ever knowing it. Church growth offers the church a challenge to re-examine its theology, philosophy, and practice of mission. It calls for a frank and open appraisal of what is presently being thought and done. In other words,

> The missionary should periodically assess every agency, institution, ministry, expenditure, and program by the burning question, "Is it causing the church to grow?" A negative answer should bring corrective adjustments. (Broom 1976:102)

There is a realization that such self evaluation may be extremely painful, but there is also the understanding that without it, the situation cannot be improved.

Church growth challenges the church to evaluate its own evangelistic success and offers simple sociological measurement skills to facilitate that evaluation. For example, Church A reports a growth of 300% over a 10 year period. This report is made from Sunday morning attendance records kept by some member of the congregation. The statistically minded persons read the report and are satisfied that they are members of a growing congregation with an active evangelistic outreach. Others, less interested in statistics have the same feeling because all the pews are filled that were empty 10 years earlier.

Someone familiar with church growth digs a little deeper into the situation and discovers that almost all of the 300% growth was due to the attendance of college students from a nearby Christian college. He discovers that baptisms from the community are almost non-existent and that very few of the members' children are being baptized. Under this kind of critical analysis the 300% growth figure is recognized as an inflated figure that does not represent outreach, soul saving, evangelism, and true church growth, i.e., many students are finding a temporary church home, which is good, but few lost souls are actually being saved.

Consider the hypothetical situation of missionary A who has been working with a particular African tribe for 20 years. He has established a training school for preachers, has 13 preachers on his payroll, and has been reporting about 20

converts per month for the past 5 years. Having been challenged
by some church growth material, he makes a survey of the tribal
area and discovers only 85 faithful church members where he had
expected to find a thousand.

Shaken by this finding, missionary A must decide whether to
defend his past methods and his choice of a place to work or
gird up his loins and face the possibility that there might be
a better way or a better place. If he becomes defensive, he
can use the presence rationale to justify his past works. If
he choses to critically examine his past efforts, he faces
many options.

He may decide that his methodology was wrong and then set
out to change it and evaluate the results of that change. He
may decide that the evidence favors the conclusion that he has
been working in a resistant field where an insincere acceptance
of baptism was confusing the true picture. In this case he has
several more options, i.e., to stay and continually test that
population with a view to reaping a harvest when that population becomes receptive; to leave someone else there to lightly
hold on to that field while he seeks more receptive fields;
or to leave and seek new fields but return periodically to
re-test the receptivity of the old field.

These illustrations are used to emphasize the need for
dedication to honest evaluation and criticism. The church
growth philosophy does not demand that men leave present fields
or give up on resistant populations, but it does insist that
they keep soul saving uppermost in their minds and know why
they are doing what they are doing.

Finally, the church growth philosophy capitalizes on the
contributions of modern science and education. Just as men
welcomed the airplane which speeds them into mission fields,
the radio which carries their messages into private homes, and
the myriad of modern discoveries that facilitate more effective gospel dissemination so man should also welcome the contributions of the social scientists that have given Christians
new and effective tools for doing better mission work.

Some Misunderstandings

Misunderstandings are bound to surface when an enthusiastic
promoter tries to attract people to a new idea or viewpoint.
Church growth has been no exception. Dr. McGavran, himself,
admits that there are those who do not accept the church-growth
philosophy because they "fear that, if they accept it, they
will be forced to abandon resistant fields (McGavran 1974:229).

1. *Abandonment of resistant fields.* *"Abandonment is not called for. Fields must be sown* (Italics added). Stony fields must be plowed before they are sown. No one should conclude that if receptivity is low, the Church should withdraw mission (McGavran 1974:229).

The idea is not to undo all that is being done nor to cast reflection on those faithful servants who have given their lives in difficult fields but to assure a more Biblical and intelligent effort in the future. Yesterday's work may have been all that yesterday's insights were capable of performing, but we need not cling tenaciously to yesterday's insights when today's are far more dependable and accurate.

2. *Emphasis on numerical growth.* Church growth deals so very much with the numerical growth of the church that many critics claim that the emphasis is on numbers regardless of how they are won or how genuine their faith. Advocates of church growth would, of course, deny this. They are also concerned with qualitative growth but feel that they are faced with a monolithic 20th century church that is so disinterested in bringing *many* to Christ that it has become necessary to give special attention to that area of general disinterest.

3. *Opposition to institutional mission work.* There are those who resent the church growth philosophy because they feel that it is opposed to all institutional approaches to mission work. Though missionaries and sponsors are advised to critically evaluate any contemporary methodology, there is no intention to blanket out all schools, orphanages, and self-help programs.

Are institutions valuable to the missionary enterprize? McGavran answers that *if* they contribute to the growth of the church . . . "Yes, Yes, Yes!" (McGavran 1974:229). (Institutions will be discussed at length in chapter VII, page 201.)

The Ripe Field Concept

Church growth is aimed at ripe fields and this is considered unscriptural by some who, basing their ideas on the commandments, "Go ye therefore and make disciples of all nations" (Matt. 28:19), and "preach the gospel to the whole creation" (Mark 16:15), feel, somehow, that the gospel must be preached *evenly* over the entire globe.

This could be the defensive reaction of missionaries or sponsors who feel threatened because they are working with unresponsive peoples. It is doubtful that anyone holds rigorously to the ideal of even or equal proclamation. If this

were true every missionary would have to go where someone else
had never gone, and it would not be correct to have three
missionaries in a given area until all other areas of equal
size had two missionaries.

The fact is that many missionaries use little objective
judgment in selecting their fields. When this writer is asked
what influenced him to go to Korea, he usually replies that it
was God's guidance. That answer seems necessary because the
only other alternative is to call it a matter of pure chance.
He did not search for the best place, ask the advice of
responsible elders, study the literature, or use any of the
tools and resources available but merely accepted an invitation
to go to Korea and trusted that it was God's will. He is not
ashamed of that decision to go to Korea because it was honest
and based upon all that he knew back in 1957. Today, however,
he feels that it would be extremely rash to ignore the many
avenues of help that are open and blunder into a field without
any preparation or selective planning.

Ripeness is a criterion for selecting a field that is
certainly as reasonable and acceptable as any other. When any
missionary selects a field, he makes a decision to go to one
place and to by-pass the rest of the world. Unless he believes that he has selected the single most important place in
all the world, he must admit that his selection was somewhat
arbitrarily based upon more or less important criteria, i.e.,
opportunity, ease of access, curiosity, personal association,
urging of family, chance, or the interest of his sponsor.

Side by side with these common reasons for field selection,
ripeness or receptivity stands pretty tall. The following
hypothetical story has been constructed to illustrate this
point.

Suppose that in country A there is one missionary and in
country B one missionary. The missionary in country A is
baptizing an average of 50 people per week and has calls from
many surrounding towns that he has no time to answer. The
missionary in country B is converting an average of one person
per month and has to look for opportunities to teach. With
these two fields in mind imagine a sponsoring church with a
desire to send a new missionary into the field. Where should
they send him? By what criterion will the church be justified
to ignore or deny the call of those begging for the gospel and
concentrate only on those who are rejecting it? It is this
basic impulse to share the gospel with all who will accept it
that underlies the church growth philosophy of mission.

Some Limitations

Some limitations of the church growth concept should be understood. Remember that this philosophy was developed by educators, anthropologists and sociologists who were using the tools of science. Thus their findings must be viewed in light of the limitations imposed by the scientific method.

Church growth is sometimes called a theory and certainly it has many of the characteristics of a scientific theory. It explains that populations are sometimes receptive and sometimes resistant and that these times are predictable. On this basis, hypotheses can be, and are being, developed which assert such facts concerning certain populations.

Evangelistic teams can conceivably go to such areas and test them with the gospel to determine the accuracy of a given hypothesis. To the extent that the hypothesis is substantiated by the test, the theory is re-enforced and to the extent that it is not substantiated the theory must be modified.

Of course, this is an oversimplification of an extremely complicated process. The variables are as numerous as the people involved and time is itself an important factor. Right now church growth is on that vague dividing line between a guiding philosophy and a practical scientific theory (one supported by much empirical evidence). In the social sciences the variables are so many and the proper controls so difficult to achieve that real progress toward sound theory is extremely difficult.

When a church determines to move ahead with a church growth philosophy, this does not mean that all the questions have been answered. There may be direction and concrete goals determined but there are still men to train, cultural barriers to overcome, languages to master, personalities to consider, and results to interpret.

Also, church growth tries to deal with measurable entities, i.e., numbers of baptisms, number of church members, and numbers of congregations. Although such entities are important, they are valid only if they are genuine and it is extremely difficult to determine what is genuine from what is not. It is the emphasis on numerical growth, the fallibility of man and the difficulty of evaluating qualitative growth that demands a critical analysis of all church growth reports.

There are numerous ways of getting names on church rolls or getting great numbers of churches in certain populations. Give away programs, hired preachers, emphasis on small house churches (when larger ones might be better), and vague definitions of what constitutes membership, are a few of the common methods. Since quantity lends itself to measurement while quality sometimes seems to defy measurement, it may take considerable time and creativity to determine whether encouraging statistics are truly meaningful or subtly deceptive.   This does not mean that they cannot be used but only that the people involved (the missionary himself, the sponsoring church, or mission committee, etc.) can be deceived unless they are capable of interpreting the statistics critically and accurately.

The simple *growth curve graph* or *bar graph*, used extensively by church growth researchers, is subject to a number of weaknesses which must be understood by the consumer of church growth statistics. The construction of the graph may be arbitrarily determined by the researcher. As he accidently or purposely determines to use a set of units with a particular interval, he determines the visual impact of the final product.

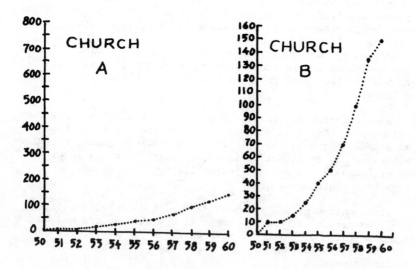

Figure 2.   Church Attendance Graphs for the Years
            1950 to 1960.

For example, in both graph A and graph B (fig. 2) one can see church attendance plotted over a ten year period, 1950–1960. It is natural to assume that the church represented in Graph B enjoyed the greatest growth during the 1950's. However, a closer look will reveal that the two churches had identical growth patterns from zero in 1950 to 150 in 1960. They look different because of the difference in the intervals between the units of measurement that were used. In graph B each line on the vertical axis represents ten people while on the vertical axis of graph A each line represents fifty people. Also, on the horizontal axis one line represents one year on graph B but only six months on graph A. Thus the growth curve on graph B is almost vertical while the growth curve on graph A is almost flat.

Another consideration has to do with the term *attendance*. What does attendance mean? Attendance figures may include only those present for worship services, only those who came to Bible classes, all those who come for any portion of any service, only adults, only members, etc. Without knowing such information the graph loses much of its power to convey meaningful information.

This does not mean that graphs are bad but only that they must be used intelligently and honestly if they are to give a meaningful contribution to the missionary activity of the church. Used carefully and objectively the graph can point out weaknesses, strong points, trends, and a host of things that can help the church improve its mission work.

Although these dangers are listed under the heading of limitations, this should not imply that church growth advocates are unprofessional or unscientific in their use and promotion of measurements, statistics, and graphs. They generally handle these items with commendable sophistication in the literature they produce.* However, as more and more people become involved with the church growth philosophy, there is a serious danger that misuse of the basic tools of research and analysis will follow. To be aware of this danger is to be prepared to deal with it promptly and intelligently when it does occur.

Finally, theories as well as philosophies tend to change with time. If it is to be of any real value, church growth must be refined regularly so that today's books and articles will become obsolete and better concepts developed in the days ahead. Twenty years from now church growth, as a philosophy

---

*See Ebbie C. Smith, *A Manual for Church Growth Surveys* (Pasadena: William Carey Library, 1976).

and theory may wane, to be replaced with a new or greatly modified philosophy that will meet the challenge of the 1990's.

POLICY FORMATION

Understanding one's philosophy of mission means a great deal more than just having an awareness of a certain set of attitudes and feelings. By translating his philosophy into a policy a prospective missionary can develop a practical approach to mission that will be consistent with his philosophy. Likewise, a sponsoring church can avoid all manner of confusion and frustration by agreeing on, compromising on, or in some fashion determining an acceptable philosophy of mission and then using this as a guide to the development of a stated mission policy.

It is very easy for a congregation to become involved in a type of mission work that is in opposition to their philosophy of mission if they have never taken the time to consider what philosophy they hold and what kind of policy it suggests. With a written policy statement it is a simple matter to compare new programs, program modifications, and all manner of new ideas with the policy statement to see if they are compatible. Of course, a policy statement need not fetter a congregation because it can be modified at any time; however, as long as it represents the philosophy of the congregation, it stands as a guide for that congregation's missionary involvement.

Below are samples of policy statements that might be formulated by churches or missionaries as a guide to their personal involvement in mission work. These policy statements are by no means exhaustive but are given as examples of policy statements built upon various philosophies of mission; i.e., for each philosophy two examples have been suggested.

> *Church Growth*
> 1. By *evangelism* we always mean the *intentional persuasion* of persons to accept Jesus Christ as Lord and Savior. Indirect and incidental witness is beautiful but cannot absolve any Christian from the joy and duty of intentionally proclaiming Christ as the Divine and only Savior and persuading men to become responsible members of Christ's church (McGavran 1967:1-3).
> 2. We understand *evangelism* to be the purposeful attempt to persuade (II Cor. 5:11) all persons (II Pet. 3:9-11) to become reconciled to God through Christ (II Cor. 5:19) on the part of individual saints (II Cor. 4:7) who become all things to those persons that they might save some of them (II Cor. 9:22) and be instrumental in guiding them into active and productive fellowship in Christ's Church.

Presence
1. By *evangelism* we mean the whole life of the church
and every aspect of Christian living. Giving a cup of
cold water, adding up accounts in the office, and setting
a good public example are all methods bearing witness to
Christ and fulfilling the important responsibility of
preaching the gospel.
2. The goal of evangelism is the whole world and no man
in the world has the right to hear the gospel twice
before some other person has heard it once. Our evangelistic responsibility is to spread the word everywhere
and trust God to give the increase.

Social Service
1. A sermon seen is worth many sermons preached;
therefore, good deeds done in the name of the Christ are
more significant than mere words. As we heal the sick,
care for the orphans, and feed the hungry, we are evangelizing in the most complete sense of the term.
2. God has made man a steward of all the elements of his
environment. God's man is one who accepts this commission
seriously and becomes a truly effective steward. Evangelism, therefore, means teaching man not only to know God
but to become an effective steward of all that God has
intrusted to him.

A church's policy statement would be much more specific and
complete than any one of these. Donald McGavran discusses
mission policy at length in the first four issues of the
Church Growth Bulletin.* Whether long or short, complicated
or simple, formally adopted or informally implied, a policy
statement bridges the gap between the abstract and the concrete. The statement is definitive and exclusive, that is, it
admits some missionary plans and rejects others. In this way
a direction is established which emotional appeals or irrele-
vant factors cannot easily change.

The mission policy of a church then determines the actual
mission goals based upon the three philosophies mentioned and
then goals are used to determine appropriate methodology.**

---

*The first five volumes of the *Church Growth Bulletin* were
published in bound form: *Church Growth Bulletin, Vols. I-V*,
edited by Donald McGavran (South Pasadena, California: William
Carey Library, 1969). This volume is now out of print, but may
be found in libraries.

**See page 180.

SUMMARY

Social Reform, Presence, and *Church Growth* are three popular philosophies of mission now guiding most of the mission work
around the world. Sponsors and missionaries should be able to
identify and defend their own philosophies. Knowing where we
are is significant in and of itself and is also the first step
toward bettering our stance and improving our positions.

(1) Service or social reform dominates much of the missionary
thinking of the day. Regardless of what brings it about, a
significant portion of so-called mission work has very little
relationship to soul saving. It is not a bad activity and may
well be justified on its own merits but, if it becomes so important that soul winning is forgotten or neglected, then a
problem exists.

Many people have a social reform philosophy of mission.
Whether their goal is ultimately soul winning or service, for
its own sake, the social reform philosophy should be carefully
analyzed and appraised lest it lead the church away from its
mission to reconcile man to God through Christ.

(2) There may be various reasons for the development of a
presence philosophy of mission, i.e., resistance, dependence
on improper methods, rationalization, etc. In the case of
resistant populations the presence philosophy may be the very
best. However, due to the fact that presence is frequently an
excuse for improper methods or just the habit of a lifetime, it is essential that it be viewed with suspicion and
continually subjected to honest re-evaluation.

(3) Church growth is dedicated to seeking and saving all the
lost of the world who will respond to the gospel of Christ.
The primary aim of the church is viewed as the reconciling of
men to God in Christ. All other ministries of the church are
considered to be important and critical but definitely secondary to soul winning.

The tools of the social scientist are used to investigate
the various tribes, nations, or societies of the world to
determine where the people are responsive to the gospel.
Though the unresponsive populations are held lightly, the
maximum evangelistic energies of the church are turned to those
receptive areas. Church growth, as a philosophy, has an ever
increasing following and is doubtless one of the most significant forces in missions today, even though it has its critics
and its limitations.

Finally, the various philosophies were translated into possible mission policies which bridge the gap between theory and practice.

3

Personal Variables

Do we not have the right to be accompanied by a wife, as the other apostles and the brothers of the Lord and Cephas?   I Corinthians 9:5.

I want you to be free from anxieties. The unmarried man is anxious about the affairs of the Lord, how to please the Lord; but the married man is anxious about worldly affairs, how to please his wife. I Corinthians 7:32-33.

Now you are the body of Christ and individually members of it. And God has appointed in the church first apostles, second prophets, third teachers, then workers of miracles, then healers, helpers, administrators, speakers in various kinds of tongues. I Corinthians 12: 27,28.

When discussing mission work there is a tendency to emphasize the things a prospective missionary should do to become an effective servant of God. He must study the scriptures, study anthropology, study cross-cultural communication, study language, and do a host of things that the experts think are necessary for successful mission work. Very little if any attention is given to the man himself.

Who is he? What is he? What does he think? How does he respond? What are his needs? These are all singularly important questions about the missionary because they deal with the real crux of the missionary enterprise. God has created, Christ has overcome death, the Comforter has come, and finally the message of reconciliation has been entrusted (II Cor. 5:19) to earthen vessels (II Cor. 4:7).

Missionary activity involves people, not the least important of whom are the missionaries themselves. The following is an attempt to isolate certain aspects of the missionary's personality and background and treat them as variables which will effect not only his own work but which should also affect the sponsoring church as it trains, sends, supports, encourages, and directs him in his missionary activity. The variables are admittedly somewhat new and perhaps untested. Thus they should be treated with due flexibility and tolerance. However, as guidelines they should prove extremely helpful to the missionary as well as his sponsoring church.

Three important factors should be borne in mind when dealing with these variables. First, they demand a high degree of introspection on the part of the missionary and introspection is admittedly difficult. Second, they demand some careful analyses by church leaders who may unconsciously misinterpret the missionary's attitudes, feelings, and personality; however, until better sources of measurement are made available, each missionary and/or sponsor will have to do the best that they can with the skills they possess. Third, it must be clearly understood that value judgments are not to be made with regard to these variables, i.e., variables are not intended to run from good to bad or right to wrong. Each variable is nothing more nor less than a dimension of background or personality, the understanding of which can aid both the missionary and his sponsor as they go into the missionary enterprise. Though a knowledge of these variables might help in matching the right person with the right field, it must be understood that Christians are frequently called upon to do things they are not prepared to do or are not comfortable doing. At such times necessity may demand that hitherto untapped reservoirs of talent be opened. The missionary learns to improvise, turn to God for needed strength, and do whatever needs to be done. Of course, *if* the right man can be placed in the right position at the right time, there may be much less stress, frustration, and failure.

In this chapter four personal variables are discussed: (1) the synergistic variable, (2) the marriage variable, (3) the economic variable, and (4) the adaptability variable. The use of psychological testing precedes the discussion of these variables because, though each psychological test has its own categories which may differ considerably from these, there may be information elicited from the psychological tests that will prove valuable in completing an analysis of these variables.

It should also be understood that these four variables are not intended to represent a total picture of man's background or personality. In some cases they tend to overlap each other while in other cases they are uniquely different and, at best, they represent only a limited view of the missionary. They have, however, been selected because of the importance they seem to have in the adjustment of a missionary to service in a foreign culture.

PSYCHOLOGICAL TESTING

Psychological testing has been used by some churches for many years. Such testing is used to determine whether or not a particular applicant is likely to succeed or fail as a missionary. For those to whom missionary work is an idealized concept far removed from actual practice or experience, the idea of psychological testing may seem, somehow, cold and mechanical. However, to those who have sent or been sent, it is one more handy tool to aid in a very difficult task.

It has been suggested that man should confer with God and not with flesh and blood. However, those who have seen frustrated missionaries return home prematurely, visited missionaries on the field who were suffering from nervous breakdowns, or tried to explain to supporting congregations why a $40,000 missionary project had to be cancelled due to missionary failure, are well aware of the value and practical use of psychological tests.

Most sponsoring churches use a crude form of evaluation before they sponsor a missionary. They invite him to speak, visit with him in committee meetings, have him over for dinner, and even require him to work with the church for a period of time. They do all of these things so that they can get to know him and develop a feel for his personality.

If they find him unfriendly, disorganized, unprepared, or unchristian in attitude, they may reject him as their missionary. They do this on the basis of *feelings, vibes,* or *intuition.* The psychologist does virtually the same thing, but he does it more systematically, objectively and professionally.

Each psychological test is designed to elicit information of a specific nature. Though there may be some overlap, each instrument is different and expert advice should be sought when determining which one to use. However, it is likely that most instruments will supply, not only information concerning a prospective missionary's general aptitude or suitability for mission work, but also information that might be helpful in identifying certain aspects of the variables which follow.

Psychological testing helps in the collection of information about prospective missionaries from at least three important areas: general academic ability, emotional stability, and
vocational interest. Even though God never required his people
to have a specific IQ before they could preach, one's ability
to learn may be very critical in certain areas of missionary
training. Also, regardless of how academically adept one
might be, if he does not possess a high degree of emotional
stability, the pressures of life in a foreign culture may be
so overwhelming that his ministry will suffer. Finally,
vocational interest is important in that the missionary whose
interest pattern is so markedly different from the people-
oriented pattern of the Apostle Paul and others like him will
be pulled and distracted from his mission. Interest inven-
tories, though poor predictors of job success, are excellent
predictors of job satisfaction.

Instruments which are commonly used include (1) the
Minnesota Multiphasic Personality Inventory or the *Rotter
Sentence Completion Test*, both of which explore in the area of
emotion and personality, (2) the *Strong Vocational Interest
Blank* or the *Kuder Preference Record*, which deal with vocational interests, and (3) the *California Test of Mental Maturity*
or the *Wechsler Adult Intelligence Scale*, which aim at intelligence. These by no means exhaust the field of psychological
tests but do provide an introduction to the names of a few of
the instruments presently being used by churches who are engaged in mission work.

No psychological test is so powerful that it can absolutely
guarantee that subject A is good, upright, honest, strong,
resilient, and will succeed as a missionary whereas subject B
is bad, untrustworthy, dishonest, weak, inflexible, and will
fail as a missionary. Testing does not give global measures
of a man's personality, character, or capabilities. Tests do,
however, give insights into various aspects of one's personality
which, when added to the other things that are known about that
person, may aid in the formulating of important decisions
concerning him.

Psychological testing must involve a qualified psychologist
who can procure, administer, and evaluate the tests.* Information concerning such testing may be obtained from a nearby

---

*More and more Christians are becoming qualified psycho-
logists and this is important because the psychologist selected
to help with the church's mission program should be interested
in mission or at least sympathetic to the program and to
Christianity itself.

college or university. There they will have a testing service,
counselling service, and perhaps a department of psychology.

Untrained personnel should not administer psychological
tests nor attempt to interpret the results. Improperly interpreted test results can be as dangerous and unreliable as
the opinion of the elder who spends fifteen minutes with a
prospective missionary, makes a snap judgment about him, and
then concludes that the man is, or is not, qualified to be a
missionary. Such methods of selection and rejection are very
suspect and can do great harm to the missionary work of the
Lord's church.

Used correctly and wisely, the psychological test can aid
the missionary and the sponsor as they determine their future
in the Lord. Needless to say, prayer and the guidance of the
Holy Spirit must remain a common ingredient in this selection
process. Everything else is merely man doing his part with the
tools and methods which are available to him.

THE SYNERGISTIC* VARIABLE

Man is a social being and thus destined to associate with
and cooperate with his fellow beings. Though psychologists
disagree as to whether man is basically cooperative or
basically competitive, the fact remains that regardless of
whether it is inherited or learned, each individual seems to
have some sort of inclination to cooperate with his fellow man;
but the force of this inclination varies from individual to
individual.

The synergistic variable** is the result of an attempt to
analyze man and categorize him on the basis of the strength of
his *inclination toward cooperative activity*. Where this inclination is maximal the person is definitely group oriented
and may be referred to as a *group dependent* individual. On
the other hand, when the inclination toward cooperative activity is minimal the person is more self oriented and may be
referred to as a *self sufficient* individual.

Self Sufficient

The individual with minimal inclination toward cooperative
activity is not one who must always work alone but rather one

---

*Cooperative, cooperating, or yielding to another.

**For a more complete discussion of the development of the
synergistic variable, see the appendix.

Self Sufficient   Intermediate   Group Dependent
(minimal inclination   (maximal inclination
toward cooperative   toward cooperative
activity)   activity)

Figure 3. The Synergistic Variable.

who can successfully work with others only when he is serving
in a leadership capacity. With our democratic ideals this
might seem like a rather undesirable type individual but quite
the contrary such individuals are as popular as they are in-
dispensable. Most great leaders fit this category very nicely,
i.e., presidents, military leaders, great evangelists and other
dynamic leaders. To understand the frustration of a self
sufficient individual trying to function as a mere group
member, one need only imagine a president exchanging roles with
one of his cabinet members, a general switching places with his
aide, or a Billy Graham exchanging places with his appointments secretary.

The self sufficient individual is the one who has enough
charisma to attract attention and become the focus of attention. He seldom hesitates to offer solutions, propose action,
and initiate innovations. His self confidence is quite obvious
and he expects others to follow his lead. If his dreams are
ultimately realized, he is recognized as an effective leader
and may become increasingly dynamic, confident, and successful.
On the other hand if his dreams fail to materialize and he is
unable to mobilize others to achieve his goals, his potential
leadership qualities may deteriorate, and people will place
less and less confidence in him.

The self sufficient missionary is not uncommon in the history of Christian mission. In fact, he may be more the rule
than the exception. Christ, Paul, Apollos, and those rugged
individualists who have carried the gospel to the world from
the first century are all examples of self sufficiency.* It
was likely the self sufficient nature of Paul and perhaps Barnabas, too, which resulted in their argument and subsequent
separation (Acts 15:36-41).

---

*Remember that *self sufficiency* is used here as the name of
a type of personal variable and should not be confused with
selfishness, pride, or selfrighteousness. Paul's self sufficiency was manifested in his life of Christian leadership and
sacrifice; however, the source of his confidence was God,
toward whom he felt absolute dependence.

During the early years of the 20th century many missionaries were examples of self sufficiency because no other kind of individual could break out of the sluggish negligent church and go to foreign fields where the needs were so great. They had very little encouragement and frequently rather forceful discouragement from their own brethren. They raised their own funds, made their own preparations, faced culture shock at a time when returning home was difficult if not impossible, and planted the seeds of the gospel under trying circumstances.

Needless to say, they sometimes had disagreements. They did not doubt their methods and were quite dogmatic when faced with challenging methods or practices. Then, as foreign mission became more popular and the fields began to be more crowded, these disagreements became more frequent and sponsoring agencies sometimes had to go into fields and carefully lead their missionaries home or into other areas.

This can be illustrated by the missionary who was working with several co-workers in an educational program. His personal sponsoring church was also the sponsor of the total educational program. During the preceeding year, elders from the sponsoring church had visited the field personally and had made some very firm policy decisions with regard to the entire program. However, the missionary that they were sponsoring was definitely the self sufficient type, and he had a constant stream of great ideas concerning how the program should be operated, how the missionaries should cooperate, and how the stateside churches should support the work.

As time passed a terrific strain developed between the sponsor, this missionary, and the others on the field. The missionary was so sure that he was right in his judgment that he refused to go along with the established policy. He resented both those who had formulated it and those who agreed with it. The situation ultimately degenerated into such a problem that friendships were broken, the work was scarred, and a sponsor-missionary relationship was terminated.

The important thing here is not that the missionary was wrong and the church right or vice versa. The problem was, first, that conflicting ideas about methods were allowed to become so paramount that more basic Christian virtues such as patience and love were violated. Yet, the greater problem was caused, at least in part, by the sponsoring church's failure to recognize that their missionary would be very hard to fit into the mold they had fashioned for him, i.e., role conflict resulted when the sponsoring church was not careful in bringing the right man and the right work together.

Both the missionary and the sponsoring church should know
something about the synergistic variable. The self sufficient
individual will then represent, for the church, a potential
leader or a potential problem depending upon his other leadership qualities and also upon his choice of a place to serve.

The proven leader can be given a leadership role and will
likely be a great asset to any program. The probable leader
can be sent to fields where he will not be frustrated by
restrictive programs and organizations and where he can grow
and prove himself. Finally, the loner who cannot seem to
function in a group nor mobilize others can be used in situations that require a free lance worker who can take care of
himself under difficult circumstances.

To misplace the self sufficient missionary by forcing him
into an organizational mold that does not permit him to function in his own natural manner may result in his complete
frustration as well as his physical and mental breakdown. It
can also prove damaging to the organization or program which
needs cooperation and help rather than frustration and conten-
tion. Of course, dealing with these variables in this manner,
it may be well to remember that the self sufficient missionary
need not be completely frustrated if forced into a group mold,
because Christ is a power source that can help him overcome
even the most trying circumstances. The discussion of these
and other variables is not intended to result in inflexible
rules that will be rigidly followed in all mission programs.
Rather, they are suggestions that may help both the missionary
and the sponsor as they make decisions concerning mission work.

It is sometimes very helpful to the missionary or his sponsor if they are just aware of sources of frustration. Once
it is evident that a missionary is involved in a work that
does not fit his personality it helps him to recognize,
analyze, and solve his particular problems. He may not be
able to make an immediate change, but at least he can better
understand the nature of his challenge and work with God to
overcome it.

For example, in 1960 in Seoul, Korea, two young missionaries
were entertaining guests from the church in America. As they
talked, they explained that they were holding down some rather
demanding positions in a local seminary until such time as the
church could send more qualified personnel. After listening
to this kind of talk for a few days, the visitors (older and
wiser men) gently shattered the young missionaries' dreams by
informing them that *no one else was coming*! The idea that
better trained or more qualified workers would soon come was
nothing more than a vain hope.

The two young men, therefore, girded up their loins and did the best that they could and even surprised themselves at what God could do through them. They were not really cut-out for the work they had to do and they paid for this discrepancy in physical and mental fatigue. Jobs which would have been pleasant to someone else were unpleasant to them, and their old skills had to lie dormant while they developed new ones.

With God's help these two men, like many who have gone before them, did what had to be done. Certainly, in the future, other of God's children will be called upon to do jobs that they will not be psychologically nor educationally prepared to do. Nonetheless, with God's help, they will do them. However, just because things can be done the hard way does not mean that one ought to try and do everything the hard way. Work could be done more effectively, efficiently, inexpensively, and enjoyably if missionaries could become involved in work suitable to their personalities and characters. A knowledge of the synergistic variable will aid the sponsor or the missionary as they consider the work the missionary is best suited to do.

Group Dependent

The missionary with a maximum inclination toward cooperative activity is also a challenge to the sponsoring church. He is the willing follower, without whom the leader would be unable to function. He is the individual who sees the challenge of a good idea and draws satisfaction from getting involved in the activity necessary to bring the idea into fruition. He is the individual with the genius capable of transforming a dream into a reality. However, he works best in a coordinated effort with others. Not only does he function more efficiently when guided by a dynamic leader, but he feels much more comfortable following than leading. He may advise presidents, keep generals out of trouble, or keep some famous orator organized, but he has little inclination to make the decisions they have to make, face the pressures they have to face, or bear the responsibilities that are theirs.

Since mission work frequently involves rather unattractive working conditions in far away places, it is not famous for attracting large numbers of candidates. Thus missionaries are often alone in strange and even hostile cultures far from sponsoring committees or churches. It is not unusual for the missionary to be forced to make *on the spot* decisions, provide some form of leadership, and, in various ways, rely on his own judgment.

To the group dependent individual, decision making can be a
real headache. If this type individual is continually called
upon to make such decisions and fulfill such a role, he may
soon break down under the strain. He would much prefer to work
with others who would share with him in the decision making
process.

A few years ago in Korea a missionary was in charge of a
mission station which included a feeding station, a clinic,
missionary housing, and a middle school. As a mission station
director, this man had several good qualifications. He was
dependable, spiritual, industrious, frugal, and had a good
grasp of both the language and the culture of Korea. However,
he leaned toward the group dependent side of the synergistic
variable. He was not a dreamer nor a visionary and had only
limited success in raising funds or stimulating the home church
to become active in collecting funds for the program. When
some rather serious financial problems developed and there was
a need for positive action, the director began sending special
delivery letters to his sponsoring church asking for advice
and help. After six months of writing and waiting, with
absolutely no response from the home church, he was forced to
make decisions which are still questioned by some people today.

When he finally returned home for a furlough, he visited the
offices of the sponsoring church and found that no one seemed
to be aware of his problems. After a bit of searching he discovered at least part of the problem. His letters, six months
of them, were neatly filed *unopened* in the church office.

The leaders of this church had not intended to supervise
their program closely. Their past workers had always taken
care of everything without asking for anything more than
regular financial support. The new man, however, was different.
He was a group worker and could have functioned much more
effectively and enjoyably if he could have discussed things
with the sponsors, arrived at some group decisions, and then
carried them out.

In this case one can see evidence of the problem that results when a group dependent missionary is placed in a situation where he cannot function naturally and enthusiastically.
He did his job the very best that he could and it is quite
possible that no one (even those who question his decisions)
could have done any better, but the fact is that he was not
doing a job that really fit his character.

The church, on the other hand, had been delegating full
responsibility to missionaries for years and never dreamed that

any missionary would actually want interference from home. They
were ideal sponsors for a self sufficient missionary but had
taken on the responsibilities of a group dependent missionary
without realizing that such a difference existed.

Persons at the extreme end of the group dependent category
are so completely inclined toward cooperative action that they
can hardly function on their own. These are the hard core
followers who rely completely upon the group for guidance,
fellowship, and security. They fit well into established on-
going programs where the limits of their responsibility are
firmly established and their job is clearly delineated.

Intermediate

Self Sufficiency and Group Dependency represent opposite
extremes of a single continuum and, by definition, extremes
are rare and not representative. The majority of missionaries
are going to fall somewhere between these extremes.

At this time, however, it seems rather strained to attempt
to develop intermediate steps. The two extremes are clearly
defined and every missionary can be evaluated to determine
whether he falls more toward one side than the other and then
whether he is nearer the extremes or nearer the center.

Also, evaluation must be very subjective and susceptible to
considerable error. As a sponsoring church has dealings with
a man, they should be able to learn something of his attitudes
and ideas, and if he falls near one of the two extremes, this
fact should be rather obvious to the alert observer. If a
decision concerning this variable is difficult to make, it may
mean that he is near the center of the continuum with broad
potential in either direction.

THE MARRIAGE VARIABLE

As the synergistic variable is one dimension of man's
personality that has to do with what he does or how he behaves
as far as cooperative activity is concerned, the marriage
variable is concerned with the individual and how he may be
affected because of what he has done as far as marriage is
concerned. Part one deals with the fact of marriage and the
added responsibilities that a married person has while part
two deals specifically with one aspect of family life, i.e.,
the unity that exists between the marriage partners.

Marital Status

The Apostle Paul set an example for unmarried evangelists;
however, it seems that the majority of the missionaries in the

world today are married, and since marriage has such a profound
impact upon the personalities and activities of those who are
married, it becomes an important variable itself. Though Paul
advised those who were capable of living outside of marriage
to do so, he also reminded his readers that if they had wives
and children, they had to fulfill their responsibilities
toward them (I Cor. 7:1-5; Eph. 6:4). Reasoning from this
point, it is natural to assume that as a family increases in
size, the responsibilities of the parent increases propor-
tionally.

One obvious area that lends support to this assumption is
finance. A family of ten will cost more than a family of
three. Missionaries with large families incur greater transportation expenses, educational expenses, and living expenses
than missionaries with small families. Expense, however, is
not the most important area of responsibility. The family
man must also be concerned about his family's health, education, socialization, and spirituality.

It is not the intent here to set a maximum size for missionaries' families nor to encourage people not to marry. The
purpose of this discussion is merely to call attention to the
fact that a person with greater responsibilities may need
more funds, more encouragement, more prayer, and in general,
more help from a sponsor than an individual with fewer personal
responsibilities.

The following 4 point scale has been designed to allow the
missionary or his sponsor to rank him according to family
size. Numbers are used so that part one and part two of the
marriage variable can be combined into a single variable
measure.

Numerical Value	1	2	3	4
Criterion for evaluation	Married couple with 4 or more children	Married couple with 3 or less children	Married couple (no children)	Single (unmarried person)

Record a score by placing a check in the small box at the lower
right of the appropriate response. Note the numerical value of
that column and place that number in the space provided at the
extreme right of the scale.

Figure 4. Marital Status.

Family Unity

The term family unity is used, to indicate that commonality
that is so important to the well being of a family. It represents the wife's involvement in her husband's work, the husband's interest in his wife's activities, the parents' interest
in those things of importance to their children, the children's
interest in their parents' lives, and any common interest shared
by members of the family.*

It might be surprising to learn that some preachers' wives
know very little about the Bible. These are the women who
"coattail" their husbands as far as religion is concerned. The
weakness of this "coattailing" may not be revealed until a time
of crisis when a wife is called upon to show her real spirituality. In some cases the problem does not surface until the
preacher and his wife grow so far apart that they no longer have
anything in common.

A missionary recently told of his experience at a school of
missions. He studied hard and dug enthusiastically into the
literature of mission and was filled with excitement. However,
his wife, who was filling in as both mother and father at home,
was unable to keep up with the mission studies. Finally, they
became so far apart in their understanding and interest in
mission that this subject was carefully avoided when they were
together. This little experience all took place in a very
short period of time and illustrates the reality of the family
unity variable.

A missionary will sometimes excuse his failure as a father
or husband on the basis of his commitment to God. He has
little or no time for his family because he gives all of his
time to local preachers, local church problems, or institutional work. This rather common attitude is illustrated by
the missionary who promises to take the family on an outing on
Friday afternoon but fails to keep that appointment because a
local preacher comes to his office to rehash minor church
problems. Emergencies do arise and, now and then, everyone
finds a situation that is so important that appointments have
to be changed. But when broken appointments with one's family
become the rule, then priorities are obviously being misunder-
stood and family unity is being threatened.**

---

*In the present discussion Family Unity is primarily limited
to the husband/wife relationship.

**Dr. Carl Brecheen, in his section of the *Marriage Enrich-
ment Seminar* places one's vocation third in a list of four

Sometimes churches contribute to this lack of unity in the home because even before a family goes to the field, they emphasize the preparation of the husband and father but forget to prepare his wife and children. Culture shock hits wives and children just as hard, or harder, than it does husbands and fathers. And, unless they are prepared along with the husband and father, the problem of disunity is going to be compounded in the missionary family.

No attempt has been made through this discussion to determine how much common activity and interest there should be in a missionary family. It is not even the purpose of this discussion to predict success or failure on the basis of such activity or interest, but rather to create an active awareness of certain potential problems so that steps can be taken to avoid or solve them.

With this idea in mind a four point scale has been formed which roughly measures the degree of family unity which is suggested by four different areas of commonality.

Numerical Value	1	2	3	4
Formal Education	Different Levels	Different Subjects Similar Levels	Similar Subjects Similar Levels	Identical
Mission Study	Very Different	Different	Similar	Identical
Enthusiasm for Mission	Opposite	Different	Similar	Identical
General Interest	Conflict-ing	Different	Similar	Identical

Record a score by placing a check in the small box at the lower right of each appropriate response. Note the sum of the numerical values of the columns checked, divide by 4, and place the answer in the space provided at the extreme right of the scale.

Figure 5. Family Unity.

priorities. The church work of a preacher or missionary fits this category and this priority: (1) God, (2) Family, (3) Vocation, (4) Self.

THE ECONOMIC VARIABLE

It is generally emphasized by those who have worked in foreign cultures, and well understood by all persons, that standards of living are much more easily improved than lowered. In other words, it seems easier to adjust to a salary increase than to a salary decrease.

On the basis of this understanding, it should be reasonable to assume that adjustment to a standard of living will be greatest where the decrease in material conveniences is the greatest. Thus an extremely affluent person might have more difficulty adjusting to life in a primitive hut than a slum dweller who has experienced life with insects, rodents, and imperfect sanitation.

A kindly missionary couple, in their late 50's, was deeply respected by their co-workers who marveled at their ability to manage so beautifully with very inadequate living conditions. Their tiny house was overflowing with relief clothing, cartons of Bibles, and various and sundry missionary paraphernalia. This couple seemed to thrive on conditions that would have driven others to distraction.

Some years later, while visiting this same couple in their permanent home in the United States, their fellow missionaries discovered that they lived in a small inconvenient house which was filled to overflowing with cartons of clothing, books, old Christmas cards, etc. It became obvious, then, that their style of living had not changed very much as they had moved from their Stateside home to a foreign mission field.

Still another missionary couple, with a large family, seemed to get along very well in a living situation that fellow workers considered intolerable. However, the family seemed to have adjusted beautifully to very cramped living in close quarters. It was not until this same family was visited while on furlough in the United States that their associates discovered that they lived in strikingly similar circumstances in their Stateside home. In fact, they expressed a longing for the overseas experience where there had been the added benefit of a fulltime house girl to help with the children.

In contrast there are those numerous examples of families who have become so frustrated with living standards abroad that they have made the adjustment to them with great difficulty. Children who have always had private rooms may find it quite distressing to be forced to share a room with one, two, or three siblings. The city bred wife who has always enjoyed an all electric kitchen may have greater difficulty adjusting to

kerosene stoves, gas lamps, hand laundry, and an ice box, than
her fellow missionary who was raised on a farm where such
things were taken for granted. Here again, it is not suggested
that the latter person will make the best missionary nor that
the former one should not try. This kind of analysis is nothing
more than an attempt to understand the problems facing different
individuals so that intelligent steps can be taken to solve
those problems.

Another factor that should be considered in determining the
nature of this variable is the amount of time an individual or
couple have been engaged in housekeeping outside of their
parents' homes. Though opinions on this subject might vary
considerably it is generally understood by young people that
when they leave their parents and set up housekeeping on their
own, they will probably not be able to move immediately into
a living situation on an equal with their parents.

It is after people have lived on their own for a period of
time that they purchase a home, have all of their own furniture,
and develop a somewhat uniquely personal standard of living.
Before that standard is reached, it is easier to move away
from one's own culture and into a new one. Newly married*
couples who know that they will be going into the field in the
future are generally careful *not* to get too firmly settled
before they go. Then, when they arrive on the field, they can
make their home right in the new culture with few habits to
break or patterns to relearn.

The wife who has cooked with Bisquick, cake mixes, frozen
foods, and T.V. dinners for several years will find it more
difficult to adjust to cooking from scratch than the wife who
starts out cooking from scratch. At a recent missionary seminar, several young missionary wives used this rationale to
urge young couples to go into the mission field before they
became too settled at home.

With these various ideas in mind the following chart has
been designed to determine the extent of the frustration to be
expected when going into a developing nation or primitive area
where one's living style will have to be lowered considerably.

---

*Cultural adjustment is a very serious challenge that faces
every foreign missionary and it can be compounded if marital
adjustments also have to be made at the same time. The term
newly married should not suggest that newlyweds rush onto the
mission field. The marriage adjustment should be made first
and then plans made to go to the mission field.

The first category involves general background information
while the second category is concerned specifically with the
amount of time one has been away from parents and engaged in
establishing his own life style.

Numerical Value	1	2	3	4
Economic Background	Affluent	Improved rural or upper middle class Urban	Slightly improved rural or lower middle class urban	Unimproved rural or urban ghetto
Own Home Establishment	Old Established (6 or more years)	Established (3-5 years)	Newly Established (1-3 years)	Not Established (Newly-wed)

Record a score by placing a check in the small box at the
lower right of each appropriate response. Note the numerical
values of the columns checked, add the numerical values, divide
by 2, and place the answer in the space provided at the extreme
right of the scale.

Figure 6.   Economic Background.

THE ADAPTABILITY VARIABLE

In a rapidly changing 20th century it has frequently been
said that the only constant is change itself. Certainly the
citizen of the modern world has change thrust upon him continually. Many educators feel that an ability to cope with
change is the greatest need of all students today (Phenix
1964); however, in spite of this constant presence of change
all persons are not equally adept at facing and adjusting to
change. Some meet changing situations with due balance and
poise while others seem to hesitate and stumble.

Since so much of the change that people normally face requires a degree of cultural adjustment, it is reasonable to
assume that success in adapting to change, in general, should
be a predictor of success in adapting to specific cross cultural changes. For this reason, Cleveland (Cleveland 1960:172)
has suggested that when choosing people for overseas jobs, it
is wise to select (a) persons who have experienced environmental *mobility*, i.e., people who have been exposed to many kinds
of people at different levels of society, (b) *resilient* people,

those resourceful and bouyant persons who snap back rapidly
from discouragement and frustrations, and (c) persons with
intellectual curiosity that goes beyond minimal academic requirements.

The missionary who enters a new field with great determination to win souls to Christ may face terrific pressures if he
has no real interest in the new culture itself. For him, the
learning of language and the adjustment to cultural differences
will be a distasteful chore and, though he may succeed, it will
not be without great difficulty.

If this missionary is especially morose and uncomfortable
when trying to do things differently than he would ordinarily
do them, his evangelistic task may well be completely thwarted.
If he can never begin to feel *at home* in another culture, it is
doubtful that he will ever have that intimate relationship with
others that Paul suggested when he wrote that he had become all
things to all men (I Cor. 9:19-23).

The following variables have been designed to provide a
simple guide for evaluating one's *adaptability*. It should not
be implied that the person low on the rating chart (figure 7)
cannot succeed as a missionary but it should be understood that
such a person will need sufficient training, time, and encouragement to overcome the cultural barrier.

Mobility

A long term missionary from the Southwestern United States
tells of his decision to become a missionary while serving the
church in the Southeast. His parents had moved to the Southwest some years earlier and had lived in several towns during
that time. He had grown up in three different towns and was
presently over a thousand miles away from his last home. Many
of his current Southeastern associates were still living in
the same houses where their fathers and grandfathers had lived.
Their roots reached far down into that soil and they had no
clear idea of what it would be like to live anywhere else.

When this man determined to become a missionary it was a
relatively easy decision to make. He had already moved a lot,
had no deep roots in his home state, and looked to the foreign
culture with anticipation and eagerness. However, his friends
not only could not identify with him in this anticipation but
indicated that they actually did not believe he would ever go.

Later as he watched other missionaries come from various
parts of the United States, he noticed that those who were from
stable, non-transient, older sections had a more difficult time

making adjustments. They had never been mobile before and
mobility was still strange to them.

In filling out the mobility section of the adaptability
chart (figure 7) , it is suggested that the military family
that has lived in various countries of the world, the construction work family that moves frequently with employment, the
diplomat's family, and the corporation family, be used as
examples of *much* mobility. From this point it is a matter of
subjective judgment to determine whether a particular missionary
has experienced mobility aptly described as *some*, *little*, or
none.

Resilience

It is sometimes amazing to witness the pressures that are
brought to bear on missionaries. One family tells of getting
medical advice via a two way radio when one of the children was
sick. Somehow, there was a mixup and medicine that should have
been diluted was given full strength. The result was near fatal
burning of the child's mouth and throat. Then followed the
agonizing train ride to a hospital where medical help could be
reached.

Others tell of wars, revolutions, imprisonment, and even
death. There are also the internal difficulties, church
division, unfaithful workers, financial problems, and a host of
trials that eat away at the missionary's faith, assurance,
patience, and health. It is this kind of pressure added to
cultural frustration and general overwork that demands resi-
lience in the missionary.

It might take a period of time or at least some in-depth
interviews to determine whether or not a given individual is
truly resilient. Of course, if he works with a church for a
few months prior to doing missionary work for them, there will
be sufficient opportunity for the church leaders to see him in
action and to evaluate his ability to handle discouragement,
frustration, and other problems. Even in a relatively short
time it should be possible to determine his bouyancy. The
smile, alertness, positive attitude, and general optimism of
the bouyant spirit cannot go unnoticed; so, likewise, the
frowning, dull, negative, and generally pessimistic attitude of
the depressed spirit.

Intellectual Curiosity

The mastery of some languages may take as much as many years
of serious study (see page 79). To adequately analyze and
learn to appreciate a new culture will likely involve a

lifetime of study and research, and the establishment of self
perpetuating indigenous churches may require extreme self
discipline, patience, and well planned strategy. Under these
conditions it is heartbreaking to see a missionary entering
into a foreign work with absolutely no real interest in language, culture, and planning. He may sometimes study long and
hard without finding even the slightest joy in that effort.
Someone who does enjoy the study and the learning can still get
so tired that he can hardly stand to keep going and may truly
pity those who hate every minute of it but still go on.

There is no real short cut to language mastery and cultural
understanding but to the intellectually curious individual,
the road will seem less frightening and the future less bleak.
Thus the assumption is that the intellectually curious individual will find it much easier to spend time in preparation and
study than the person who, for example, is interested only in
preaching the gospel.

Again, subjective evaluations will have to be made and only
marginal help can be expected from educational records. Those
records might show that the prospective missionary has a wide
range of interests, although an educational transcript showing
that many fields have been sampled may indicate indecisiveness
and frustration rather than intellectual curiosity.

Numerical Value	1	2	3	4
Mobility	None	Little	Some	Much
Resilience	None	Little	Some	Much
Intellectual Curiosity	None	Little	Some	Much

Record a score by placing a check in the small box at the lower
right of each appropriate response. Note the numerical values
of the columns checked, add the numerical values, divide by 3
and place the answer in the space provided at the extreme right
of the scale.

Figure 7. Adaptability.

Perhaps a more important area of investigation might be
into one's hobbies and interests. The kinds of books one has
in his library, and the community service he renders, can
contribute to an understanding of this aspect of his personality.
Finally, as he meets and talks with people, he will display

an interest in what they are doing if his interests are really
broad. Thus, in conversations and friendly visitation, the
leaders of a church can get a feel for a prospective missionary's intellectual curiosity.

SUMMARY

With respect to the variables discussed in this chapter a
prospective missionary can be systematically evaluated by a
missions committee with a view to helping him find his rightful place in God's plan. A battery of psychological tests
administered and analyzed by a sensitive Christian psychologist will have helped both the prospective missionary and the
committee understand more about their options, challenges and
advantages. As the prospective missionary, with the help of
his committee, determines his place on the Synergistic Variable Continuum, yet another dimension is added to the understanding of the role he can best fulfill as a missionary.*

The marriage, economic, and adaptability variables each have
a contribution to make as they reveal areas of strength and
weakness that can be dealt with prior to facing the actual field
situation. Prayer, training, counseling, or any combination of
the three can be used to assure all involved that the new missionary will be prepared to meet the challenges of his calling.

Figure 8 shows a sample rating chart for a hypothetical prospective missionary. It must be understood that the score of 12
can have no intrinsic meaning but will only have value for the
missionary and his sponsor as it indicates relative strengths
and weaknesses. For this reason, the subtotals are very important because they pinpoint the limitations, problems or challenges that should be attended to before the prospective missionary enters the mission field. For example, in this case,
the fact that he has a wife and family means that careful attention must be paid to the housing, education, and health of his
family. Second, the fact that the husband and wife have had
quite different introductions to mission education and that
their degree of enthusiasm is quite different may indicate that
one of them needs some special training to bring their interests
more in line. Third, the fact that they scored quite high on
the last two variables gives encouragement to the sponsors who
can assume that their cultural adjustment will be made easier
and that they will be able to adapt whenever it is necessary.

---

*The following chapters contain information concerning other
critical variables which will relate directly to the synergistic
variable, i.e., Chapter V, Mission Field Development Levels, and
Chapter VI, Missionary Control Structure.

Numerical Value	1	2	3	4
Criterion for evaluation	Married couple with 4 or more children	Married couple with 3 or less children ✓	Married couple (no children)	Single (unmarried person)

Marital Status 2

Numerical Value	1	2	3	4
Formal Education	Different Levels	Different Subjects Similar Levels	Similar Subjects Similar Levels	Identical ✓
Mission Study	Very Different ✓	Different	Similar	Identical
Enthusiasm for Mission	Opposite	Different ✓	Similar	Identical
General Interest	Conflicting	Different	Similar ✓	Identical

Family Unity 2.5

Numerical Value	1	2	3	4
Economic Background	Affluent	Improved rural or upper middle class Urban	Slightly improved rural or lower middle class urban ✓	Unimproved rural or urban ghetto
Own Home Establishment	Old Established (6 or more years)	Established (3-5 years)	Newly Established (1-3 years)	Not Established (Newly-wed) ✓

Economic Background 3.5

Numerical Value	1	2	3	4
Mobility	None	Little	Some	Much ✓
Resilience	None	Little	Some	Much ✓
Intellectual Curiosity	None	Little	Some	Much ✓

Adaptability 4

Figure 8.   Sample Use of Four Personality Scales.

4

Environmental Variables

And he said to me, "Son of man, go, get you to the
house of Israel, and speak with my words to them. For
you are not sent to a people of foreign speech and a
hard language, but to the house of Israel (Ezekiel 3:4,5).

I have become all things to all men that I might by
all means save some (I Corinthians 9:22).

Many books and articles have been written which deal with the
problems a missionary will likely face when he enters a mission
field. However, very few attempts have been made to synthesize
the existing fund of knowledge in a manner that would permit a
prospective missionary or his sponsoring organization to
develop a model, graph, or profile of either the field or the
man that would permit a general evaluation of the difficulties
to be expected.

If such a synthesis could be made, imagine the value it
would be to a man going into a particular mission field.
Suppose he could calculate a relative measure of the difficulties he would meet, the culture shock he might experience, or
the problems he would have to overcome. Such might influence
a man to study harder, re-evaluate his attitudes, select a
different field, or even reconsider his decision to become a
missionary.

Important as such a measure might be, one fact must be
clearly understood . . . such a measure at this stage in the
development of mission theory will be, at best, a very rough

and inaccurate one. However, once the idea for such a measure has been suggested, it can be refined and revised so that it becomes increasingly more accurate and reliable. In the meantime, the rough measurement should serve as a kind of stimulus to those planning a mission program, i.e., it should stimulate an awareness of and call attention to the problems inherent in missionary activity.

Figure 9 is called the *culture contrast scale* (CCS) and is a model that can be viewed in several different ways. After filling in the appropriate cells, the result is a graph that indicates the areas of greatest similarity or difference between the missionary's background and culture, and the background and culture of the people with whom he plans to work. By giving a numerical value to each cell it is possible to calculate a number or percentage that will represent a global measure of the overall similarity or difference between the man and his chosen field.

One basic assumption of this chart is that culture shock and related problems increase in direct proportion to the difference between the background and culture of the missionary's home and the background and culture of his chosen mission field.* The differences listed on the chart include the two extremes, *identical* and *exotic* (very different to the point of being awesome or fascinating) with four intermediate levels. These levels are further divided to give a total of eleven different levels (see figure 9, page 54).

It may occur to some that although each category is given equal value or importance in the chart, it is quite likely that some categories are considerably more important than others. The writer is aware of this possibility but does not feel capable, at the present time, of making a reasonable evaluation of the relative importance of each category. Here again is a challenge for future study.

-----

*This basic assumption is subject to challenge. For example, one might draw the conclusion that when the differences are slight, the chance of culture shock being a problem is negligible. Actually, the very opposite may be true. A man going into an exotic country will probably be very much aware of the differences he is facing and thus in a position to deal with those differences intelligently. The man going into an almost identical society might feel that the high degree of similarity absolves him of the need for concern about culture shock (see pages 71-72 and 122). However, aside from this unique circumstance the assumption should hold.

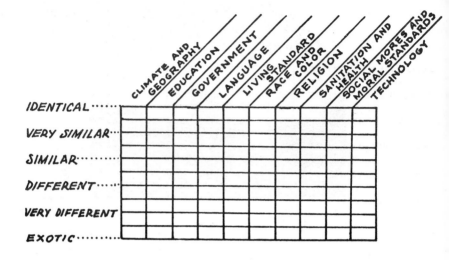

Figure 9.   Culture Contrast Scale.

To use the chart one must first determine, using one category at a time, the degree of similarity or difference between
his own culture and the culture to which he is going.   Then,
for example, if the climate/geography category is determined to
be exotic, no marks are made on the cells of that category
since exotic is the bottom line.   However, if that category is
determined to be similar, then the cells are all colored in
from the exotic line to the similar line.

In this manner, a bar graph is constructed with the taller
the colored-in bars, the greater the similarity.   Also, the
number of colored-in cells can be divided by the total cells in
the chart.   The resultant number or percentage will represent
an overall measure of similarity or difference.*

The two charts (figures 10 and 11) are filled out by prospective missionaries.   According to the information in the scale
labeled figure 10, five categories are similar, three categories are very similar, one category is between similar and very
similar, and only one is different.   The total number of cells
colored in is 65 (65 divided by 100 equals .65 or 65%).
According to figure 11, four categories are exotic, three are

*Since there are a total of 100 cells, one need only count
the colored cells and that number is the correct percentage.

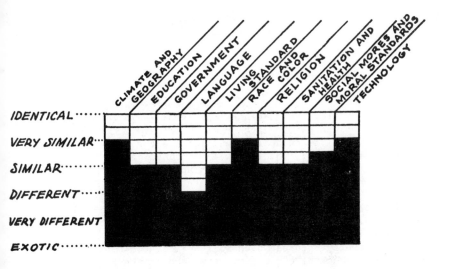

Figure 10.   Culture Contrast Scale (Mock). Missionary
from the Northeastern United States comparing
his background with Central France.

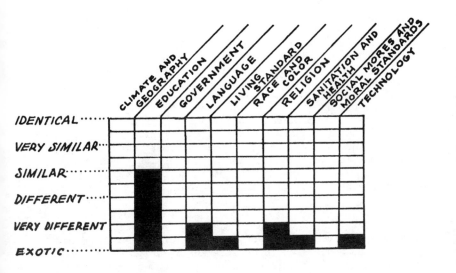

Figure 11.   Culture Contrast Scale (Mock). Missionary
from Ohio, United States, comparing his background with the Ashanti of Ghana, Africa.

between exotic and very different, two are different, and one
is similar. The total number of cells colored in is 13 (13
divided by 100 equals .13 or 13%).*

Note that the charts become graphs that show areas of similarity and difference. Such graphs should help the prospective
missionary pinpoint the categories where he might find encouragement as well as those that will demand the greatest preparation and attention. The following sections deal with the
categories of the chart and suggest some guidelines for
measuring the similarities or differences.

The potential of the scale should be noted at this point.
If, for example, one prospective missionary completes a scale
for each of two or three different countries, he will have
three percentage scores which will suggest the relative degree
of culture shock he can expect from each country. Turning,
then, to the bar graph profile he can see which categories in
each scale are going to present the most difficulty. This
information plus the understanding he can have about his own
personality (see chapter III) will provide him with valuable
information as he makes that final decision concerning his
future mission work.

Before reading the following sections which cover each of
the ten categories suggested in the Culture Contrast Scale
(CCS), keep in mind the comparative nature of the chart. Value
judgments concerning the merit or inferiority of any of the
items in the chart must not be confused with similarities and
differences. For example, the fact that the educational level
of the people of a given mission field is high or low has no
significance except insofar as it differs from the educational
level of the missionary himself. The difference or similarity
is important, not the level. Thus the chart does not serve,
in any manner, as an evaluation of any nation or culture,
but merely as a measure of the difference between one man and
the people he is going to try to teach.

---

*The percentages 65 and 13 must be interpreted very sub-
jectively due to the subjective nature of the measurements
themselves. Precision in measurement is still a challenge to
be met and in the meantime, the limitations of existing
measures must be clearly understood. The charts in figures 10
and 11 are included only as examples of how the chart is to
be filled out and not as norms or standards for the cultures
they compare.

CLIMATE AND GEOGRAPHY*

Though human beings are among the world's most adaptable animals, they still tend to have preferences that were determined by association early in life. The Southwesterner from the mountains of New Mexico will likely feel hemmed in and crowded in the hills of Tennessee. The Tennesseean, on the other hand, may feel alone and lost in the seemingly empty vastness of the Southwest.

Since the United States is large enough to have almost all ranges of temperature and climate in a variety of geographical settings, it is necessary for each prospective missionary from the United States to determine just how different the climate and geography of his selected field will be from that to which he has been accustomed.

One missionary to Korea heard such awful stories of the cold weather in Korea that he had himself and his friends back home worried when winter approached. When December rolled around and it was not yet as cold as in his own hometown, he began to investigate the reports he had heard. Some were from people who had previously lived in very warm sections of the United States and others had come from ex-servicemen who had spent many cold nights in pup tents several miles further north where the temperature was much colder.

Personal reports from friends and relatives are valuable but temperature charts, humidity charts and a topographical map will help one get a more accurate view of a strange country. If the summer months have thirty or forty inches of rainfall with temperatures in the 80° to 90° range, then the visitor from a dry or cold country will have some real adjustments to make.

Since climate and geography have such a great influence on the way people build their houses, dress, move from place to place, and transport things, the impact of an exotic change may be greater than a person would think. Hot weather in the midwestern United States may be countered with air conditioning but in Africa or South America, the answer may be windowless homes and fewer clothes. The wife who cannot stand a fly in the house may find great frustration in these areas of the world where lizards and other crawly things are commonplace.

The missionary who has never considered the possibility that climate and geography can have an impact on his work in a given

---

*Alphabetical order determined the location of each category on the chart and thus the order in which they are discussed.

area may meet with serious physical problems as well as damaging
mental frustrations as he walks blindly into the unexpected.
A missionary to the Philippines was engaged in some pretty heavy
outdoor work and his fellow laborers tried to get him to wear a
hat or head covering of some sort. Not being accustomed to
wearing headgear and of the opinion that the local men looked
rather ridiculous with towels, scarves, turbans, and frequently
worn out hats on their heads, the missionary ignored the warnings until he had a bout with sunstroke.

The visitor to Southeast Asia from some cooler climate to
the north may find that his or her light summer clothing is not
light enough. A double knit suit will be fine in Northern
Japan even in the summer but that same suit may be completely
inappropriate for the hot humid summers in Thailand or Malaysia.

As a missionary seeks to find out information about a
certain foreign country, he should be very careful to be as
specific as possible concerning the exact location in that
country that he wants to study. It would be improper to de-
scribe Malaysia or the Philippines as simply hot countries
because in both nations there are upland areas that are quite
cool all year around. The missionary who cannot survive the
oppressive heat of Manila might find himself quite content in
cool Baguio City just a day's ride away.

Missionaries are sometimes forced to adapt their workloads
or schedules to changes in climate. In countries where the
siesta is customary the new missionary may be well advised to
change his own habits to accomodate not only the siesta itself
(which might improve his temper, health, and general attitude)
but also synchronize his activities with the activities of the
local population.

Those going as missionaries will do well to examine the
climate and geography of their target area and then make as
much preparation as possible so that the change (if there is a
difference) from one climate and geographical setting to another
can be made as smoothly and painlessly as possible.

Elders and church leaders also need information concerning
climate and geography because it will help them give the
missionary the proper training, proper living allowance, and
proper encouragement as he goes into his work. They need to
know, for example, that it takes a great deal more money to
live in Alaska than in central Texas or that the winter fuel
bill for a family in Northern Michigan will be considerably
higher than the fuel bill for a similar family in Arkansas.

Suggestions for Scaling the CCS

How does one rate a difference in climate and geography on a scale from identical to exotic? Though no definitive measurement is available at the present time, the following examples might suggest how the difference could be rated.

The accompanying world map (page 60) indicates three major temperature divisions based upon isotherms rather than the traditionally used parallels of latitude. If a person from a *cold* zone plans to work in the *tropical* zone (or vice-versa), it is suggested that the expected difference would be on the exotic end of the scale, i.e., somewhere between *very different* and *exotic*. Comparisons of zones bordering on each other would be expected to reflect differences somewhere between *different* and *very different*, and comparisons of areas within a zone would be expected to reflect differences on the similar end of the scale.

More precise measurements might be determined by considering two other factors, precipitation and terrain. Differences in these factors would move one's selection more toward exotic while similarities in these categories would indicate a selection closer to the similar end of the scale.

For example, someone going from Alaska (cold) to Africa (tropical) would look to the exotic end of the scale. Since Alaska has heavy precipitation and rugged terrain, if the area under consideration in Africa were dry and flat, the difference would definitely be exotic. If the terrain were similar, the mid-point between *exotic* and *very different* might be best and if the part of Africa under consideration also had a high precipitation, then *very different* might be the best level.

In this manner each evaluation can begin with the zone differences, then refine the measurement on the basis of precipitation, terrain, and any other significant information that is available.

EDUCATION

Education has been selected as a variable because of the important place that education holds within any society, and *formal education* is given special treatment because of its unique influence on most of the people who are presently interested in doing mission work. Education is defined as the process by which the members of a society pass on the obvious as well as hidden aspects of culture to their children (Goldschmidt 1960:178). Thus education includes not only what

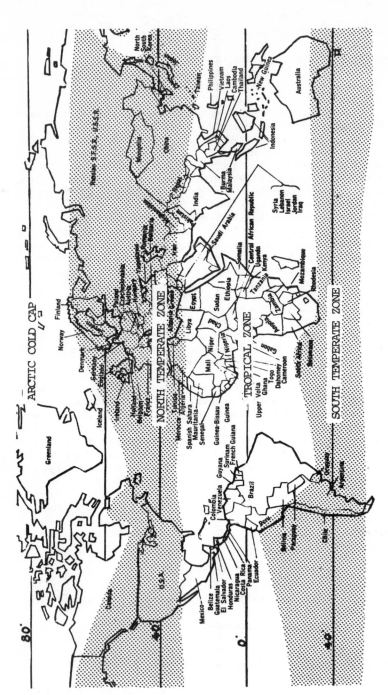

Figure 12. Isotherm Map.

one learns in a formal "school" situation but also the totality of things that are passed on by any number of means within the society.

In the United States as in many nations, formal school education deals primarily with technological training. In schools, students learn to communicate, study the past, and develop mathematical skills. Regulatory, moral, or spiritual training is generally considered the responsibility of the home and church (Kluckhohn 1960:181). However, due to the importance of the technological in western cultures, formal education is extremely important and people often ascribe status on the basis of school achievement alone.

It is this preoccupation with formal education that makes it important as a variable to the missionary. Formal education also provides a convenient means of measurement since it can be broken down into educational levels.

It should be noted that the following discussion does involve only *formal* education. However, it should be emphasized that formal education is not to be confused with general cultural education, knowledge, or wisdom. A bushman in Australia may have all the education and knowledge that his culture demands without having any formal education. Also, a man can have considerable formal education but lack the wisdom to apply what he knows. However, due to the present day emphasis on formal education, any variation in levels of education between the missionary and the people of the host country will likely call for some form of adjustment on the part of the missionary.

Since systems of education vary from nation to nation, it is not always easy to determine exact levels of education. Students in some countries have to decide rather early in life (by personal choice or by way of competitive examinations) whether they will study toward an academic or vocational career.

In some countries, the philosophy of education seems to support the thesis that every student should get a college education and the system tends to push all students toward college. In other countries only the elite are considered college material and only a certain type of student can qualify for higher education.

Thus a college degree from one country may mean something quite different than a college degree from another country. The same is true with graduation from other levels within the educational systems. In the United States, a university education is available to a wide spectrum of high school graduates and may include science (chemistry, physics, biology, etc.), professional training (for doctors, lawyers, economists, etc.), as well as teacher education, Bible study, and vocational or technical training. On the other hand, in Canada a university degree is limited to a certain segment of high school graduates and does not include ordinary teacher training, vocational or technical training, or religious training.

If enough insight is available, it may be possible to determine comparative educational levels with a relatively high degree of precision and even if information is scarce or one's ability to evaluate such matters is limited, the degrees or graduate levels achieved are good *rule of thumb* measures.

To aid in comparing educational levels between cultures, the following benchmarks are given for the reader's consideration. Beginning with illiteracy, several steps have been formulated ending with college doctoral study. In determining which levels are significant to the reader, remember that it is not unusual in any city from New York to South Africa to find illiterate and literate people rubbing shoulders with each other daily. Thus, to make the chart meaningful, the prospective missionary must determine the type of people he is going to try and reach during his missionary work.

If a man knows that he is going to be working primarily with people living in slum or poverty areas, he may discover that the poor people of the nation he has chosen are generally illiterate. On the other hand, if he is going to work more with professional people, he may find that he is entering a group with a high level of formal education.

If he is not sure what kind of people he will be working with, it may be a sign that he has not yet analyzed his chosen field closely enough. Or it may be that he intends to have a wide range of contact. In that case, he may need to evaluate the overall educational level of the nation in question and compare it with the overall educational level of his own nation.

Illiterate (Preliterate)*

For comparative purposes this term refers to people who have not yet learned to read and write. Since it may be assumed that a person studying this book is literate, it may also be assumed that if that person plans to engage in mission work

---

*Preliterate refers to people living in a society which does not have a written language. In such societies people are not illiterate by choice but by circumstance.

among people who are generally illiterate, he is going to face some unique problems. Literate people who study books, read papers, and browse through magazines pick up many kinds of information that may remain a mystery to the illiterate.

The literate person generally relies heavily upon the written word and certainly Christians place great stock in the Bible which is the "written word of God." Communicating the gospel to people who cannot read or who may not even have a written language is a terrific challenge in itself and many missionaries have devoted their lives to such mission endeavors.*

Preparation for work among illiterate people should include those studies that help the missionary to accept illiterates as significant persons and not look down upon them because of their lack of formal education. There is no place for snobbery in the Christian religion and certainly not among those who carry the gospel into other nations or cultures.

One word of caution: When determining education levels, seek professional advice whenever possible. A chamber of commerce, ministry of interior, bureau of information, department of education, or similar agency can supply statistical information on their nation's educational levels that are far more accurate than the prejudicial guess of a friend or relative who may have visited the country at one time or another.

Borderline Literacy

The second benchmark is that of borderline literacy. Though different nations may have slightly different methods of determining literacy, they generally agree that literate people have the ability to read daily papers or certain portions of them, are able to use Bibles and other literature, and are able to communicate through the written word even if their written communications may not be grammatical or correctly spelled. This category is limited, however, to those who are literate but not elementary school graduates. This limitation is necessary because when a government announces that 80 percent of its citizens are literate, this does not necessarily mean that 80 percent of the population can just barely read or write. Rather it means that 80 percent of the people can read

---

*The slogan of the Wycliffe Bible Translators, Inc., suggests that they will have the gospel translated into the language or dialect of every tribe by 1985. See also, Joyce Hardin 1975:2,3.

or write but it does not tell what percent have been educated beyond this minimum.

In the United States where free public education is readily available to almost all of the population but where some people fail to take advantage of the educational offering due to economic or social reasons, observers tend to link literacy with prosperity and middle class urban standing.

Americans visiting in some developing nations may see poverty, deprivation, and struggling rural economies and assume that the people must be illiterate. Such judgments can be very false for literacy rates in some underdeveloped nations may be very high (equal or nearly equal to that of the United States). This may be due to a number of factors (the nature of the language, availability of printed material, etc.) not necessarily related to economics.

As in the case of illiterate people, the missionary must evaluate his personal feelings regarding borderline literates and know how to identify with and fully appreciate those who have never received anything equivalent to his own formal education. Motives are very important in mission work, and it is distressing to see missionaries who choose to work with borderline literate people simply because they feel superior when surrounded by such persons. This attitude is not only disgusting in its obvious implications but may also prove to be very impractical because a lack of formal education does not indicate ignorance, stupidity or even naivete. People in the borderline literate category may be wise, sophisticated, and fully aware of the motives and weaknesses of others.

Elementary School

The ages at which children are permitted to start to school will vary from country to country and even the method of determining age may vary, i.e., in Asia it is common to consider a child one year old at birth and two years old on the following new year. Thus a child born on the day before New Year's Day would be considered two years old the day after his birth.

Regardless of how age is determined, there is rather general agreement that children are ready for school at the age of 5, 6, or 7. Schooling is generally divided into levels and the elementary level covers the first four to six years of study. In developing nations, free public education may be limited to elementary school though, as economies improve, the trend is to include more and more grade levels under the public education system.

The missionary from America should understand that the American concept of continuing education for all (in California, education through junior college is virtually free to all students) is actually a social experiment that has not yet been thoroughly evaluated. Other nations have not always considered it necessary or even advisable to educate *all* the people to the extent that America tries to do.

In some countries, an elementary education may be afforded as much status as a high school or college education in the United States. Thus people in those countries with only an elementary education should not be considered drop-outs or failures as some might label them according to United States' standards. In any case, the missionary who elects to work with people in this category or level of education should be prepared to face a society that differs from his own even if it is only with regard to the status afforded elementary school graduation.

Junior High or Middle School

There is considerable variety in the divisions of a child's education and the period between elementary and high school may vary from two to four years. Traditionally, the schools in the United States have followed a 6-2-4 system (six years elementary school, two years of junior high school, and four years in high school). However, today the 6-3-3 and 4-4-4 systems are gaining in popularity as is the non-graded system (where students move forward in each subject matter area at their own rate).

Junior high or middle school may vary in length but generally covers a period of two to four years including grades 7 to 8, 7 to 9 or 5 to 8. The very fact that this level of education is labeled *middle* or *junior high* (as opposed to senior high) suggests the idea that a higher level of education is available. This may account for the strange fact that middle school graduates who cannot go on into high school may feel more frustrated than elementary school graduates who cannot take advantage of a middle school education.

Frequently a missionary will find that a nation is continually improving or at least extending its educational system so that today's students have more educational opportunities than the children of past generations. Thus the educational level of the adults with which he is working may be on a middle school level while the young people with whom he works are presently in or have recently graduated from high school.

High School

Whether this level of education covers three or four years
is not as significant as the implications that a high school
education has for the individuals of a nation. In the United
States, a high school education is considered a must for almost
every youth. And from high school a student may move on to a
junior college, college, university, vocational school, or a
job.

In other nations this is not always the case. By the time
the students of some countries have reached high school, they
have already been placed on a track that will lead to a future
in either a vocation or an institution of higher learning. In
some countries such decisions are virtually irreversible and
transfer from one track to another impossible.

Where high school graduates in America must consider four
or six years of college study if they want to teach in the
public school system, the normal schools (teacher training
schools) of other countries are only on a high school level.
Thus public school teachers may be graduates of only a high
school, rather than a college.

In other countries, high school may be divided into different
kinds of schools, i.e., technical high schools, vocational high
schools, and college preparatory high schools. These differences may be found in American high school programs but they
are not as restrictive and rigid as similar systems in some
European and Asian nations.

Therefore, a chance to work with a high school class in one
nation might bring one into contact with a different type of
student than the same opportunity in another country. Also
associating with high school teachers in one country might be
quite different (in terms of their educational level) than
associating with high school teachers in another country.

Of course, there may also be differences in the students of
different schools. In the United States, a high school student
may drive his or her own car, wear stylish clothing, go on
dates, and in many ways display behavior that is generally
considered by those students to be adult and mature. A high
school student in Korea, however, will wear a school uniform,
have a standard hair cut, wear no make-up, go on no dates and,
in general, behave in a manner that an American youth would
consider immature or childish.

College and University (Undergraduate Levels)

   The baccalaureate (bachelor's) degree is a fair indicant of
a certain generally understood level of education. However,
this degree represents a wide range of academic excellence even
within the educational systems of a single nation.

   The holder of a B.A. degree from a state university might
be slightly more awed at the thought of teaching a Bible class
of Harvard graduates than teaching a class of graduates from a
city college. Each nation has its own system of education and
there are internal differences found in every system as well as
the differences between countries.

Advanced Degrees

   Some prospective missionaries may be surprised to know that
missionaries frequently have opportunities to contact persons
with very high levels of education. The American missionary in
the Twentieth Century has often found himself in the company
of socially and educationally prominent people. The economical
and technical superiority of the United States has been responsible for this situation and the lone missionary in some exotic
nation may find that, as the representative of his particular
religious group, he is on the V.I.P. list. Determining which
fork to use at a "western style" royal banquet may be more
frustrating than eating with chopsticks at a local restaurant.
And, carrying on a casual conversation (in English) with half
a dozen national congressmen may prove more of a challenge than
talking in the local language with the taxi driver or fish
peddler.

   The missionary who has not considered the possibility of
contact with the upper classes where education levels are
particularly high may have robbed himself of the preparation
necessary to take the best advantage of such opportunities.
The preparation for such contacts does not necessarily include
advanced education for the missionary but rather an ability
to meet and associate with such people in a natural, poised and
comfortable manner.

   Perhaps the greatest disaster comes when the missionary from
middle or lower class American society feels socially superior
to middle or upper class members of the host culture. Imagine,
for example, the missionary who has been introduced to the host
country's most famous painter. The next day, the missionary
goes to the artist's home, hands him a cheap paint-by-number
set and asks him to paint it for the missionary's new office.
Such things do happen when missionaries fail to understand the
status and sophistication of the people of the host nation.

Whether the missionary feels uncomfortable in the presence of another person or superior to that person, the results can be detrimental to the missionary's preaching of the gospel.

Suggestions for Scaling the CCS

Using the formal education bench marks as discussed above, one can conclude that if he has a graduate education (M.A., Ph.D., etc.) and plans to work among illiterates, the educational difference will be exotic. To work this into a simple formula, first note that there are seven levels discussed:

```
        Advanced (graduate study)----- 7
        Undergraduate------------------ 6
        High School-------------------- 5
        Junior High (Middle School)--- 4
        Elementary School------------- 3
        Borderline Literacy----------- 2
        Illiterate-------------------- 1
```

1. *Identical:* Using the numbers as listed above, any comparison within a number (1:1, 2:2, 4:4, 5:5, 6:6, 7:7), would indicate identical on the scale unless, of course, something of the differences in the educational system is known which would influence this rating slightly. An M.A. degree holder, planning to work with people holding M.A. degrees (7:7), etc., could conclude that his educational background is *identical* with the educational background of the people to whom he is going. However, if he had information that an M.A. in the host country was more prestigious than an M.A. in his own country, he could adjust the rating to *very similar*, etc.

2. *Very similar:* Using any number and any number next to it (1:2, 2:3, 3:4, 4:5, 5:6, 6:7) would indicate a *very similar* relationship. For example, the 4:5 (High school missionary going to work with middle school graduates in a mission field) would select *very similar* on the scale unless he had further information which might indicate a step up or down *(Identical or Similar)*.

3. *Similar:* Using any number with another number once removed (1:3, 2:4, 3:5, 4:6, 5:7) would indicate a significant difference in education and thus a mark on the scale somewhere between *similar* and *different*.

4. *Different:* Using any number twice removed from a given number (1:4, 2:5, 3:6, 4:7) would indicate a mark on the scale between *different* and *very different*.

5. *Very Different:* Using numbers three times removed (1:5, 2:6, 3:7) would indicate a measure of *very different*.

6. *Exotic:* Using numbers four or more times removed (1:6, 2:7, 1:7) would indicate extreme differences and suggest the *exotic*.

In each case, the exact location of the measurement would be determined by more specific knowledge of the cultures and educational systems involved.

One word of caution: No confusion should exist between educational background as a variable on the CCS and one's knowledge of psychology, sociology, or education. A student of anthropology with a Ph.D degree might be better equipped to deal intelligently with illiterates than a high school graduate who has never considered the problems involved in such relation-ships; however, even though training in anthropology might have an important part to play in a missionary's success in over-coming cultural barriers such training represents a separate factor not to be confused with or included in this educational variable.

Also, though the measurement device suggested includes all possible levels in contact with each other, this does not mean that the author expects to see many illiterate missiona-ries coming in contact with illiterates on some mission field, (1:1 relationship). Theoretically, this is conceivable and for the sake of simplicity the total range of relationships is included.

GOVERNMENT

Temper has been called the vice of the virtuous and if that is not an accurate concept, then a more accurate one might be that temper is the vice of the missionary. Nothing can stimu-late a missionary's temper more quickly nor more frequently than the red tape and bureaucracy of a foreign government.

A man who merely complains about how his local government operates will likely feel like pulling his hair when faced with the inefficiency that *he thinks* he sees in other govern-ments. The man who has enjoyed the freedom of saying almost anything he wants to say about anyone including the president may be shocked to find that in some nations, such behavior can result in severe reprimands.

Our government has been responsible for molding our thinking and attitudes, intentionally or unintentionally, all of our lives. We have learned how to live within its framework or to

suffer its sanctions. Whether we respect it, pretend to ignore
it, or hate it, we are all a part of it, and most important,
it is a part of us.

When placed in the framework of a new and strange government, we can be momentarily or even permanently confused and
frustrated. These frustrations, in turn, can be modified by
the local people, especially the local officials. If our
nation enjoys a place of respect and privilege among our host's
list of friendly nations, then we may be given that extra help
that seems to solve even the most perplexing problems. On the
other hand, if we are resented or merely tolerated, then even
little problems may turn out to be insurmountable.

Not infrequently, the smaller struggling nations turn out
to be the most frustrating to the foreign visitor. The customs
check at the international airport of many powerful nations may
be perfunctory while the customs inspection at a small airport
in a developing nation may be extremely thorough. Likewise,
the procedure for doing something in America might be quite
simple whereas doing the same thing in a small Asian nation may
involve days of complicated paper work and numerous visits to
government offices.

Of course, there are reasons for these differences between
nations. The small developing nation may be new at the business
of self government. It takes time to develop efficiency in any
operation and governments are certainly no exception. Also,
the developing nation may be faced with unique problems that
demand a more careful investigation of all requests for entry,
exit, or permission to import.

The currency of a small nation probably has no value on the
international money market. Thus that nation may be completely
dependent upon American dollars, English pounds or German marks
for its international trade. If such a nation has no valuable
trade goods which bring in these needed foreign monies, then
the control of the foreign money on hand may be extremely important. Suppose that a given country has only a limited
number of U.S. dollars to use in its foreign trade. In that
country there may be literally thousands of people who have
the wealth to import automobiles from abroad. However, if
the government allows the uncontrolled import of thousands of
vehicles (all of which must be purchased with U.S. dollars)
the total number of dollars on hand would be used up buying
automobiles leaving nothing for defense spending, developing
industry or purchasing food. In such a country, the purchase
of an automobile may be extremely difficult and thus extremely
frustrating to the American who has always considered an automobile as a standard family necessity available to anyone with
a few dollars for a down payment.

The proximity of the national government can also be an important factor in adjustment. Though Americans may read about the congress and president almost every day, the average citizen rarely deals directly with the government on a national level. However, especially in smaller nations, the national government may be as close to the citizen or visitor as a state or county government in the United States.

A missionary planning to establish a school or hospital may deal directly with a ministry of health or education and, from time to time, speak directly with the ministers themselves. Thus the impact of another government's policy and regulations may seem much greater than they actually are.

Then, too, the American may just feel that he will be more comfortable in a democratic nation where the nature of the government is similar to his own. However, this evaluation must be made by or according to the feelings of the individual. The conservative American, over 39, who feels that America is getting to be too permissive may enjoy a slightly more totalitarian form of government where regulations against long hair and unusual clothing are rigidly enforced. There are probably many Americans, for example, who would feel more comfortable in a society where there is less individual freedom, more direct control of young people and less interference with police activities. At least they would feel more comfortable until their own personal freedoms were challenged. However, generally speaking, a foreign government will likely serve to frustrate the missionary to the extent that that government is different from his own.

The impact of culture shock generated by governmental factors can also be considered on the basis of the official and unofficial relationship between one's home government and the government of the country to which he wishes to go. The American might be an unwanted but tolerated guest in one country, officially welcomed but unofficially resented in another country, and warmly accepted in yet a third country. Obviously, adjustment and identification should come more easily in the culture that is warm and receptive.

During a recent trip through Southeast Asia, a missionary evaluated the attitudes of various governments as projected by the customs agents at the airport. This one measure proved to be extremely accurate when compared with the opinions of long time residents of those countries. Those attitudes included rude disdain, icy indifference, tolerant acceptance, friendly courtesy, and warm hospitality. Though simple measures of this sort may have some validity, they are definitely subject to error. The customs agent's personality could reflect his own

early morning grouchiness, a Monday morning hangover, or his
private knowledge that he holds a winning sweepstakes ticket,
rather than the climate of the government with regard to a
visitor. Nonetheless, the generalization has some validity and
might help someone determine the extent of resistance and frustration he will have to face in any given country.

One insight into nations of the world can be gained by
discovering the policies of each with regard to missionaries.
Some countries welcome almost all Americans and/or their dollars
while others make it almost impossible for an American to serve
as a missionary. A missionary's first hint as to the attitude
of a country's government may be the simplicity or difficulty
with which a visa is obtained. In some countries an American
can stay for lengthy periods without a visa whereas another
country might refuse entry altogether. Some missionaries live
continually under the threat of expulsion while others enjoy
almost total freedom and security.

One method of determining the possible attitude of a given
nation toward missionaries involves noting the relationship of
that government to some dominant religion. State religions
are very common and if a government supports a religion or is
supported by a religion, it is difficult for other religious
groups to come into the country and teach their doctrines. If
the state religion is truly evangelistic and/or militant,
missionaries may find entry almost impossible.

In one Southeast Asian nation, for example, there are three
major nationalities: the indigenous group, Chinese, and
Indians. Although the Chinese and Indians feel that they represent a majority of the people, the government is controlled by
the indigenous group or, as they call themselves, the *sons of
the soil*. The sons of the soil are Muslims, and Christian
missionaries are forbidden to preach to them. They can preach
to Indians and Chinese and, of course, these make up the bulk
of the Christian population in that nation. Recently that
government has added further restrictions by refusing to renew
certain missionaries' visas. There had been a threat of this
type action for some time but now it has become a reality and
missionary visas are fast becoming a thing of the past.

Even friendly countries may have quite strict visa regulations due to their own international problems. Thus ease of
obtaining a visa cannot be used as an absolute criterion for
determining the government's attitude toward a guest unless it
is further supported by other evidence.

Magazines and newspapers are a good source of information on
government policies; however, the real analysis of a newspaper

may require some previous knowledge of the type of government it represents. For example, paper A may carry an editorial complaining about the national leaders (Watergate is a good example) while paper B (from a different nation) has nothing but praise for its government. On the basis of newspapers alone one could not conclude that everyone is happier in nation B or that nation B has a better government.

The complaints in paper A may represent the fact that the people of that nation have the freedom to say what they think whereas the praise in paper B may be the result of totalitarian suppression that forbids criticism of the government. Therefore, analysis of governments must not be made casually.

Even reports of government suppression of religion may be deceptive. Late in 1974, foreign missionaries became involved in anti-government demonstrations against the authoritarian regime of the president of South Korea. The premier of Korea, in November of 1974, reminded the religious leaders in Korea and especially the foreign Christian missionaries of the great freedom given to Christianity in Korea. He pointed to a 210 percent congregational growth between 1960 and 1973 with an accompanying 593 percent increase in clergymen. He then called upon the foreign missionaries to pay more attention to their primary religious missions and refrain from becoming involved in local politics (Kim 1974:2).

Perhaps those missionaries involved in the political demonstrations felt that they were justified in trying to bring about a change in government policy but certainly the premier was within his rights as an official representative of the government to remind the missionaries that they were guests of his country and had been granted visas for the purpose of preaching the gospel and not for demonstrating against the government.

From this illustration it is clear that even reports of government suppression of religion may be inaccurate or at least subject to critical evaluation. Also this illustration touches upon the problem of missionary involvement in local (host country) politics. If one's religious beliefs permit such involvement, he should certainly be aware that the result will likely be general alienation, deportation or even imprisonment.

Suggestions for Scaling the CCS

All of the above information emphasizes the fact that governments are different, that those differences are significant, and that the accurate measurement of differences is difficult. In concluding this section it might be well to make some very general suggestions as to possible methods of applying differences in government to the CCS.

1. *Exotic:* A very liberal American missionary planning to do mission work in a militant Moslem nation (see page   ) would probably be justified in selecting *exotic* as the measure of difference.

2. *Very Different:* That same missionary comparing his nation's background with the government of an authoritative but not anti-Christian nation could select the *very different* level of difference.

3. *Different:* The middle of the road American going into a friendly but totalitarian type government would probably be able to say that the level of difference is *different*.

4. *Similar:* The American going into a newly emerging democratic nation may select *similar* even though the actual functioning of the two governments might be quite different. The developing nation, in Asia for example, might have all the forms of a democratic government but still function along the lines of an age old monarchy.

5. *Very Similar:* The American going to Australia, England, France or Canada would probably be justified in selecting *very similar* although a careful analysis of these governments might indicate that this selection is rather naive. Also this measure might serve for the extreme right or left wing American who travels from one section of the United States to another. A move from the north to south or east to west would involve significant differences.

6. *Identical:* The middle of the road American with little interest in politics visiting Guam or some other Trust Territory might feel that the closeness of these places to statehood (they do have congressional representation in the U.S. Government) makes them almost *identical* to the United States as far as government is concerned.

LANGUAGE

During the past few years linguistics and language study have played an increasingly important part in the preparation of missionaries. The day of the interpreter (or interrupter as some prefer to call him) is fast fading away as people learn that they must communicate the gospel within the linguistic and cultural framework of the listener.

This is an especially difficult responsibility for some
people who fear the task of learning another language. Americans, as a rule, have considerable fear along this line; not
because they are less intelligent or linguistically talented
than any other group of people but because they are psychologically unprepared to learn another language.

Asian, Europeans, and others who have become accustomed to
communicating in more than one language can easily approach a
new language with an understanding that it is merely a tool
that will work if properly applied. The American who is accustomed to everyone else speaking English approaches a new
language with a kind of awe and disbelief.

Students in language classes or travelers in other countries
demonstrate this generalization. The Japanese student studying
Korean or the Japanese visitor to Korea will hear the new
sounds and strange words, practice them a few times, and then
expect a native speaker to understand him when he speaks. The
American hears the new sounds, practices them a few times, and
then uses them in a state of acute embarrassment with no confidence that he will be understood.

People may be very unrealistic as they consider language
study. The embarrassed speaker above has no real understanding
of the objective reality of language, and to him it is not a
tool to be picked up and used but an inborn part of self,
something that he has always accepted as a part of himself.
The attitude of others may be overly simplistic or overly
problematic. The latter throw up their hands before they begin
study or even after a few weeks or months of study and declare
that it is impossible, the former casually assume that they
will "get" the language next month or next year. There are
missionaries on the field today who have been there for many
years but still do not speak more than a few stilted phrases.
Some have completely given up any hope of settling down to a
serious study of the language while others are still optimistic
and plan to pick it up next summer.

The problem is that languages not only can be learned but
must be learned if a missionary is going to be doing his best.
However, it cannot be mastered overnight, in six easy lessons,
in one year, or perhaps not even in three or four years. Just
as our own language must be polished and improved year by year
as long as we live, so must a foreign language be learned little
by little for as long as one is willing to study.

Before going further it might be well to consider what is
meant by the term *mastery*. Different people have different
ideas and the one selected by the writer was received in a

letter from Frank Robbins, Vice President of the Summer Institute of Linguistics. He defines mastery as the "complete
internalization (both in understanding and in automatic production) of the sound system and of the grammatical patterns, with
sufficient vocabulary so that the student can proceed to ask
intelligent questions (and understand the answers) about almost
any aspect of life in the target culture." Certainly, the
preacher of the gospel should at least aim at such a grasp of
a language if he is going to be able to understand the people
and communicate the gospel to them effectively.

Others have suggested that there are different levels of
proficiency that a person might acquire and that each level
takes more study time. The Brewsters suggest five general
levels which they ultimately break down into 11 levels ranging
from no understanding to complete understanding (Brewster 1976:
370-373). This is an important concept because an evangelist
can certainly communicate and preach in a second language long
before he might consider himself a master of that language.

Of course, language study, like any other study, is easier
for some than for others. There are those who seem to have a
propensity for languages who develop conversational proficiency
in a surprisingly short time, while others have to study longer
and try harder to make equal achievements. However, every
prospective missionary has demonstrated his ability to learn a
language by the very fact that he speaks his own with reasonable fluency. He may have acquired mental blocks, poor study
habits, or strong personal doubts, all of which may negatively
effect his mastery of a second language, but even these
obstacles to learning can be overcome. Thus, anyone who has
learned one language can learn another.

The suggestion that language learning is a continual,
never-ending process may be frustrating to time conscious
Westerners who want to see a clear beginning and ending point
with regard to any activity. Therefore, the following information has been compiled for the purpose of suggesting concrete
(though flexible) time periods for sufficient mastery of any
given language. This information is offered with the full
understanding that it is quite general in nature and perhaps
overly simplified. However, it is intended as a guide to
laymen who are faced with sending someone or themselves going
to a place where a different language is spoken. It should
sober the thinking of the individual who takes language learning too lightly as well as encourage the individual who looks
upon language learning as impossible.

The time suggested for the study of each language is, of
course, subject to reconsideration in the light of contemporary

advances in the teaching of language, individual motivation and
determination, and the specific training program involved.
Linguists are generally quite optimistic and one recently
reported on an individual who mastered English (as a foreign
language) well enough to do graduate level college work in
less than a year.

Others, while admitting that the grammar of any language
can be learned in a period of six months or so, are less sure
about the mastery of a large vocabulary in such a short time.
It has been suggested that language learning is still "memory
work" (Pei 1957:312 and Sweet 1964:65), and, of course, it
takes time to memorize and fluently use the grammar, vocabulary
and sounds of a new language.

One assumption that has been made with regard to the
following information is that similar languages are easier to
master than exotic languages. Some linguists share this
feeling and point out that similarity may prove to be psychologically advantageous because the learner is less awed by a
foreign language that is spelled with familiar symbols and
even has similar words, i.e., Spanish, Italian, French, and
English all use the same Roman alphabet and some words have the
same meaning: English--*enter*; Spanish--*entrar*; French--*entre*.

As one develops proficiency in a foreign language that is
similar to his own, he will likely discover that cross-asso-
ciations are a great hindrance (Sweet 1964:54). For example,
the Spanish word *embarazar* (pregnant) looks, sounds, and also
has a second meaning similar to the English word, embarrassed.
Likewise, the Spanish verb *asistir* has a primary meaning of
'presence' or 'attendance' though it looks and sounds like
the English word, assist. Both of these cases illustrate the
problem of similarity. If the speaker thinks he knows the
meaning of a foreign word while in reality he is substituting
a meaning for a sound-alike from his own language, it may
prove to be very frustrating. Such cross-over problems would
not exist for the learner of an exotic language because similarities are quite rare.

In further defense of the time levels suggested in the
following section is the very real difficulty one can encounter
when searching for avenues of study for certain languages. The
American who wishes to study German may be able to find numerous
text books, dictionaries, grammars, and even qualified instructors no matter where he lives in the United States. However,
if he wishes to study Korean or Finnish, it will be extremely
difficult to find either the written materials or qualified
teachers. Korea has produced many good books to help speakers
of English learn Korean but these books are not easily found

in the United States. Likewise, there are excellent Finnish
language books but the best ones are written in Swedish rather
than in English.

During the past few years language enrollment in the popular
language courses (French, German, Russian, Spanish, etc.) of
United States colleges and universities has declined while
enrollment in exotic language courses (Chinese, Japanese,
Arabic, Swahili, etc.) has increased (*Houston Post* 1973).
However, the exotic language courses are still hard to find and
study in these languages will, therefore, be more difficult.

Donald Larson and William Smalley have developed a very
sophisticated language study program which is based upon a
thorough knowledge of linguistics, languages, Bible transla-
tion problems, and foreign mission. They clearly state that
languages and individuals differ to the extent that no one
program or time span can possibly suit all circumstances but,
given a language with a relatively easy writing system, they
recommend a program that requires seven hours of study per day
for a period of three years (Larson & Smalley 1972:81-83).

If a language with a difficult writing system is considered,
the three year period might have to be stretched. Also, it is
important to understand the nature of a good language study
program. It is much more than a native speaker coming into
your home each day to tutor or even an intensive course at a
local university. A real language school should have that 7
hour daily study period backed up with:

(1) a fully organized and controlled program so that no
    time is lost, effort duplicated, nor individual differ-
    ence ignored,
(2) an educational psychologist to design the overall pro-
    gramming, and testing,
(3) all the necessary books, tape recorders, and props,
    that might be needed,
(4) a staff that is sensitive to individual differences,
(5) professionals who can help learners understand their
    learning problems,
(6) actual daily contact with community life in the new
    language (Larson 1972:74,75).

If this *ideal* learning situation is not available, then it
is reasonable to add some more time to the period of intensive
study. The church leaders, or elders, who send missionaries
must be aware of the time needed to master a foreign language.
Under ideal circumstances it may take three years and under the
circumstances that face most new missionaries, it will likely
take longer.

Language Mastery Time Guide

Since many church leaders and prospective missionaries do not have any first hand knowledge of foreign languages the following division of languages has been made to provide a flexible guideline as well as introduce some of the major* world languages. It is assumed that study time needed for mastery, the relative difficulty of the language, and the difference between the learner's language and the foreign language he is learning are all highly correlated. Thus the language that is most exotic to a given missionary will be the one that is most difficult for him to master and thus the one that requires a longer period of study.

1. Dialects of English (1 year of study): Languages in this group might not be considered "foreign languages" but they still demand some attention and perhaps present a subtle challenge that is often completely overlooked by the potential missionary.

(a) Within the U.S.A.: While visiting for the first time in the Southeastern United States the guest did a double-take when his host said that he had *carried* his wife home from a party. The guest asked for a recap of the story because he felt he must have missed the part where the wife became ill and had to be carried. Slowly the light dawned and the guest realized that *carried* did not mean *carried in the hands;* but only that the man had *taken* his wife home.

This rather humorous confusion of simple American English may seem altogether too insignificant to be given serious consideration but think for a moment of the attitudes you or your acquaintances have concerning regional dialects or idioms. A strange accent or dialect can render a speaker's message meaningless because people pay more attention to the *funny way he talks* than to the ideas he may be trying to communicate.

Quite recently some Christians in the Northeast began a training school for preachers. One of their reasons for dupli-cating training presently being given in several Southern states involved dialect and customs. Although Southern prea-chers could adjust to the Northeast they felt that the adjust-ment problems were so great that it would be best to train local men who would not have to make the adjustment.

---

*Only 40 or so of the world's 5,000 languages are mentioned by name in this section.

Any time a preacher goes from one region of the United States to another, he should be aware of the subtle differences in language. The wrong words can cause real misunderstanding and humorous blunders while dialect differences can psychologically turn people on or off.

(b) In other countries: A prospective missionary came to the writer's office recently and stated that he wanted to do mission work in Canada. When pressed for a reason for selecting Canada, he responded that he wanted to go there because it is so similar to the United States. A surprising number of Americans* hold a rather naive view of other English speaking nations. They tend to be considered extensions of the United States in some general way, and the American visitor to Canada, Australia or England, if he notices at all, may be surprised to learn that there is a certain resentment against him on the part of some of the people he meets.

Even if the people warmly accept him, and many will, he is still different and one of the ways that this difference is communicated is in his speech. He speaks English but to the Englishman, it is American English and not too deeply appreciated. To illustrate the difference between American and English the following hypothetical story has been written:

The old *victualler,* with a warm *vest* worn under his shirt and his *bags* securely fastened to his *braces,* walked to his *lorry,* paused at the left front *wing* to wipe his brow with a *face flannel.* A few minutes later he was on his way down a *tarmac road* with his *silencer* bouncing from side to side. He drove up to the *zebra* shouting, *"shove over"* to pedestrians enjoying a *bank holiday.*

If the story sounds a bit strange, it might help to substitute American words for the following English words:

---

*The term *American* is not well received in Canada as a term to designate citizens of the U.S.A. because the entire land mass from Ellesmere Island of Canada's Northwest Territories to the southern tip of Chili is America (North America, Central America, and South America) and all peoples on this land mass can be called Americans. Of course, the United States of America faces a problem because *United Statsers,* or *U.S.ites,* etc., are not very good names for the citizens of the U.S.A. Thus *American* becomes the reasonable and generally accepted form of designation.

British	American
victualler	saloon keeper
vest	under shirt
bags	slacks
braces	suspenders
lorry	truck
wing	fender
face flannel	wash rag
tarmac road	asphalt
silencer	muffler
zebra	crosswalk
shove over	gangway
bank holiday	legal holiday

An American warehouse worker was working side by side with men from several English speaking countries and he was having his own form of culture shock. As he entered a room carrying a heavy package, a scotsman looked up and casually said, "Eresaplaztapudidon'ta." Baffled by this statement, he stood momentarily speechless. It took the Scotsman three more tries before the dense American realized that he was saying, "Here's a place to put it onto."

Thus regional differences in American English as well as national differences in the English language must be given some attention by the missionary who would cross these barriers. Though they might not be illustrative of extreme differences, they should not be considered identical (See the CCS, Fig. 9). Finally, even slight differences can have far reaching consequences. The great danger is not that the missionary will be unaware of the differences mentioned here but that he will consider them insignificant (for more information, see p. 124).

Although a course in some regional United States dialect may not be available to the person planning to go into that area, he should still plan to spend at least a year's time studying the dialect so that he can speak to the people in a natural manner. The same is true when going to England or Western Canada.* In filling out the CCS, it is suggested that

---

*Of course, if one goes specifically to the Ukranian or French populations of Canada, English will not be quite as important as Ukranian or French. And if he goes to one of the Indian tribes or Eskimo villages, he faces very different, if not exotic languages. This emphasizes the danger of rash generalizations when discussing nations. Accuracy in analysis and understanding depends upon a specific knowledge of where one wants to work.

the *similar* level be marked (not the *identical* level) when planning mission work in one's own language.

2.   *German* (2 years of study):   Since English is a Western branch of the Germanic subfamily of languages, it has a very close relationship to the modern German language. Many high school and college students have studied German in school and it is one of the major foreign languages taught in the United States.

Assuming a strong motivation to learn, a good learning situation, and adequate teaching materials a missionary to Germany should be able to carry on a conversation in one year. By the end of two years, he should be able to speak freely and manage the language in such a manner that he can quite ade-quately teach himself. At this time and as he moves on into the third year, he should be able to begin teaching the gospel and making the necessary progress toward more effective preach-ing. An American (unfamiliar with the German language) would probably consider German as *similar/different* on the CCS.

3.   *Romance Languages* (2 years of study):   Those languages which can be linked to Rome are also quite well known to most English speaking people and the influence of these languages on English has been great. Italian, French, Spanish, or Portuguese may have been studied in high school or college and thus may seem somewhat familiar even though *mastery* was probably not the outcome of that language study experience.

As with the German language, two years of intensive study should open the door to preaching in the Romance languages. Of course, preaching ability does not indicate language mas-tery. Since sermons can be written, re-used, read or even memorized, a missionary might be able to preach acceptable sermons long before he is able to talk freely without notes or special preparation. An American (unfamiliar with a Romance language) would probably consider it as *similar/different* on the CCS.

4.   *Teutonic and Celtic* (2 or more years of study): Since English is a Western branch of the Teutonic or Germanic subfamily along with the closely related Celtic subfamily, other languages of this branch should be somewhat familiar to the speaker of English. These include Irish, Swedish, Danish, Norwegian, Dutch, Flemish, and Scottish.* These languages are

---

*German might also be included in this list but due to the popularity of German in the United States, it will likely be easier to find places to study German, good dictionaries, text

somewhat familiar to most English speaking people and certainly many of the words of these languages will look and sound
quite familiar to the American. This should not indicate the
mastery of these languages will be easy but only that the
familiarity of a few of the words may make the task of language
study somewhat less awesome.

Perhaps the greatest single obstacle to learning the languages of this group is opportunity. Courses in these languages
are not found in every high school and college. Dictionaries,
text books, and other study aids may be quite difficult for the
layman to locate. Thus it is assumed that the typical missionary setting out to a country where one of these languages is
spoken will need at least the two year course mentioned above
and will likely need an extra year if he attempts to learn the
language without the benefit of a highly professional language
study program. It is suggested that the missionary planning to
study one of these languages mark the *different* level on the
CCS.

5. *India to Russia* (3 years of study): For most Americans
the languages of India, Afghanistan, Iran, Armenia, Yogoslavia,
Russia, Czechoslovakia, and Prussia, are all somewhat unusual,
to say the least. Though there are Americans from all of these
places, and areas of the United States where these languages
may still be spoken, they are generally not as well known as
the Romance languages or German.

A glance at the bulletin of almost any language school will
generally reveal that the course in Russian, for example, requires more time than Spanish or German. However, remember
that these measures are relative to people who only speak
English. A citizen of Poland would probably find Czechoslova-
kian easier to master than Spanish.

Here again, generalizations are difficult because factors
that influence this *time* problem are constantly changing.
Remember that in 1973 the *Houston Post* carried an article
("Language Barrier," Sept. 30, 1973) that noted the changes
that were then taking place in American college level language
offerings. French, German, Russian, and Spanish classes are
experiencing enrollment drops and exotic languages like
Chinese, Japanese and Swahili are on the upswing. At any
given time some of these less familiar languages might be
offered at some nearby college or university while more common
courses might be cut.

---

books, instructors, etc. Thus German was placed ahead of
group (4).

It is still likely that the students of the languages in this group will need more time for mastery than the students of the first four groups. Of importance to this conclusion is the fact that all of these languages require the mastery of new written symbols. Therefore, even written sermons cannot be preached until the learner is quite familiar with all of the written symbols.

It should also be borne in mind that of this group, Russian may be easier than Armenian because of the popularity of Russian in the United States for the last few years. Thus, it is assumed that mastery of these languages will require four or five years as a minimum and perhaps longer if ideal study opportunities are not available. On the CCS, the person going into one of these language areas would probably mark the *different/very different* level.

6. *Semitic and Ural-Altaic* (3 or more years of study): These two language families are combined, not because of any particular relationship but because they are probably equally unfamiliar to the average American. Included are the languages of Arabia, Egypt, North Africa (Semitic); and Finland, Estonia, Turkey, and Mongolia (Ural-Altaic).*

The arbitrary grouping and categorizing of languages is always subject to correction and experts in the various languages of this group might argue that some of these are likely to be more difficult for the typical American missionary than others. The problems still involve the seeming strangeness of these languages, the difficulty of mastering the written language, and/or the difficulty of finding texts, dictionaries, and teachers.

The typical missionary planning to go into one of these areas will likely need more than three years of study to master these languages. As with any of the world's languages there are those persons who seem to be able to gain amazing proficiency in a relatively short period of time, however, this is not typical. Whatever the reason might be, there seem to be few missionaries who have gone into these areas and mastered the language in less than three years. Again the written forms are difficult and must be learned before one can even read a sermon or lesson. Therefore the *very different* level is suggested for persons going into areas where the Semitic or Ural-Altaic languages are spoken.

---

*Korea and Japan may have been influenced by this family but will be included under the Indo-Chinese group.

7. African, Austronesian, and American Indian (4 years of study): The Bantu, Sudanic, Coptic, Berber, Cushitic and other tribal languages of Africa; the Indonesian, Polynésian, and Melanesian of the Pacific Ocean area; and the various languages of the Indians of North and South America are listed together for the sake of simplicity.*

Sometimes limited to single tribes, these languages or their dialects are frequently considered too limited to demand mastery. For example, a person could spend many years learning the language of one pueblo in New Mexico and not be able to communicate in that language with any person outside that pueblo. Considering the fact that most of those pueblo members also speak English or Spanish has influenced missionaries not to be concerned with the mastery of that language.

Such reasoning is subject to a number of criticisms. First, a local dialect is the first or native language of a tribe or clan. It is in and through his own dialect or language that his most intimate and meaningful thoughts and feelings are communicated. His second language, though quite aptly handled, is still a second best method of communication and may not lend itself to the deepest expressions of his heart. Therefore, it is strongly recommended that a missionary going to a specific tribal area determine to master the language of that tribe as a first step toward serious gospel communication. Where second languages or national languages are also used, it may be very wise for the missionary to learn the national language first and then the tribal dialect. In many of these tribal situations two languages may have to be learned, thus the need for several years of study.

Second, some tribes have no written language and thus no way of studying the Bible on their own. One of the first jobs of a missionary to an area like this might be the developing of a written language for the tribe. This requires some linguistic skills that might be studied as a part of one's general preparation for mission work. Even if the missionary does not feel adequate to the task of developing a written language, he must learn the language and be a good resource person when the professional translators come.

Third, unless the missionary can talk face to face in a very intimate manner with the people he is trying to convert, he can never really know how well the work is going. Reports

---

*The writer hesitates to even make an attempt to isolate and discuss individually the hundreds of tribal languages in this grouping.

of success by missionaries who do not speak the native language
of the people they are teaching are always suspect. It is too
easy to be deceived and to misunderstand when one cannot understand the most intimate communications of the people he is
teaching.

Fourth, as one studies language he really begins to study
the culture of the people. Language is a reflection of culture
and through the language the customs, ideals, and beliefs of
a people are revealed. Through a second language the missionary gets only the impact of the culture that gave birth to that
language and not the impact of the people he wants to teach.

Of course, there are those colleges and universities where
some of these rather obscure languages are being taught but
considering the general difficulty of access to courses in
these languages and frequently the absence of any written
language at all, it is assumed that five or more years of study
may be needed by the typical missionary. If a second (national)
language must be learned first, then the time might be
stretched to six or more years.

Donald Deer, a missionary in Zaire (Belgian Congo) asserts
that missionaries who do not "stick it out," trace their failure to their inability to communicate. He recommends that
French (one of five official languages) be mastered before
coming to Zaire and then one of the 250 tribal languages be
studied after arrival (Deer 1975:87-91).

In a discussion with a colleague, a missionary to Africa
was mentioned who seemed to get a pretty good grip on Swahili
(in Kenya) in a matter of eight or nine months and then went
to the Kipsigis, and in a few more months seemed to be making
rapid progress using Swahili as a bridge to Kipsigis; however,
a co-worker who has spent more time in study is just barely
getting along in Swahili and has not yet made any progress in
any tribal language.

This is, of course, unofficial information based upon very
limited first hand observation by a person who does not speak
either of the African languages. Therefore, degrees of mastery
are really not known. The report, however, does point out two
important possibilities: (a) some people seem to develop language proficiency much more rapidly than others, and (b) many
ideas that we have about language learning come from "unofficial," "unverified," or "undocumented" sources.

It is suggested that complete preparation for work in many
of the languages of this group may take four years. It is

recommended that persons planning to go to any of these language groups select *very different/exotic* on the CCS.

8. *Indo-Chinese* (5 years of study): To the non-Asian American, the languages of China, Thailand, Tibet, Burma, Japan, and Korea probably seem to be among the most exotic. Though they form a vast language group that covers a sizable portion of the globe, they have only recently begun to be studied by the people of the West.

The complicated characters of the written form and the tones of the spoken form of the Chinese language make it a very unusual and difficult language for Americans. Likewise, the glottal sounds and aspirants of Korean can quickly frustrate the student of Korean language.

Although language schools are available for most of these languages, it is the rare missionary who becomes fluent in a short period of time. Since many of the citizens of these nations speak some English, there is a strong temptation to rely upon English when doing mission work in some of these countries. Even the language student may find his learning hampered by the continual presence of those who do know some English.

Concerning Korean, Chin-Wu Kim, Professor of Linguistics at the University of Illinois, says that,

> Among a few dozen languages that the Peace Corps teaches to its trainees, Korean was found to be one of the most difficult . . . . I'm sure that those . . . who have tried Korean . . . will agree. In order to comfort a student complaining of the bitter difficulty of learning Korean, I used to say with some delight that yes, Korean is indeed a complicated language, and that only geniuses and demigods can speak it (Kim 1974:11).

This tongue in cheek comment does serve to illustrate the feeling that even a Korean may have about the Korean language. Whatever the reason, the student of Korean generally finds it very difficult to gain fluency in the Korean language.

In 1949, Eiichi Kiyooka, Professor Language at Keio University in Japan and Columbia University in the United States, prepared a Japanese language book for speakers of English. In the foreward he makes a statement with significant implications concerning the mastery of Japanese:

> Japanese is one of the richest languages in the world. Naturally the *full mastery of its elegant uses is very*

difficult even for a native. (italics added). However,
the grammar of the spoken Japanese is very simple. For
a beginner learning to speak it for daily purposes, the
Japanese should be easier than any other language
(Kiyooka 1953:x).

Though simple every day conversation may be quickly learned in
the Japanese language, full mastery, Kiyooka asserts, is very
difficult even for a native. Add the written language with
Japanese syllabic script plus 4,600 Chinese characters and
Japanese, too, becomes a real challenge to the language student.

A "Teach Yourself Book" for Chinese by H. R. Williamson
introduces the Chinese language beginner to a total of 409
different sounds, not including the contour tone feature which
could multiply this list to 1,636 or 3,272 sounds depending
on which Chinese dialect is being learned. He also suggests
the difficulty associated with the tones by the following
statement (Williamson 1972:2-21):

> Don't let the difficulty of intonation* unduly dis-
> courage you. For your comfort, let me say that intona-
> tion varies considerably in different parts of China,
> and that the Chinese themselves experience difficulty
> in this respect as they move about the country.

This brief introduction to the study of Chinese is sufficient
to alert us to the potential difficulties to be met in studying
the Chinese language. Pronunciation, tonemes, and written
characters all contribute to make this language a real challenge
to the Western missionary. Thus it is suggested that the
missionary going into any of these countries mark the difference
as *exotic* on the CCS and consider at least five years for
mastery.

Suggestions for Scaling the CCS

Language is perhaps one of the most important culture
barriers that the missionary must cross because it is fundamen-
tally the means by which he must determine, analyze, and overcome all other barriers. To measure the difficulty involved
in mastering a second language, the missionary will also be
measuring the difference between his own language and that
second language. This assumption underlies the above discussion where eight groups of languages are ranked according to
the expected study time needed for mastery.

---

*Williamson uses the term *intonation* for that which Pike
would call *tonemes*. (See Pike 1957).

The suggested study times, and levels of difficulty, for each group are as follows: (1) Dialects of English (1 year)--*similar*; (2) German (2 years)--*similar/different*; (3) Romance Languages (2 years)--*similar/different*; (4) Teutonic and Celtic Languages (2 or more years)--*different*; (5) Languages from Russia to India (3 years)--*different/very different*; (6) Semitic and Ural-Altaic Languages (3 or more years)--*very different*; (7) African, Austronesian, and American Indian (4 years)--*very different/exotic*; (8) Indo-Chinese (5 years)--*exotic*.

These times and levels of difficulty are, of course, highly generalized and may be modified by the student's motivation, study habits and special skill with language as well as the opportunities he has for study, the sophistication of the program, the hours per day spent in study, and numerous other factors. They are, however, sound guide lines to help the prospective missionary and his sponsoring church understand the seriousness of the language study challenge.

LIVING STANDARD

There is probably nothing about a culture that is as generally well known as information concerning its standards of living. However, such standards are usually presented in U.S. dollars equivalents on a per capita basis. For example, a 1969 yearbook shows that the per capita income of India was $73.00 in 1968 (United Nations 1970:557-562). This information actually means very little to the person who reads it unless he is especially familiar with the nation of India. Here are several reasons why such statistics fail to communicate adequately.

(1) Unless the method of arriving at an average or standard of living is understood, it is virtually meaningless. For example, ten men have yearly incomes as follows: one gets $10,000, one gets $5,000, and eight of them get $1,000 each. What is their average income? If we add all the incomes together and divide by ten, the average income is $2,300. If we take the modal income (income received by a majority of the people), it is $1,000. If we take the income of the middle class person, we will end up with an answer of $5,000.

(2) Unless we know something of the value of a U.S. dollar in a foreign country, as well as the buying power of a specific number of dollars, we cannot understand how well a man can live on a given number of U.S. dollars.

(3) Countries with large rural populations are difficult to analyze according to per capita income since the farmer may not turn much of his produce into cash. The farmer who is

self-sufficient may be impossible to classify because no cash
flows through his hands.

(4) The very nature of living standards will vary from
country to country and age to age. In the early 1900's, a
well-to-do American family had such status symbols as a hand-
pump right in the kitchen, an ice box (ice delivered twice a
week), a wood range in the kitchen, a hand crank milk separator,
and a glass butter churn. In 1975, Americans measured status
by color television sets, college educations, electronic equipment, and before the energy crisis, the length of their automobiles. For the majority of citizens there was no suffering in
either period, it is just that 1975 offered many more work
saving gadgets, luxuries, and opportunities.

The technology and energy necessary to operate the standard
of living that many Americans enjoy is completely beyond the
resources of most nations. Yet the people of these nations
are not necessarily suffering from lack of food, clothing,
shelter, recreation, and education. Thus, the relative dollar
expenditures by members of different nations may not be true
indicants of differences in essentials but only differences in
non-essential luxuries.

The technology of the 20th Century has brought all nations
closer together and thrown many new wrenches into the machinery
of traditional culture and life style. A recent magazine had
a picture of a very primitive tribesman in traditional garb
catching spilled fuel from an airplane to use in his modern
cigarette lighter. This confrontation of the past with the
present is evident in many parts of the world today and makes
it increasingly difficult to determine relative standards of
living.

From the United States to Europe, Asia, and Africa, poverty
and privation dwell in the shadow of luxury and wealth. From
almost every exclusive housing district, one can view the
ghetto or tenement. Thus, the missionary, when considering the
standard of living in any country, must determine just where
he will plan to fit into the society of that country.

A few years ago, the term "going native" was used by missionaries to describe any foreigner who was trying to live in a
grass roofed hut or hide tent. However, going native need not
demand a sacrifice at all. In most countries it would be
rather relaxing and comfortable to "go native" like the *rich*
nationals. In other words, there are rich and poor in every
country, and we can try to identify with either or both of
these groups; and the standard of living of one will be quite
different from the other.

Frequently there will be quite a significant difference in living standard or style between city and rural dwellers. The missionary planning to work in a large metropolitan area will likely find things much less strange or different than a man who chooses to work in a rural area (especially if the missionary came from an urban background in his own country).

It is not the purpose of this section to deal with the pros or cons of any missionary's living standard on the field. As a missionary attempts to identify with a specific sub-culture in a given country, he will have to determine what he should and can do to bring about the greatest amount of identification. However, regardless of how he plans to live (in a primitive hut or exclusive Western style hotel), he will still be facing a culture that is different from his own with respect to general living standards and this difference will effect him regardless of how or where he chooses to live (Nida 1960: 167-169). The man living in the hut, as well as the man in the hotel, will both see the starvation, hunger, crowded conditions and poor sanitation (if, indeed, these do exist) that surround them, and it would be difficult to say which one would be affected the least.

Some missionaries have gone into the field with beautiful ideas of what they feel to be "real down to earth identification" with the people. One family, for example, goes into a village in Africa, Asia, or Latin America, and moves into a local thatched hut. They eat all local foods, prepare the food in the local manner, and suffer the same sores, parasites, and illnesses as the local people. To aid identification (and there is no guarantee that identical living will result in identification), they have "gone native" in the common sense of the word. Though they may feel that they have done their best and thus feel no sense of guilt, they will still suffer from the change that they have made. Their adjustment will be a very real one.

Another family goes "pseudo native" in a similar village situation. They live in a local hut but they shore up their living situation with a gas burner, some canned foods, some chocolate bars, and frequent trips to town where they can relax in more familiar surroundings and recuperate from the past three months in the village. They have frequent respite but must continually make the physical and psychological readjustment to the culture each time they return to the village.

Of course, the third missionary in his typical frame house overlooking the thatched roof village dwellings has his own problems. He may live in a style more familiar to him but this, in itself, may be quite frustrating. There is nothing quite so

unnerving as refrigerators without constant electricity, ice
boxes with no ice, trucks with no spare parts, and radios
without a full complement of tubes. The development of a little
America in another culture may increase the frustrations of
living in that culture rather than ameliorate them.

Therefore, with regard to the *living standard* category on
the CCS, the difference between one's familiar living standard
and the standard of the nation or sub-culture where one plans
to work is significant regardless of how or where he plans to
live when he arrives on the field.

Suggestions for Scaling the CCS

To aid in determining the level of difference as suggested
by the CCS, the following suggestions are made. The base for
measurement will be a middle or upper middle class American
standard of living. This would be a family owning a house full
of the standard gas and electric gadgets; one or two good
cars; recreational equipment; and a home in a neighborhood
where lawns are well tended, houses well kept, and the household members well dressed. (Persons not fitting this standard
should adjust their measurements on the CCS accordingly.)

1. *Exotic:* An urban low income area or isolated village
where there are few if any household gadgets (no electricity,
ice, canned foods, or shopping centers) would be exotic to the
family described above. There might be some significant
differences between living among low class dwellers in a
crowded city where higher class houses and sections are visible
than in living among mud huts in a village that offers nothing
better. But, the fact remains that both situations would
present the missionary with an exotically different environment
regardless of how he chose to live.

2. *Different:* The standard family (above) moving into an
area where there are houses with some gadgets, electricity or
gas, and similar styles of clothing but where the gadgets are
quite inferior to those at home, the electricity is not as
strong nor dependable, automobiles are reserved for the very
wealthy, and where canned foods lack pure food controls, will
find the situation to be different, though not exotic.

Living standards like these are to be found in almost every
high class section of every developing nation in the world.
At first glance, it appears to be similar but after trying it
for a while, the differences become quite noticeable.

3. *Similar:* The American standard of living is one of the
highest in the world so it is certain that wherever the American

goes, he will find that things are not quite the same as he has experienced them at home. The person going from middle class America to middle class Europe may find that the living standard is similar but not identical. The similar level should probably be reserved for those areas that are very much like home because living standard differences seem to have so much impact on people, especially when they move from a higher to a lower standard. Missionaries from those thatched roof huts may be surprised to hear missionaries from France or Germany explaining how difficult it is to adjust to the living standards in Berlin or Paris.

With these three levels as a starting point, the prospective missionary should be able to consider his own standard of living (making allowances for the differences between his own standard and that given above) and the standard of living of the people to whom he is going and determine a measurement of difference. He might even evaluate his own feelings about the way he lives and raise or lower his measurement on the basis of the impact he feels that such a difference will make.

RACE AND COLOR

During the past few years, the American people have been made aware of the problem of racial prejudice. The knowledge has not come easy and there are those who are alarmed at the course that race relations in America have taken. However, one thing is sure, almost all Americans have been forced to face the problem and deal with it in a more or less open manner.

Majority groups have been alerted to the fact that there are *many* minority groups who feel that they are not getting equal treatment or equal rights. Minority groups are facing the fact that prejudice works both ways and that they may be equally prejudiced against each other or against the majority. People on both sides have discovered prejudices that they really did not know they had.

Therefore, the problem of prejudice has changed from one of determining who is prejudiced to determining how to cope with the prejudice that all seem to have. One must decide to ignore it, rationalize it, control it, encourage it, or overcome it, and this decision is especially important for the future missionary because, wherever he goes, his prejudices will go with him. Most important in this respect is the fact that a prejudice against one group of people will likely be projected to another group of people as one moves from place to place. The missionary who was prejudiced against the Blacks in the United States will likely find that he harbors the same feelings against Orientals when he becomes a missionary in Asia.

The problem is compounded by the typical American's misconceptions concerning foreigners. Americans are just beginning to outgrow the provincialism of the pre-revolutionary period when they were dependent upon England and Europe for most quality products. Precision machinery, china, glass, fine furniture, and clothing were imported because America was not able to reproduce the workmanship of the old country.

An appreciation for imported items has continued into the twentieth century. The Swiss watch, German clock, set of English china, or Scandinavian glass will be displayed proudly by the American who knows that there is something special about imported items. And, though these things may be quite well made and worthy of appreciation, there have also been thousands of other items sold from the shelves of the *imported* sections of department and grocery stores that have no claim to value except that they are imported.

Along with this provincial fondness for imports has been a special feeling toward people in or visitors from other countries. American minorities from these same countries have frequently become the victims of intense prejudice but as long as they are in those other countries or recently have come for a visit from those countries, they have been looked upon with a kind of awe.

Note the dark skinned exchange student attending college in the United States. He boldly wears his turban (or she wears a sari) because this is the badge that proclaims, "I am imported, do not treat me like a domestic product." This idea that being a foreigner makes a person somehow better or less subject to our prejudice can be a very serious misunderstanding for a missionary, because it is really an illusion or dream based upon the fact that we tend to idealize the foreigner, with whom we have not had any close contact. However, once that contact is made and we find that he is human, like everyone else, then prejudice is free to rear its ugly head and rearrange our feelings and attitudes.

Since racial prejudice frequently operates near the unconscious level, it reveals itself in subtle ways. For example, the parents of adopted foreign children (when the children were adopted as infants and are completely American) can spot a prejudiced person very quickly. The person will soon ask some or all of the following questions: "What about marriage?", "Does he speak English?", "When he is older, will he go back to his own people?".

One does not have to be an adoptive parent to see these subtle signs of prejudice. At a recent college missions' workshop, one of the featured speakers was Black. Those in charge of the program asked a Black faculty member to make the introduction. Most people thought it was quite the right thing to do except the speaker who alluded to it as a "remarkable coincidence in programming." Again, at a predominately white public school a white teacher was assigned a Black student teacher from a local college. She tried so hard to be casual and do the right thing, and her first action was to take the student down and introduce him to the only Black faculty member in the school.

In both of the above illustrations, people were trying not to be prejudiced, but it slipped out in spite of their efforts. This is not to belittle those efforts but merely to show that race and color do effect people very strongly and the missionary is among those so affected. One does not have to travel far to hear missionaries say things that indicate their prejudices. Rash generalizations such as, "Mexicans always . . . ," "You know how Koreans are . . . ," "Why don't the Sudanese . . . ," or "Over there, the people . . ." are clues to strong racial feelings that frequently surface among missionaries.

Perhaps the most subtle of all clues to those hidden feelings that tend to separate people or reveal the separation that is already there is the *tattle tale they*.* This is the little *they* that creeps into everyone's conversation now and then. *They* are those church leaders who do not do things the way we would, the neighbors who don't keep the neighborhood as neat as we would like, or the local people who leave missionaries frustrated. It is especially common when other colors or races are involved. Rudyard Kipling says it this way:

> Father, Mother and me,
>   Sister and auntie say,
> All the people like us are *we*
>   And everyone else is *they*
> And they live over the sea
>   While we live over the way,
> But, would you believe it...they look upon us
>   As only a sort of *they*?

If it seems somewhat presumptious to attach so much importance to race and color, do not forget that adjustment is a two-way street. Though a missionary may not be overly prejudiced against a people of a different race, there is a strong

---

*Those old enough to recall the fact that certain soaps that failed to get clothing clean left a "tattle tale gray," will understand the significance of this concept.

likelihood that members of a given race may be prejudiced
against him.

Also, color is important because it seems to be the most
distinguishing mark of individual difference. Scientifically,
races are difficult to determine and even color is a very un-
dependable criterion. Kroeber defines only three races in the
world, i.e., caucasian, mongoloid, and negroid (Kroeber 1948),
whereas Coon, et., al., defines a total of thirty (Coon 1950).
(See Figure 13).

Thus, even the experts cannot agree on the exact basis for
distinguishing race. However, for the average individual, the
first and foremost distinguishing characteristic that indicates difference is color (not withstanding that there are
albino Blacks in Africa and sun-blackened whites in California).

Suggestions for Scaling the CCS

In filling out the *race and color* category on the CCS it is
suggested, on the basis of the above discussion, that differences in race or color between the prospective missionary and
the people to whom he is going be used as a criteria for
selecting an appropriate measure.

1. Exotic: Extreme differences in color, for example,
would indicate the selection of the exotic level. A Black
missionary going to a white population or a white missionary
going to a black population would be advised to consider this
difference in race and color as exotic. Of course, this might
be modified somewhat by personal feelings, attitudes, and
background.

2. Different: The so called brown, yellow or mulatto
peoples would comprise an intermediate step between the white
and black extremes. Any relationship between these intermediate colors and either of the extremes would be considered
different, as far as color is concerned, but not exotic.
Again, this type of measurement is based upon very general
understandings and might need extensive modification depending
upon the individual missionary involved.

3. Similar: The similar measure has been reserved for
those missionaries going to people of the same or similar race
and color. Remember that this category is not measuring real
differences between individuals but only the race or color
differences which seem to harbour potential problems of prejudice. The Black missionary to black Africa may develop very
strong negative feelings toward the local black population,
however, this type of prejudice develops in spite of color
similarity and not because of it.

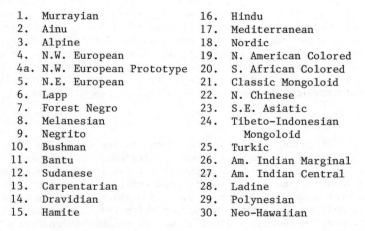

1. Murrayian	16. Hindu
2. Ainu	17. Mediterranean
3. Alpine	18. Nordic
4. N.W. European	19. N. American Colored
4a. N.W. European Prototype	20. S. African Colored
5. N.E. European	21. Classic Mongoloid
6. Lapp	22. N. Chinese
7. Forest Negro	23. S.E. Asiatic
8. Melanesian	24. Tibeto-Indonesian
9. Negrito	Mongoloid
10. Bushman	25. Turkic
11. Bantu	26. Am. Indian Marginal
12. Sudanese	27. Am. Indian Central
13. Carpentarian	28. Ladine
14. Dravidian	29. Polynesian
15. Hamite	30. Neo-Hawaiian

Figure 13. Races of the World.

RELIGION

   Though some who call themselves Christians believe that
Christianity is simply one among many genuine religions, the
typical evangelistic Christian missionary has a goal of
supplanting any non-christian religion that he encounters. He
may respect the moral or ethical principles of Hinduism, Islam,
or Buddhism but believes that salvation comes only through the
Lord and Savior, Jesus Christ.

Since religion is such an intimate part of man and so pro-
foundly affects his culture this attempt to introduce a new
religion will be met with varying amounts of interest, doubt,
skepticism, and resistance by those who already hold their own
religious beliefs. Though no one can predict with absolute
accuracy how a given individual will respond to the hearing
of the gospel there are some valid generalizations that can be
made which will help the missionary by giving him an idea of
what reception he and his message are likely to receive by the
various peoples of the world.

Among the major world religions discussed will be Christianity itself. This is necessary because many of the nations
of the world have already been introduced to one form or another
of Christianity. Thus, when the latest missionary arrives he
will find, not only a culture influenced by some non-christian
religion but also influenced, to some degree, by a form of
Christianity itself. Whether or not he agrees with the
Christian message that preceded him, he must still do his own
work in the shadow or light of that message.

The religions covered in this section in the order that they
are discussed are, (1) Christianity, (2) Hinduism, (3) Buddhism,
(4) Islam, (5) Confucianism, and (6) Animism. The discussion
of each of these religions will also involve a brief mention
of some other religions that are associated by virtue of an
actual relationship, similarity of ideas, or geographic location, but which are so limited in size or influence that a full
discussion was not deemed necessary, i.e., Judaism, Shintoism,
Zoroastrianism, Taoism, Jainism, Sikhism, and Communism.

Christianity

The influence of the various forms of the Christian religion
is widespread in the world today. Missionaries have been
teaching people about Jesus Christ for two thousand years, and
the impact of that teaching is frequently quite evident
wherever a new missionary goes. The missionary may face not
only Animism, Buddhism, and Confucianism but also Presby-
terianism, Methodism, Catholicism, Seventh Day Adventism, and
a host of different Christian denominations.

Each missionary will have to determine his own attitude
toward and relationship with these Christian groups. In Korea,
for example, the Presbyterians, Methodists, Lutherans, Baptists,
etc., usually send their children to one of two English language
mission* schools. Also these missionaries themselves study

---

*The term *mission* is commonly used to designate the private

language at a Presbyterian University. Seventh Day Adventist
missionaries, on the other hand, have established their own
system of educating their children and the Catholics have
developed their own language school. The missionary population
in Korea forms a very distinct sub-culture with its own inter-
denominational "union" church and each new missionary must
determine his relationship to that sub-culture. In Italy the
non-Catholic missionary faces a highly Catholic oriented
society while the missionary to some parts of Latin America
may face a unique mixture of Catholicism and Animism. So, the
various forms of Christianity that have already made their
presence known in the world present the new missionary with a
wide range of challenges. To help understand the specific
challenges that various of these groups might present, the
following classification has been prepared.

1. Catholicism: The Catholic religion may offer the non-
Catholic missionary some of his strongest opposition especially
in those countries where Catholicism is or has been the state
religion. Anytime that the government of a nation is closely
tied to a particular religion, the missionary can expect the
government officials, the national laws, and the citizens to
be rather firmly opposed to any religious change.

The Catholic religion has also been subject to all manner of
syncretic involvement. A recent T.V. film report showed
Southwestern United States Indians performing a traditional
tribal dance which was concluded with a mass inside the local
cathedral. In other places Catholicism has become mixed with
animistic practices (for a discussion of Animism, see page 119)
to the extent that the Christian influence has been all but
lost.

With the dialogue that has lately been established between
Catholic and Protestant leaders, there have developed some new
relationships between the missionaries on the mission field.
Missionaries from these divergent Christian religions may belong
to the same social work organizations, serve on the same local
government committees, and attend the same social functions.

Thus the impact of Catholicism may range from virtual control
in one nation to casual comradeship in another. There may be
an obvious hostility in one population and a friendly acceptance
in the other. The exact influence will depend upon the place,
the time, and the history of Catholicism in that society.

---

schools although they are by no means limited to missionary
children or completely supported by missionary funds.

2. *Old Line Episcopal* Churches:* The Presbyterian,
Episcopalian, Methodist, and Lutheran churches, like the
Catholic church have been able to exercise considerable power
in certain nations of the world, i.e., the Lutherans in
Germany, the Episcopalians in England, and, to a lesser extent,
the Presbyterians in Korea and the Methodists in Korea and
parts of India. Though in the past these forms of Christianity
may not have been quite as militant as Catholicism in their
opposition to other Christian groups, their influence has been
undeniably significant.

Of course, early forms of Christian influence are not always
nor even generally in opposition to the newer forms, but are
none the less significant. For example, McGavran notes that
Jamaican society is composed of upper classes and the masses
and the upper class people are generally Methodists or Presbyterians (McGavran 1970:196-197). This distinction began in
the 1800's when the white estate owners became members of the
Anglican church, the mulattos were converted by Methodists, and
the black slaves were reached by the Baptists. Once this
distinction was made it was impossible to reverse the process
or change it significantly. The Baptists and later the
Disciples who began with the lower classes or masses were
never able to attract any significant portion of the upper
class population.

The Methodists in India and Korea have been closely associated with local politics and have, from time to time, been
criticized for this particular involvement. Once nationalis-
tic feelings arise against a strongly organized Christian
denomination and it is accused of undue involvement in local
politics the whole attitude of the government can be colored
against all Christian groups. Thus the late comer may find
that he must labor under constraints brought on by the activities of those who preceeded him.

Influence may be positive as well as negative and the influence of early efforts to Christianize, more often than not,
have opened doors that favor the new missionary. One may find
that laws have been passed which pave the way for easy entry
into the country, simplified registration procedures for a
religious organization, and protection of personal or church
assets. Unless one has had to face a government that is
strongly resistant or simply unprepared to meet the church's
needs, he cannot fully appreciate the blessing of a way that
has already been smoothed by those who have gone before.

---

*Churches governed by a hierarchy of bishops or presbyters.

3. *Evangelical Churches**. Baptists, Disciples, Nazarenes, and various Pentecostals can be found in almost every country, and the influences that they have had is significant. However, these groups, as a whole, do not exercise as much control over politics and government as those mentioned previously.

The missionary in a given country may have opportunity to join a club or similar organization made up of missionaries from some of the evangelical churches; however, it is doubtful that government officials, customs inspectors, accrediting bureaus, and the like will make things difficult for him because he is not a member of a particular evangelical group.

During the past few years the evangelicals have tended to band together and mutually support one another especially in areas where independent activity is too expensive, i.e., inter-denominational missionary training centers, resource centers, and language schools. These groups have also taken the lead in mission work and many of the latest advances in missions bear the mark of evangelical Christianity (Wagner 1973:11).

Churches in this group, generally speaking, have had less involvement in large scale institutional mission work than some of the episcopal churches. Likewise, many of them are relatively new to some of the mission fields. Thus, they have not developed as obvious and tangible a sub-culture as the episcopals. However, they are there, they have had rich and rewarding experiences, they have good advice to offer, and their influence cannot go unnoticed by the new missionary.

4. *"Commune" Type Churches***: The Mormons, Seventh Day Adventists, Jehovah's Witnesses and Mennonites are examples of this type church. Generally speaking the missionaries with these groups tend to stay with their own fellow missionaries and do not socialize regularly with the missionaries of other churches. They tend to operate their own schools, recreational facilities, scout troops, and printing presses.

Though these groups are seldom large enough to influence entire nations, they sometimes exert tremendous influence on

---

*These are the groups who believe in the inspiration and authority of the Bible, the deity of Christ, the person and work of the Holy Spirit, the centrality of the Church, heaven, and hell. (Wagner 1973:11.)

**These are the people who actually exist in communes or that tend to disassociate themselves from other *Christian* groups to the extent that contact is quite limited.

individual communities. Once a community is predominately
composed of members of one of these churches, it becomes
difficult for a non-member to make much headway in that community especially if he is vocally in favor of a different
religious viewpoint.

Other "commune" type churches are the indigenous Christian
movements that have developed in some countries. In Korea
one can visit Christian Town, a self-sustaining community composed of followers of Elder Park, a type of latter day John
the Baptist. Then there are the followers of another Korean
named Sun Myung Moon. This man's following includes people
all over the world, and he has a sizeable following in the
United States.

The influences of these churches is rather spotty and may
be confined to a single village, province, or region. They
tend to work quietly and unobtrusively (relying on people to
people contacts) and may escape the notice of the new missionary. However, they are on the mission fields of the world,
they may provide a rather rich resource to anyone who will seek
their advice, and from time to time their influence will be
felt by the new missionary.

In Korea, for example, one might purchase Bible School
material from an evangelical book store, buy fresh milk from
the Seventh Day Adventist's dairy, buy sweet rolls from Park's
Christian Town, seek agricultural advice from the Mennonite
agricultural school, and collect statistics on door to door
evangelism from the Mormons.

To review briefly, then, the various Christian churches in
existence today have made their impact upon the world in many
ways. As a new missionary goes out into the mission field,
he will meet, not only the non-Bible religions of the nation
to which he goes but also the influences of Christian missionaries who have preceeded him. The Christian community in a
given location may form a very significant sub-culture with
which he will have to deal, i.e., he must determine whether to
join it or try to avoid it.

The Christian influences can be beneficial, having paved the
way for his ministry or very frustrating, having created negative feelings or attitudes of hostility. The failure to
acknowledge the Christians already in an area can be detrimental to one's own efforts. For example, following World War II,
missionaries from many of the smaller evangelical churches began
doing mission work in areas where previously only the old line
episcopal churches had labored. In some cases the experiences
of the earlier programs had alerted their missionaries to the

importance of planting indigenous churches, avoiding elaborate
financial entanglements with local churches, and learning
language and customs before trying to evaluate the sincerity
of local converts. However, when some of the newer groups
came, they blithely accepted into leadership positions persons
converted through interpreters; put new converts on the mission
payroll as preachers, interpreters, and clerks; and extended
missionary control over their converts from the very beginning.

Today some of these groups are struggling to extract themselves from binding financial obligations, end contractual
agreements with very unsound persons, and work toward true
indigenousness in their fields. Had they taken the time to
ask a few questions, listen to the advice of those who had
already traveled the same road, or even read the literature
produced from the field at the time of their arrival, they
might have saved time, energy, money, and most important of
all, souls.

In other cases the new comers tried to copy the methods of
those who had gone before without careful investigation and
evaluation. In Africa some older missions were able to extract
themselves from unproductive medical and educational programs
by selling their facilities to new mission groups who were
enamored by the programs even though they were not resulting
in any converts to Christ.

For better or for worse there will likely be missionaries
who have preceeded the one who goes out tomorrow. They may
offer him help and encouragement or present him with problems
and frustrations. He can choose to join with them, openly
oppose them, ignore them, or whatever but he must somehow
cope with their presence. To be unaware of the Christian sub-
culture in a given nation is to be robbed of valuable insights
into cultural adjustment and mission methodology.

The CCS should be scored on the basis of the predominant
religion in a given area and then that score somewhat modified
after considering the secondary Christian work that has gone
before. If those who are already on the field will likely
make it easier for the new missionary, then his score on the
CCS might move upward one level. If those already there may
prove a problem, then the score might be lowered slightly.

Judaism: Judaism is, of course, one of the major living
world religions. However, to the Christian, it is the stem or
tree of which Christianity is the flower. Jews can be found in
almost every country in the world and, for the past three decades, have struggled to build a nation of their own in the
middle east.

Some Christian missionaries work exclusively among the Jews in America, Europe, or Israel. The number of Christian missionaries to the Jews is as small as the Jews' resistance to Christianity is firm. For this reason Judaism will be touched only very lightly in this section on Christianity.

By the end of the 5th century A.D., the Jews, in spite of strong persecution, had compiled a massive religious work called the Talmud. This collection represents an exhaustive and authoritative guide to orthodox Jewish practice and is still used today. Therefore, the Jew of the past fifteen hundred years has not been guided solely by the Old Testament and the Christian wishing to learn about Judaism must study from the modern standpoint and not try to rely on his knowledge of Biblical Judaism.

The persecution of the Jews has been continuous, and it was not until the 19th century that they were granted general equality in most nations of the world. It has only been during the past 150 years that Jewish doctors, lawyers, politicians, professors, and scientists have poured forth into the communal life of Europe, and the result of this newfound freedom and acceptance has had a profound effect upon Judaism itself.

The educated Jews in a modern world sought to change or rejuvenate Judaism and in 1843 declared that the Talmud was not authoritive, no Messiah was expected nor wanted, etc., and as might have been expected these Reform Jews were bitterly challenged by their Orthodox brethren. At the present time the Reform is strongest in the United States, having been successfully halted or modified by Orthodoxy in other nations (Noss 1961:550).

Persecution of the Jews did not cease in the 19th century but continued to plague the Jews from time to time in every decade and in every country. This continual persecution led to a rising nationalism that ultimately resulted in the establishment of the Jewish state by the United Nations in 1947.

Recently there has been a renewed interest in Christianity on the part of numerous Jews; however, the extremely strong Jewish nationalism reenforced by persecution from many sources has made the Jew extremely hesitant to accept Christianity with its traditional Gentile cultural trappings. Therefore, there is an attempt being made to establish or develop Messianic Synagogues where the converted Jew can worship God through Christ the Messiah in a cultural milieu that does not reflect undue Gentile influence (see Sobel 1974:388 pp.; Goble 1975). Since the terms *Christ* and *Messiah* are synonomous and since both the terms *church* (ekklesia) and *synagogue* originally meant assembly, a Messianic synagogue is just a church or assembly of Christ (or Christians).

Hinduism

Hinduism is an ancient religion that has given birth to many other religions including Jainism, Buddhism, and Sikhism (see Jainism, p. 108; Buddhism, p. 109; and Sikhism, p. 108). Hinduism is almost exclusively confined to India because in its orthodox form it is not a missionary religion, natural birth being the only avenue into membership (Cattell 1967:189).

A brief discussion is quite difficult because, like other religions including Christianity, there are many variations, sects, and doctrines. Hinduism is very tolerant of any religious belief and has absorbed many ideas from many different religions; however, there are a few beliefs generally accepted by most Hindus.

1. Caste: Caste is perhaps one of the most obvious features of Hinduism and has also brought Hinduism its greatest public criticism. There are four main historic castes: Brahmins, the priests and intellectuals; Kshatriyas, the rulers and warriors; Vaisyas, the farmers and artisans; and Sudras, the servants (Hume 1959:19-20). These are, in turn subdivided into two or three thousand sub-castes.

Hinduism allows for great latitude in belief, ranging from monotheism to polytheism, as long as caste is not violated. Each caste or sub-caste has its own hereditary occupation, prohibitions against intermarriage and interdining, and other restrictions. If one should violently break caste rules, he can be temporarily placed outside the caste system at which time he would become an *outcaste*. In time, however, he can be reinstated if he follows a certain pattern of repentance.

Hindus have been strongly criticized for their infamous treatment of permanent *outcastes* who were also *achut* or untouchable. These could never move into the caste system and become true members of society. In modern times Indian law has outlawed "untouchability" though it still exists in practice.

2. Idol and spirit worship: A second common feature of modern Hinduism is the worship of idols and all manner of popular gods (Noss 1961:257). Although, philosophically, the Hindu accepts the idea of *Brahma*, an all inclusive being or spirit, he still worships thousands of gods or spirits much in the same manner as an animist (see page 119).

A study of Hinduism may be frustrating to the student because there is such disparity between the deepest religious
thought of the priests or philosophers and the common people
of India. Some of the former hold lofty though conflicting
or vague ideals of human worth and morality while the latter
are content to dwell in primitive superstition and idolatry.

   3. Reincarnation and Karma: Samsara (reincarnation or
transmigration of the soul) has long been a part of Hindu
thought. When a man dies, his soul does not go to some eternal
heaven or hell (except in the case of becoming one with Brahma)
but is reborn in another form as a member of the same caste,
higher caste, lower caste, animal, insect, or even vegetable.
With the exception of becoming one with Brahma this rebirth
continues endlessly.

   Of course, as man considers his present state and the state
or caste of those about him, he wishes to determine the direction of his re-birth. He would rather his soul entered the
womb of a Brahmin than the womb of a dog so he must try and
influence his reincarnation. To do this he must deal with
Karma (deeds or works).

   Roughly speaking a man's level of re-birth will depend upon
the balance between his good and evil deeds throughout life.
He must not only suffer the results of his sin in this life
but also be bent by those sins toward a lower re-birth in the
next life. Sometimes the re-birth is determined successively
in advance. A Brahmin who steals gold from another Brahmin
must pass 1,000 times through the bodies of spiders, snakes
and lizards (Noss 1961:136).

   Karma is impersonal and objective. It exists as a law which
will determine each man's future. The only way of overcoming
the harsh reality and relentless omniscience of the law of
Karma is through the attainment of oneness with Brahma. The
holy men who attempt to make their way to this oneness are the
yogis, sannyasis, and sadhu. Yoga is practiced to attain to
the other two levels. And the ascetics or sannyasis look to
ultimate attainment when they will become sadhu, persons of
great sanctity.

   Anyone familiar with the literature on Hinduism will be
quite well aware of the deficiencies of such a brief glimpse
into this highly complex religion. The surface has hardly been
scratched and only the most general and popular aspects of
Hinduism has been its acceptance of *all* religious teaching.
One religion is really no better, nor worse, than another and
the Hindu would be happy if every man would be satisfied with
the religion of his birth.

Thus, during the latter half of the 19th century Christianity was preached in India and millions of the oppressed lower castes or outcastes accepted the new way with its help and hope; however, as waves of nationalism have swept over India during the past half century, there has been a serious slowdown in the conversion rate.

To meet the challenge of more evangelistic religions like Islam and Christianity, several new forms of Hinduism have evolved. Some have tried to reform the caste system so that its obvious social evils could be eliminated, others have sought to actively win back those who embraced Christianity, and there are, in the United States today, numerous centers of Hinduism where the superiority of Hinduism is proclaimed.

Also, after receiving her freedom from foreign control following World War II, India began restricting the foreign missionary population in India. Today a missionary from the United States cannot directly enter India as a missionary. Thus, in spite of the basic liberalism of Hinduism, much of the Hindu population of the world is off limits to the new missionary.

Not all Hindus are in India, however, and a missionary to other areas may find large Hindu populations. While visiting a church in Malaysia the guest noted that the membership seemed to consist of Chinese and Indians. He asked about the absence of Malays and was informed that preaching was limited by the government to these two minority groups. The missionary who could not preach to the Malays who are Muslims had established churches among the Chinese and Indians; the latter, for the most part, were Hindus prior to accepting Christianity.

From this brief glimpse of Hinduism it can be concluded that Hinduism is different from Christianity especially in that the common people worship all manner of idols, gods, and spirits much in the same way that the animists do. Hinduism is somewhat resistant to Christianity through the laws of India which limit the number of Christian missionaries. However, orthodox Hinduism is not opposed to any religion and thus is open to the Christian message. Therefore, it is suggested that the person going to an area where there are many Hindus should mark the *different* level on the CCS.*

---

*This is a very arbitrarily selected level. Hinduism is so different from Christianity that the *very different* or *exotic* levels could have been chosen. However, due to the receptivity of the Hindu it seems expedient to leave the last four categories (from different to exotic) for those other religions which are not only different but also resistant and even hostile.

Jainism. A little known religion that grew out of Hinduism
five or six hundred years before Christ, Jainism has never
flourished anywhere except in India where its origin is traced
to Mahavira the Venerable one.* Mahavira rejected the evils
of caste, all animal sacrifice, the concept of a supreme deity,
and the exclusiveness of the Brahmins. He spent 12 years
wandering about in a search for nirvana.**

The stories of Mahavira's twelve years of wandering are
filled with incredible tales of personal self control and
discipline. He would destroy no living thing and took great
pains to sweep insects away from the path before stepping down
with his foot. People are said to have beaten, pierced, and
burned him in futile attempts to interrupt his meditations.
Finally in the thirteenth year he reached that state where
Karma was overcome and all future re-births unnecessary. He
was thus a victor and the *Jains* are those people who still
strive to become *Jinas* (victors).

Today's followers of Jainism are few and are noted because
they are strict vegetarians. They know that vegetables also
have life and thus the greatest good is to abstain from eating
until death. The Jains can appreciate the beautitudes of
Matthew 5 but are opposed to the Christian concept of a saving
God and are rarely converted to Christianity.

Sikhism. In the 16th century A.D. the Muslim influence in
India was quite strong and complacent Hinduism seemed to be no
match for the more militant Islamic religion. One Guru
(teacher), Nanak, incorporating some of the best Islamic beliefs into his own Hinduism, developed a new religion that
has since defied all attempts to turn it back into the Hindu
fold.

The Sikhs have always been confined to the Punjab in Northwest India and did not give up their fight to become an independent state until quite recently. In 1947 when India became
self-governing and was partitioned into two separate nations
(India and Pakistan), the Sikhs lost their most fertile lands
to Pakistan. Since that time even the most optimistic Sikh
leaders have quit talking of separate statehood.

---

*According to the Jains, Mahavira was merely a reformer and
Jainism was in existence long before Hinduism.

**Nirvana is the state of oneness with the supreme being.
It is the closest thing to heaven that Hinduism or its offshoots
consider.

Quite early in their history the Sikhs became a strong military force and seem to have had greater political influence in India than religious influence. Sikhs are recognized by five distinguishing marks: uncut hair, a comb, shorts, an iron bangle, and a sword. They also abstain from tobacco, intoxicants, meat (unless decapitated by a single blow), idolatry, caste, Hindu pilgrimages, etc. (Voss 1967:282).

Sikhs are still the backbone of the Army of India although the leaders, having given up hope for political gains, have turned more toward the religious aspect of Sikhism. This relatively small religion is still alive but on the decline and some believe that it will soon fade completely away.

Buddhism

Although actually an outgrowth of Hinduism, Buddhism has come to be such an important world religion that it demands an equal place alongside Hinduism. It began as a reaction to the misery and suffering found in the Hindu world of 500 B.C., and in its early form had no deity, worship, nor prayer. It was only after the passing of two or three hundred years that the founder Siddhartha Gautama*, was deified and many of the aspects of a real religion added.

Born to wealth, Gautama lived a life of luxury for twenty-nine years then became an ascetic for a half dozen more years. At the end of this time he concluded that extreme wealth as well as extreme poverty were both delusions and he gave them up as avenues for seeking the answers to life. Under the Bo Tree** he finally received enlightenment and then spent the next forty-five years teaching his disciples.

Gautama realized that the real world problem was desire. He felt that the extremes of lust and self-mortification must be avoided and the Middle Path accepted. This Middle Path, he concluded, would lead to insight, wisdom, calmness, knowledge, enlightenment, and Nirvana (Noss 1961:163).

Buddhism was not built upon a belief in a supreme being but, like Jainism, looks to man as the source of his own enlightenment. The law of Karma is retained from Hinduism although the system of caste has been rejected. Transmigration is accepted although there is some confusion as to whether or not man has

---

*The name Buddha is an honorific title meaning *the Enlightened one.*

**Maha Budhi Tree or tree of wisdom.

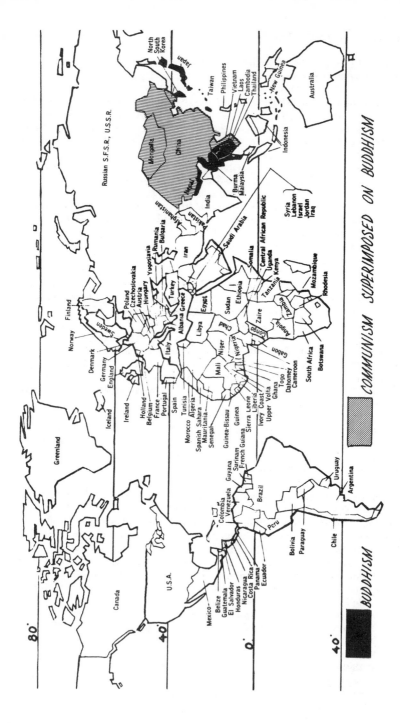

Figure 14.   Areas Influenced by Buddhism and Now
             Overshadowed by Communism.

a soul. Finally, like Jainism, Buddhism rejects the sacrifices of Hinduism and protects all animal life.

Unlike Hinduism, Jainism, and Sikhism, Buddhism moved out of India as missionaries carried this new religion to Syria, Egypt, Cyrene, Greece, and Ceylon (Noss 1961:185) in the latter half of the 3rd century B.C. After this, Burma, Siam (Thailand) and Cambodia accepted Buddhism. Several hundred years later, in the 4th century A.D., Buddhism moved to China, Korea, and Japan, and in the 7th century to Tibet and Mongolia.

Strangely enough, Buddhism all but ceased to exist in India and has found its permanent home in Southeast Asia. Buddhism reached a peak in Asia in the 8th century but had some setbacks in the North during the 15th and 16th centuries and began a decline that has still not been completely reversed in China and Korea today.

Buddhism, like Hinduism, has differing teachings and philosophies and broad generalizations are dangerous. For the Christian missionary it should be noted that the Buddhists of Thailand are extremely powerful and have pretty firm control of the political as well as the religious thinking of the masses. The visitor to Thailand will not fail to note the yellow garbed monks who, at times, literally fill the streets. Christian missionaries are permitted in Thailand but the resistance to the Gospel is great.

In Japan a militant Buddhism has developed as a part of a general renaissance of Buddhism that had its beginning in the early 50's; however, in Korea Buddhism is quiescent and monks tend to confine themselves to their quiet mountain retreats or temples. Thus, the impact of Buddhism on the Christian missionary will depend largely on the country where he goes.

On the basis of difference and resistance, the religion category of the CCS should probably be marked at the *very different* level. If the Buddhism involved is very resistant to the presence of Christian missionaries that mark could be lowered one level. On the other hand where Buddhism is tolerant of the Christian missionary, the mark could be moved upward one level.

Islam

Islam, like Christianity, has its personal founder (Mohammed), a belief in one God (Allah), and a universal appeal. It began later than Christianity but now ranks second to Christianity in terms of numbers and growth (Hume 1959:221-222).

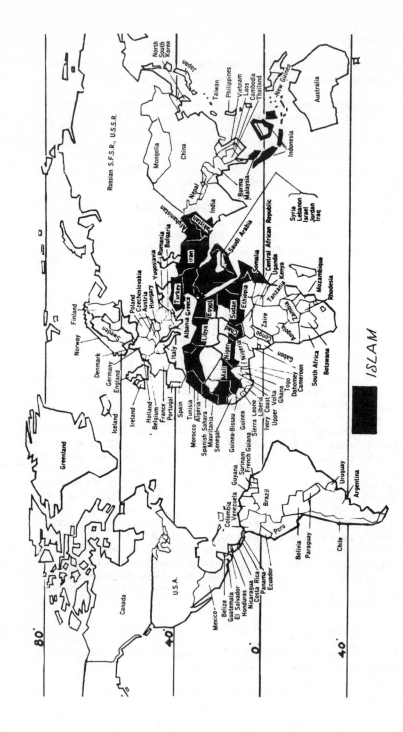

Figure 15. Areas With Predominant Islamic Influence.

Islam means *submission* and a Muslim (or Moslem) means *one who submits*. This idea of submission to rule has resulted in a tendency for Muslims to form autocratic forms of government. The largest Muslim state is Pakistan which demanded and received autonomy from India in 1954. Also a very strong nationalist spirit has developed in other predominately Muslim nations of Southeast Asia (Malaysia, Indonesia and Singapore) as well as in North Africa (north of a line running from Mauritania to Somalia) and Asia Minor (from Turkey to Pakistan and south through the Arabian peninsula).

The strong nationalism of Islam is reinforced by an important prayer schedule that is central to the life of every Muslim. Added to this is the freedom to practice polygamy and wage war. The early Muslim conquests were made by sword and fire rather than by more gentle missionary efforts. Even today Islam is not only militant in its missionary zeal but strikes mortal fear into the hearts of those who come under its control.

In some Southeast Asian and African countries where Islam predominates it is almost impossible for the Christian missionary to make a convert. In the first place he may be denied entry to the country, given a visa limited to a very short period of time, or forbidden to preach the gospel to a local citizen unless the citizen initiates the dialogue; secondly the people who are converted may come under such harsh sanctions by their extended family members, local pressure groups, and the society at large that they generally revert to Islam out of desperation. Gailyn Van Rheenen, missionary in Africa, tells of the fantastic power of a Muslim president in a predominately non-Muslim nation (Van Rheenen 1976:119).

Thus, Islam presents the Christian missionary with some conflicting insights. Basically there are some strong similarities between Christianity and Islam but these similarities are almost hidden by the obvious differences and hostility that is also present. Polygamy, warfare, and intense nationalism tend to establish a barrier between Islam and Christianity that demands the selection of exotic as a measure of difference on the CCS.

Zoroastrianism. Also out of the Middle East comes a religion that has had considerable influence on religious thought but which has never had the far reaching appeal of Islam. The religion of the early Persian kings whose names are found in the Bible (Cyrus, Artaxerxes and Darius), was built upon the concept of one God (although polytheism crept in later), a devil (some critics contend that the Christian concept of Satan or the devil was learned by the Jews while they were in captivity under the Persians), an array of good and evil spirits (similar to angels and demons of the New Testament), and other ideas that are quite familiar to the Christian.

It may have been Zoroastrians who came from the East, followed the star, and found Christ in Bethlehem; however, in spite of the influence of Zoroaster upon the people of Persia and the closeness of these people to the truth as revealed in the Bible, the influence of Islam all but obliterated Zoroastrianism and only a very small remnant can be found today. These are for the most part the Parsis (the people from Persia) who are now living in India.

Confucianism

Confucianism has long been considered the religion of China. Born in the province of Shantung, China, in 551 B.C., Confucius became a teacher and founded his own school. He was successful as a teacher and was finally appointed to a government position when he was 51 years old. In his later life he failed in his political ambitions and devoted himself to writing until he died at age 72.

Confucius discouraged any belief in a supreme being, a personal God, divine supervision over the world, or prayer (Hume 1959:111). He taught an ethical system based upon social propriety. His rule was that we should not do unto others what we do not want done to ourselves. This rule is especially important in five relationships: (1) ruler and subject, (2) father and son, (3) husband and wife, (4) elder brother and younger, and (5) friend and friend.

Though Confucianism had to violate some of its founder's basic beliefs (especially his belief that there was no God) before it could function as a religion it managed to continue with Confucian morality and ethics even while adding the worship of a supreme being. The ethical teachings, however, have had greater worldwide influence than the worship and ceremony.

In Asia, the ethics of Confucius continue to permeate the thinking of the people in spite of the presence of Buddhism, Communism,* and a host of lesser religions. In Asia it is difficult to locate groups of people worshiping at a Confucian shrine or temple but the very manner in which one person treats another will reveal Confucian ethics.

---

*Communism has discouraged the religious forms of Confucianism and no one knows what the future holds for the Chinese with respect to these two philosophies or religions. See page 117.

For example, in Korea, the five relationships (see above) are still extremely important. Politics are still influenced by the Confucian concept of a subject's rightful relationship to his ruler (even when that ruler is now an elected official). Family relationships are extremely important and the Western idea that when a man marries a wife they both leave father and mother and start a new home is foreign to the Asian who still clings to his Confucian ethic that a son always remains obedient and submissive to his father.

Americans are sometimes confused by the many names that Asians have for relatives. In America, a male sibling is a *brother* and a female sibling is a *sister;* girls have sisters and boys have sisters, or girls have brothers and brothers have brothers; however, in Korea it is all much more complicated. A boy's older brother is called *hyung,* his younger brother is called *dongseang,* and his older sister *nuni;* and a girl's older brother is called a *opah* and her older sister an *uni.* Thus a distinction is made on the basis of the sex of the subject him/her self as well as on the sex of the sibling and the *ages* of the siblings. It is the Confucian emphasis on the importance of age that calls for this complicated kinship system.

In Korea, Japan, and other Asian countries Confucianism has lost its strong religious influence. In China, Communism has attempted to replace the philosophy and thinking of the masses and no one knows just how much Confucianist thought remains. Confucianism might well be dropped from the list of world religions except for the fact that it has left such a solid imprint on the ethics and mores of so many people.

The missionary going into Asia would do well to study Confucianism to familiarize himself with the culture of the people. As a religion it will likely be overshadowed by Buddhism, Communism, or Animism; therefore, no levels will be suggested for the CCS *religion* category.

Taoism. Taoism may be as old as Buddhism although the founder, Lao-Tze, is thought by some to be a mythical rather than real person. He is dated from four to six hundred B.C. and seems to have been more of a philosopher than a man establishing a religion. There are stories of his meeting with Confucius and the two discussing their ideas together but this cannot be proven. *Tao* means *way* and Taoism is the way to the divine being. In contrast to Confucianism which placed great stress on doing the right thing and suffering for any mistakes, Lao-Tze taught that evil must be repaid by good.

Taoism has never been the leading religion in China and for the past one thousand years has been deteriorating and some scholars already consider it a dead religion. In its later forms the high ideals were lost and polytheism, superstition, and magic became central to Taoist worship.

Shinto. Shinto has long been the national religion of Japan. *Shin* means spirit and *to* (like the Tao of Taosim) means *way* so Shinto is literally the "way of the Spirits or Gods." According to Shinto tradition this religion dates back almost as early as Buddhism and Taoism but modern scholars are not so sure that it is really that old.

According to Shinto beliefs Japan is the holy land and the emperor or Mikado is a direct descendant of the Sun-goddess in heaven. The Japanese flag with the sun symbol illustrates the impact of Shintoism on the culture of Japan. Strangely enough, during the history of Japan, Shinto has been very tolerant of other religions, especially Buddhism, Confucianism, and Taoism. It was not until the last few years that Shinto sought to monopolize the religious thinking of the people of Japan.

During the period just prior to World War II the Japanese government forced all citizens to attend certain Shinto ceremonies as a part of the civic duty of its citizens even though religious freedom was legally permitted. In this manner the government hoped to solidify the feelings of religious nationalism that have always been an important factor in Japanese life. At this time Shinto was also taken to Korea, Manchuria, and China as the Japanese assumed military control of each of these lands.

Following World War II Shinto was rejected by the non-Japanese to whom it represented the hated Japanese conquerors and was forced into the background. To some extent the same thing happened in Japan when it was no longer forced upon the people by law. Today, Shintoism is still practiced in Japan although it shares Japan with Buddhism, Confucianism, and other less influential religions (including Christianity).

Shinto involves nature-worship, Emperor-worship, personal purity and patriotism. There seems to be a supreme deity concept but also tens of thousands of lesser deities. Since World War II there has been much mixing (syncretism) involving Shintoism, Buddhism, and Christianity, as Shinto has again begun to grow and prosper in its own nation.

Communism: Due to the vast amount of material available on Communism it seems unnecessary to devote much space to a discussion of the nature of Communism, the attitude of Communists toward Christianity, or the place of Communism among the world's religions. With its God (Marx), prophet (Engels), and shrine (the tombs of these two in Moscow), Communism has all the elements of a true religion. Also, since it is so violently opposed to Christianity it behooves the Christian to study it very carefully.

Not only is Communism a world religion but it is also in the forefront of the battle for the hearts and minds of the people of the world. Nowhere is this more obvious than in those areas of the world where developing nations with animistic religious backgrounds are being modernized by technology and robbed of the culture that gave meaning to their religion. Most of these nations will turn away from the religions of their forefathers and embrace Islam, Communism, or Christianity, sometime during the next twenty-five years. To Christians the victory of Communism in any area may have two meanings: (1) With the Communists in control there is little hope for any large scale Christian evangelistic effort, and (2) if the population was resistant to Christianity in the first place, perhaps when it becomes disillusioned with Communism in the future it will be ready to turn to Christianity. There may be some validity to the second point but it also has a bit of the odor of rationalization.

Already Communism controls a majority of the people of the world and much of what has already been said concerning the religions of Asia and the Middle East must be modified by the presence of Communism in so many of those countries. No one really knows the fate of Buddhism, Confucianism, and Taoism because so much of China is completely under the control of Communism.

Perhaps the most important thing that the missionary to a Communist country needs to know is how to carry on his ministry without causing undue trouble for the converts who continue to live in the Communist country. Preaching, for example, behind the Iron Curtain is no lark to be taken for the sake of instant adventure. The Western preacher can get a permit to enter one of the Iron Curtain nations, drive across in his own car, visit a convert for a few days, and then dash home with a story about how he outwitted the Communists. The problem is that unless he really knew his business he likely left behind a Christian who is now under constant surveillance by the secret police.

Americans should be especially careful because they tend to feel rather superior to other persons in other cultures anyway. They tend to rely quite heavily upon their individual rights and behave pretty much as they please wherever they are. In most nations of the world such behavior is expected of the

American and is reasonably well tolerated; however, in a
Communist country the American visitor will likely be accepted
as a spy and afforded all the attention usually associated with
that profession. In spite of what has been written, this is
very difficult for the American to comprehend.

Those slipping into Communist countries had better look and
act like tourists at all times. A husband and wife with children is much more convincing than a single man with a trunk
full of literature. Those who are now working behind the Iron
Curtain advise all prospective missionaries to Communist
countries to read the latest works by Solzhenitsyn, Dolgun, and
Kuznetsov (Solzhenitsyn 1974; Dolgun 1975; and Kuznetsov 1975).
The next step is to contact someone who has worked in the area
long enough to have developed an understanding for the situation.

First of all, *know the language* of the people you are going
to visit. Countries behind the Iron Curtain are not known for
their high receptivity and people are not likely to rush out and
embrace a religion that is disliked by their government. There
will need to be a real heart level communication that cannot be
expected when an unfamiliar language is used. Second, learn
as much about the country as possible and become a good tourist.
If the local inn keeper knows that it usually takes three days
to visit all the sights in her town, she will not likely contact
the police and give them your name unless you spend four or five
days there.

Third, be cautious of driving up to a Christian's home in a
car with, for example, a Texas license plate. Fourth, and this
really upsets the Christians behind the Iron Curtain, do not
use the Communist country ministry as a means of getting yourself undue publicity back home. Written reports, lectures,
and books may all be valid tools for communicating the truth
concerning a certain ministry to one's brothers but they can
also be misused to the sorrow of the people behind the curtain
who cannot or do not want to leave their homeland.

A strong name calling denunciation of some Communist country
by an American, for example, can add fuel to the fires that are
already trying to stop the issue of visas to Americans. The
same is true of other areas of the world. As much as a missionary might want to blast a consulate or nation through the news
media or private publications, such measures can actually limit
the preaching of the gospel in some countries.

There are differences of opinion concerning the methods that
Christians should use to get the word of God spread in difficult
fields. But however one chooses to do it, the point is that it

is a very serious business. Of course, the teaching of the gospel is always a serious business but the results of an error while behind the Iron Curtain might be much more immediate and painful than a similar error in a friendly country.

For all the talk of coexistence and friendship with the Communist block, the fact remains that Communism is opposed to Christianity and the Christian missionary is going to face a hostile government any time he tries to present the gospel to a Communist nation. On the religious category of the CCS exotic is recommended as the level of difference between a Christian missionary and a Communist society.

Animism

To some it may be surprising to see Animism* listed alongside the great world religions; however, to today's prospective missionary it is a very practical arrangement because of all the religions mentioned thus far Animism may be the most important. A look at the map on page 120 will reveal that Animists can be found in every part of the world (the United States, Latin America, Africa, Russia, India, Asia, and Oceania).

Actually, Animism is used as a single name for all forms of worship that in the past have been referred to as primitive or tribal. This is not one single religion with a specific set of literature, national home, formal organization, nor stated doctrine. Rather, it is a catch-all for those many forms of religion that involve belief in such things as *mana* (the in-dwelling power of an object, animal, or person), *magic* (words and actions that control the world), *tabu* (prohibitions of various kinds), *ancestor-worship*, and *totems* (animals with which a clan has a close relationship).

To control the mana or spirits the Animist relies on magic which may operate through sacrifice or fetishes. The profes-sional worker of magic is the witch-doctor or shaman who makes it his business to know as much as possible about the habits, desires, weaknesses, and habitats of the spirits.

Among the many spirits and forces in the world are those that belong to the dead. These generally wander about the place where the dead reside and must be mollified along with other spirits. Thus ancestor worship goes hand in hand with animal and spirit worship.

---

*For a more complete discussion of Animism see Nida and Smalley 1974.

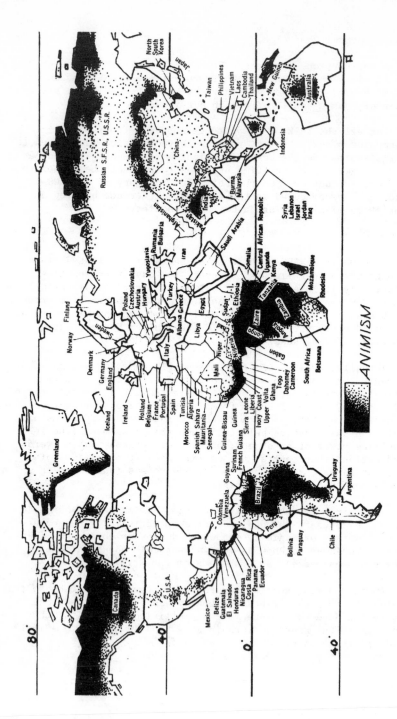

Figure 16. Areas Where Animism Flourishes.

At any given time a New Mexico Indian may dance with an ear
of corn in his hand as he attempts to insure a good harvest
while a school girl in Korea purchases a small charm from a
shaman so that she will pass her exams. Meanwhile, in Africa,
a witch-doctor gazes through the eyes of a grotesque mask as he
watches for signs of recovery in a sickroom while in India a
Hindu* adds some pieces of glass to a village shrine to insure
that her next son will be born strong and healthy.

These people all have different methods of controlling the
forces in the world around them and they all suffer from the
same haunting fears that are central to Animism. The spirits
are evil and not to be worshipped the way Christians worship
God nor respected the way Confucianists respect Confucius.
The spirit must be outwitted, appeased, or somehow temporarily
subdued until the present impending evil is passed, and then
there will be new evils and renewed attempts to escape.

Missionaries have discovered that the Animistic tribes and
peoples are frequently fertile soil for the sowing of the gospel. The reasons for this fertility, from an anthropological
viewpoint, may be the encroachment of civilization and technology on hitherto isolated areas. Old ways cannot deal with the
sudden changes and people are left with gaps in their ability
to cope.

Also, Christianity is easily accepted by the Animists at
least as far as God, Christ, the Holy Spirit, Satan, angels,
and evil spirits are concerned. He is already aware of the evil
spirits and frequently has, as a part of his vocabulary, some
name for the supreme diety.

In Korea the masses of people in the rural areas are Animists. Yet they have a fairly sophisticated concept of God
whom they refer to as *hananim*. *Hana* means one and *nim* is an
honorific suffix. Thus this monotheistic concept is labeled
by the name *one*. When a Christian missionary speaks of
hananim the people understand what he is saying and although
they may never have considered worshipping *hananim* before they
are quite willing to learn of this good super-spirit or God who
can control the evil spirits for them.

As Christianity vies with Islam and Communism for control
of the minds and hearts of men the Animistic peoples of the

---

*The common people of India may consider themselves Hindus
but still practice a kind of Animistic worship. See page 105ff.

world become the prize. The third world nations* are developing modern technologies, educational systems, and new philosophies. They are turning away from the old paths and embracing
Islam, Communism, Christianity, or some other religion.

The whole continent of Africa is an Animistic stronghold
that will soon capitulate to the Muslins who are moving in
from the North, the Christians who have a firm foothold in
South Africa, or to the Communists who are gathering strength
every year. The missionary who goes to any of the Animistic
peoples must be aware of their general philosophy and have a
specific understanding of local beliefs and customs.

Animism is, of course, different from Christianity but
generally Animists do not oppose the preaching of the gospel.
They may be secure in their tribal religion and ignore the
gospel message but they seldom refuse to hear it or make it
difficult for the missionary. Thus the *different* level on the
CCS might be best for a missionary comparing his own religious
background with an Animist.

To summarize briefly, what has been said concerning religion,
when the Christian goes into the world with the gospel of
Jesus Christ, he believes that he carries the only message by
which man must be saved. Thus, it is his desire to see all men
everywhere turn from their false religions and accept the one
true communication from God to man, Christianity. For this
reason, the Christian is a threat to the status-quo of any non-
Christian nation and an enemy to those who believe strongly
that their religion is superior.

Therefore, the Christian missionary will find other religions not only different in the things that they teach but also
resistant to some degree. Thus the prospective missionary is
advised to study the religion of the people to whom he is going
and record a proper level of difference on the religious category of the CCS.

SANITATION AND HEALTH

"Don't drink the water!" has become the motto of the American tourist. Even the American military stationed on foreign
soil issues frequent warnings against eating "local" foods and

---

*A label used by the backward but developing nations of the
world to refer to themselves. In the international struggle
for political power these smaller nations have already determined that they have the power to swing the balance. A similar
truth exists with regard to religion.

drinking "local" water. *Montezuma's revenge, Egyptian tummy,* or just *the bug* are common names used by Americans abroad to indicate the presence of diarrhea which is assumed to be caused by contaminated food or water.

The prospective missionary may have heard all manner of stories about the health and sanitation problems of the place to which he is going; however, he should be cautious in determining what he will actually find. Americans are hypersensitive where health and sanitation are concerned, and their views of these areas can be easily distorted.

Americans are especially concerned with the outward appearance of cleanliness in eating places and hospitals. Oblivious to environmental pollution, the American breathes noxious smog daily but recoils at a lunch counter that is not spotlessly clean. Hospitals, clinics, and health centers must be chrome plated and sparkling clean before the American will relax with a feeling that all is sterile and well.

Health can become such a fetish that the American missionary only trusts American doctors and will drive for miles to visit a clinic operated by a fellow countryman. This compulsion to have American medical help may be so great that qualified local medical help is completely ignored.

With all due respect to American doctors, it is still true that some are better than others, and the name one selects from a telephone book when he moves into a new town may belong to the M.D. who was tops in one of the best medical schools or to the M.D. who was last in his class at one of the little known schools. Selection of a doctor is generally a very arbitrary matter for the average American at home but when he gets overseas, he suddenly becomes highly selective.

The real problem is not in this sudden turn toward critical evaluation of doctors but the lack of judgment that is used in making the evaluation. The American missionary might be a very ordinary doctor whereas the local clinic doctor may have graduated from the medical school of his own country, passed rigid exams to enter medical school abroad (Germany perhaps, or America), graduated with honors and passed the last five years as a chief resident in the local medical school hospital. Yet, the missionary patient may refuse to be examined by the local doctor and turn instead to the medical missionary. Of course, there is nothing wrong with going to the American doctor but the illustration shows how unscientific and prejudicial one's decisions can be where health and sanitation are concerned.

On the other extreme are those rash individuals who do not seem to be at all concerned about health and sanitation. These are those adventurers who will go everywhere and eat everything. Since the human body is capable of absorbing a great deal more punishment than most people realize, these individuals frequently live to ripe old ages with seemingly no ill effects from their daring; however, there are others who have suffered and even died because they did not take even moderate precautions.

One enthusiastic missionary to Southeast Asia has his own pet theory concerning sanitation. "It is all in the mind and attitude," he says. His theory is that if you throw your shoulders back, think positively, and refuse to get sick, you can eat the foods sold by the dirtiest vendor and never worry about illnesses. Interestingly enough, this man is still going strong after spending many years eating and drinking almost everything; however, another hardy athletic type Christian with this same theory and behavior made a single trip through Asia and has never been able to overcome the amoebic dysentery which he contracted. One can become infected right in his own hometown, U.S.A., but no doubt the odds are greater as one moves into more primitive or crowded areas.

Missionaries in Korea, for example, usually exercise a little special caution by boiling drinking water and peeling vegetables in an attempt to control hepatitis and other diseases. They also use mosquito netting to avoid contact with mosquitos carrying encephalitis; however, during the late 60's and 70's, there were several outbreaks of both of these diseases in America, and missionaries in Korea began to be worried about their family members back home. But illness in one's own culture does not strike the same fear in people's hearts as that same illness would when one is in a foreign country.

The sponsoring eldership or prospective missionary should exercise caution in evaluating the health and sanitation situation of another country. They should be very critical of reports or advice from casual visitors to that country or even long time foreign residents. The sensitivity of the American can completely blind him to the reality that may present itself.

One missionary, upon his arrival in an Eastern nation, saw some children running about with butterfly nets. When he asked what they were doing, some of the older missionary residents informed him that the children caught and ate all manner of bugs and insects. This rather apalling idea stayed with that missionary until his language study carried him into fourth grade readers. There he discovered that all children of this nation studied zoology. One of their yearly projects was to catch and mount specimens of the many local insects and spiders.

The people of this nation did eat locusts (although some have
spent many years there and never had locusts served to them),
and perhaps this little element of truth was the seed for the
false concept, accepted by many foreigners, that the people
also ate all manner of insects.

Even reputable reporting agencies cannot be fully trusted to
supply the missionary with an accurate picture of the place to
which he wishes to go. A few years ago, the *National Geographic*
did a beautiful picture story of Korea. It is an accurate
story until one comes to a picture of a vendor selling live
red ants. The caption indicates that red ants are a *common*
food for the people of Korea. After sixteen years in Korea,
this writer only once saw ants for sale (dead ones) in a little
back alley in Seoul. Since that time, he has questioned hundreds of Koreans and has yet to find one that knows anything
about eating red ants. Evidently someone has a use for them
but, obviously, they are not at all common. Perhaps ant eating
in Korea is like rattlesnake eating in America. Every year,
near Sweetwater, Texas, there is a rattlesnake hunt and quite
a bit of snake meat is consumed. Yet it would not be accurate
to tell a foreigner that Americans eat beef, pork, chicken, and
rattlesnake. It is true, at least in Sweetwater, but it is not
a valid generalization.

Remember also that tourists are looking for the unusual and
colorful. The well intentioned camera man may ignore thousands
of well dressed citizens and carefully capture all the pathos
of a single beggar. Healthy children running and playing in a
park may be bypassed by the photographer who focuses on a lame
beggar boy who passes through the streets leading his blind
father.

Home from a trip abroad, a local couple may have hundreds of
slides of the strange, unusual, primitive, and morbid elements
of the nations they have visited but very few that show the
modern, ordinary, and familiar aspects of the places visited.
Therefore, the prospective missionary must be able to examine
such information critically and honestly lest he also be led
astray by photography and reports that are more sensational
than realistic.

Once the prospective missionary has all the information that
he can find concerning a given country, he must determine how
he plans to live in that country. There may be aristocratic
nationals whose standards of sanitation are extremely high as
well as slum dwellers who are appallingly dirty. He may plan
to live in town and commute to rural areas, live in a Western
house built outside a rural village, or live in a mud hut inside the village. The impact of sanitation and health problems

will likely be greater as the missionary lives closer to the
local people.*

In spite of the preparation one makes and the determination
he has, it will take some time to overcome the typical American
super-consciousness to sanitation and health. During this
period, differences will be noted by the missionary and he will
have to deal with them.

Suggestions for Scaling the CCS

For the person wishing to compare his own background with the
sanitation and health situation of another country might find
some clues in the following four areas. (1) *Climate* is a
factor in sanitation and health because where cold weather does
not destroy much of the microscopic insects, and small animal
life each year, these things become a real nuisance if not an
actual threat to man. Germs, ants, spiders, roaches, lizards,
rodents, and snakes are a constant source of concern for people
living in tropical climates. These things may be found in the
temperate zones but they are never quite as large nor plentiful
as in the tropical areas.

Numerical Value	1	2	3	4	5	6
Yearly Climate	Cold and Dry	Cold/ Warm	Cold/ Hot	Cool/ Hot	Hot and Humid (Mediter.)	Hot and Humid (Trop.)
Missionary Background						
Field Situation						

Place the numerical value in the appropriate cell for the
missionary background and for the field situation. Subtract
the smaller number from the larger number and place the answer
in the space provided at the right.

Figure 17.   Climate Comparison Scale for Sanitation
            and Health.

---

*Though true during the initial period of culture shock, the
missionary who lives very close to the people where he is working may make a more rapid adjustment than the person who never
quite comes in contact with the problem.

Figure 17 is a simple scale running from Dry Cold to Hot Humid (Tropical). The different types of yearly climate suggest varying degrees of problems with crawling and scurrying pests that carry poisons, germs, or simple disgust as far as the prospective missionary is concerned.

(2) *Living Standards* vary from culture to culture and even from sub-culture to sub-culture. As a general rule, the higher the standard of living the more preoccupation the people have with such things as sanitation and health. Of course, education and other factors are involved but many of these factors tend to be positively correlated. For example, increased education generally parallels an increase in living standard, and they both parallel a greater concern for sanitation and health.

Man seems to be very adaptable and this includes adaptability to sanitation and health standards. If he can afford to boil his water, live in a clean neighborhood, and get regular medical check-ups, he will likely do so; however, where it is extremely inconvenient if not impossible to be sanitary, man seems to be able to adapt to those conditions and live in filth. Thus, the missionary who goes into any given area will likely discover that the local population is as sanitation and health conscious as their living standard will permit.

Thus, the Living Standard Scale (Fig. 18) has been designed to permit the calculation of a comparison between the living

Numerical Value	1	2	3	4	5	6
Living Standard	Affluent	High	Middle (Upper)	Middle (Lower)	Low	Poverty Level
Missionary Background						
Field Situation						

Place the numerical value in the appropriate cell for the missionary background and for the field situation. Subtract the smaller number from the larger number and place the answer in the space provided at the right.

Figure 18. Living Standard Comparison Scale for
Sanitation and Health.

standard of the missionary and the living standard of the people
of the area to which he is going.

   (3) *Water* is not only the source of life for man but also the
medium for the transfer of various organisms from individual to
individual or animal to individual. Thus water is a necessary
element in man's survival but also the source of all manner of
disease. To avoid the transmittal of disease by contaminated
drinking water, man has developed various water purification
procedures. Water plants may chlorinate city water, wells may
be treated with bacteria killing chemicals, or individuals may
boil their drinking water to assure the destruction of most
harmful bacteria.

   Also, there is an obvious relationship between the quantity
of water available and cleanliness. Where water is scarce,
baths are fewer, living areas cannot be scrubbed and washed
frequently, and sewage cannot be disposed of effectively. This
is especially true in crowded or urban areas but is also a fair
generalization even in rural areas. Therefore the water scale
(Fig. 19) has been designed to take into consideration the
availability as well as purity of water as it relates to sanitation and health.

Numerical Value	1	2	3	4	5	6
Water	Scarce & Polluted	Limited & Polluted	Unlimited & Polluted	Unlimited, Pure & Not Running	Unlimited, Pure, Cold & Running	Unlimited, Hot & Cold & Running
Missionary Background						
Field Situation						

Place the numerical value in the appropriate cell for the
missionary background and for the field situation. Subtract
the smaller number from the larger number and place the answer
in the space provided at the right.

         Figure 19. Water Comparison Scale for Sanitation
                     and Health.

   (4) *Medical Doctors* are symbols of health and help to 20th
century man. Each culture has its own ideas concerning

physical health, and the men of each culture tend to rely most
confidently on the kind of doctors they have been taught to
trust. The Asian may go to a western doctor, but if he does
not get immediate results, he will likely see a Chinese herb
doctor or someone who practices acupuncture. Likewise, the
American wants a good doctor who practices western medicine.
Just knowing that such a doctor is close at hand is comforting
to the westerner. He may be well aware that 80% of all illness
will run its course and disappear even without the attention of
a physician, but he still feels better when the doctor prods
him a few times, looks in his ears and mouth, and tells him
that everything seems to be under control.

On the other hand when one faces the prospect of a day's
trek through the jungle just to find a doctor, it is discom-
forting, to say the least. Where doctors are not readily
available sometimes emergency help can be received if an
emergency call is made. Although it is encouraging to know
that an emergency call to a nearby city will bring a doctor by
helicopter, the missionary is still faced with the problem of
deciding when an illness is serious enough to demand such extreme measures. It is serious enough to get the family doctor
out of bed at 2:00 A.M. in the United States, but even more
serious to mobilize a complete medical unit that is already

Numerical Value	1	2	3	4	5	6
Medical Doctor Availability	None	Non-Western* (Distant)	Non-Western* (Near)	Western (Distant)	Local Western (Near)	U.S. Western (Near)
Missionary Background						
Field Situation						

Place the numerical value in the appropriate cell for the
missionary background and for the field situation. Subtract
the smaller number from the larger number and place the answer
in the space provided at the right.

Figure 20.   Medical Doctor Comparison Scale for
             Sanitation and Health.

_____

*Oriental medicine and acupuncture are examples of medical
practice that is more like western medicine than primitive
superstition.

overworked and may have little sympathy for foreigners who are
trying to teach a strange new religion.

On the basis of the availability and expertise of doctors
the Medical Doctor Scale has been developed (Fig. 20).

Finally, after the four scales have been filled out, the
scores should be added together and the total divided by four
to give a global measure. This global measure may run from
zero to five:

> 0 = Identical
> 1 = Very Similar
> 2 = Similar
> 3 = Different
> 4 = Very Different
> 5 = Exotic

SOCIAL MORES AND MORAL STANDARDS

Since the Christian missionary is so deeply involved in
moral, ethical, and similar value laden patterns of behavior,
he may be especially sensitive to what he feels is immoral
behavior. If he feels that the accepted behavior of a particular society is immoral or unethical by his own standards,
he may find that living in that society is extremely frustrating.

Of course, each prospective missionary should be aware of
that important distinction between the *ideal* and *real* standards of both his own culture and that of the culture to which
he is going. For example, his concept of American honesty may
be a part of the American ideal, but a glance at the front page
of any newspaper may give firm evidence that the real standard
of honesty in America is far below the ideal. Likewise, the
seeming acceptance of immoral or unethical practices in a
foreign country might belie the fact that the people of that
society have ideals that are quite contrary to their visible
patterns of behavior.

The importance of this category as separate from government,
education, etc., may be illustrated by the case of the conservative Christian missionary who believes in political democracy
but enjoys living in a nation with a totalitarian government
which forbids long hair, hippies, and X-rated movies. In
other words, a person may rank a government as very different
to that with which he is familiar and yet find himself very
comfortable in the society controlled by that government.

Countries where polygamy is practiced and generally accepted may cause the missionary considerable heartache. Yet, it could be that such countries show unusual tolerance toward Christianity and provide great hope for the future. On the other hand, a strongly anti-Christian government might have general standards of moral behavior quite acceptable to the missionary.

In the movie *Eskimo* a missionary became quite upset when the man he was attempting to teach offered him his wife. Although this custom has been over popularized by those who write or tell about the Eskimo culture, the fact remains that frequently people behave in a manner so strange to the Westerner that he can hardly believe it possible; however, strangeness of the behavior is not always due to the supposed immorality of the people involved. A reverse example might best illustrate this point: An American, teaching English in Asia, was trying to help his female students pronounce difficult English words. So that they might see the position of the lips and tongue as he articulated the 'th' sound, he demanded that they look at him and then demonstrate the procedure themselves. What the teacher did not understand was that for these girls to look a man in the eye was sexually stimulating and extremely immodest, if not immoral. Also, to reveal the tongue in public was in very poor taste and simply not done by girls of gentle breeding. Thus the simple command to *see* and *do* was rather vulgar and ungentlemanly in the eyes of the students, while to the teacher it was merely an innocent teaching device.

The dress or lack of dress in some cultures may seem terribly immodest to the missionary who has been raised with rather strict codes of dress and modesty; however, to the people of some hot humid climates who wear little clothing, the clothing they do wear is quite proper and they, in turn, may feel that the missionary wife's lipstick, hairdo, and eyeshadow make her look like the prostitutes they see in the nearby city.

Thus, again, the missionary must be very cautious about making judgments until he knows the people and culture well enough to see beneath his own cultural influence and into the real values of the culture itself, and as he rates a given culture as more or less different from his own in terms of mores and morals on the CCS, he must not misinterpret this as an accurate evaluation of that society. Such an evaluation could only come after months or years of careful study.

The Social Mores and Moral Standards category presents the prospective missionary some unusual problems due to the fact that as a Christian, he may be expected to have rather high moral standards of his own. Although a similar phenomenon

might exist with regard to one or more of the other categories
on the CCS, it seems quite obvious to the writer that the
Christian in many of the Western nations has had to face the
shock of extreme and rapid cultural change within his own
society during the past few years. Social mores, morals, and
habits have undergone such a radical transformation that it is
staggering to the sober observer.

Needless to say it would be an unusual society that did not
have its share of immoral and perverted behavior, and it may
be true that such behavior touches more people more frequently
than many Christians realize or are willing to admit. The fact
remains, however, that there is a vast and visible difference
between a society where immoral behavior is relegated to
secrecy, easily avoided by moral persons, and pervaded by guilt
and a society where that same behavior is openly displayed,
impossible to escape, and cloaked in an aura of respectability.

As bookstore shelves become crowded with books and magazines that are obviously pornographic, X-rated movies dominate
the movie screens, and homosexuality becomes respectable, the
Christian may discover that he is as thoroughly frustrated by
his own society as he could ever be by any foreign society.
For this reason the difference between a missionary's home
culture and the culture to which he is going may not be as
significant as the difference between his Christian moral
consciousness and the general moral impact of any culture.
Therefore, to determine a level of difference for this category
on the CCS, the difference will be between the missionary's
own moral standard and the moral standard of the culture to
which he is going.

There may be a host of things involved in the concept of
morality, but in this discussion only four are going to be
considered. These include (1) dishonesty, (2) prejudice,
(3) lax sexual behavior, and (4) cruelty. These have been
selected because they seem to represent the most obvious forms
of immoral behavior that a new missionary is likely to observe.

Dishonesty. Dishonesty has been selected because it seems
to mean so much to the Christian missionary. One does not
spend very much time around missionaries without hearing tales
of honesty or dishonesty on the part of the people in the
society to which they have gone. Sometimes such discussions
reveal shallow reasoning and inaccurate observation while on
other occasions they reveal shrewd judgment and keen perception. But, regardless of the sophistication of the judgment
made with regard to honesty, it is an important aspect of a
society and makes a strong impression on the missionary.

This writer recalls an occasion when he started to pay for a purchase in the tax free shop in the departure lounge of the Tokyo International Airport only to discover that his billfold, with over one hundred dollars in cash, was missing. The customs inspectors and immigration officers allowed him to hurry back through the various departure check points into the public lobby where he had done some shopping earlier. There he met two clerks who recognized him immediately and came running forward with his billfold. He left them a sizeable tip and rushed back through the various departure check points and was once again in the departure lobby when one of the clerks caught up with him, returned the tip, and explained that returning the billfold was normal and expected behavior and not worthy of any reward.

This kind of honesty is impressive and not always found either at home or abroad. The missionary who, while walking through town, has his camera snatched, his pocket picked, or his briefcase taken can hardly help but be negatively impressed by the experience. In some countries the members of a family cannot all leave home at the same time. A family member or at least a servant must be at home lest thieves break in and ransack the house. In other countries missionaries have no locks on their doors and virtually no fear of theft.

Even though there may be reasons why the people of a given nation or society are given to thievery (due, for example, to poverty, caste, or social dislocation), the fact remains that such behavior effects the newcomer and makes it necessary for him to make an adjustment.

Prejudice. Equality of treatment is an American ideal and whether or not it is a reality in the United States, it is generally a part of the thinking of the American citizen; therefore, when he sees behavior that indicates inequality or prejudice, it is disturbing. He may be especially sensitive to employer/employee relationships and may be appalled when a superior strikes a subordinate or in any manner treats him with contempt.

There are minorities in every nation and the treatment afforded some of them is very upsetting to visitors. Since many nations have generally homogenous populations the only true citizens are those of the single majority nationality. All other ethnic groups or nationalities are second class citizens no matter how many generations they have been in that country. Whatever its form, prejudice makes a strong impression on those who critically observe it.

Lax Sexual Behavior. Sex has become such an important element in American life that sexual morality is one of the most
heated issues of the times. With X-rated movies, pornographic
magazines, and legalized perversion encountering the American
at every turn, it is no wonder that he is sensitive to the
problem of sexual morality.

In some countries one can walk down the street and see
numerous nude pictures on magazines, calendars, night clubs,
and theaters. In other countries such pictures are not allowed
in public and can only be seen in the hands of dealers who are
working outside the law. The visibility of houses of prosti-
tution, massage parlors, public displays of affection, nudity,
and similar things are important in determining the moral
standard level on the CCS; not because these are necessarily
the most important moral issues or the most critical manifesta-
tions of them but because they are the first and foremost
factors that will effect the visitor from another country.

As with all categories on the CCS, the prospective missionary
or sponsor must be cautious and critical when evaluating other
cultures. It might be tempting to just accept standard stereo-
types and forget objective analysis. There are those, for
example, who think that the people in Sweden are all openly
immoral because of the publicity concerning nudity in Swedish
films and television. A missionary who has recently returned
from Sweden says that the first question he is usually asked
has to do with the morals of the Swedish people. He recalls
an American newspaper report of a Swedish television program
in which a man completely disrobed. The newspaper report
stopped there but the missionary recalled that the people of
Sweden flooded the TV station with calls demanding that such
exposure not be allowed on home television. This reaction by
the Swedish public was not reported by the American journalists;
therefore, it is important that the prospective missionary seek
reliable information when determining the impact that a nation's
attitude toward sexual morality will have on him when he makes
contact with that society.

Cruelty. Cruelty may seem a strange element to include
with the other three; however, it is not uncommon for a prospective missionary to find information about a country to which
he is going that strikes him as callous to the point of being
cruel. He may hear stories of the sick being deserted to the
elements until they die, of the insane wandering the streets
in a state of starvation, or of animals being slowly beaten to
death to tenderize their flesh for eating.

The writer once asked a citizen of another country how to
train a watch dog. The answer was that you should keep the dog

on a short leash, never exercise him, beat him twice a day with a stick, and underfeed him. This would likely result in a mean and alert watch dog but, to most Westerners, would be considered cruel.

Of course, some of these stories are probably fabrications completely misrepresenting the truth while others, though based upon some element of truth, may be extremely misleading. For the prospective missionary, however, his perception of the situation is the significant thing as he fills out the CCS. Misunderstandings may be cleared up with time on the field but until that clarification comes one's adjustment will be strained by the way he perceives things.

Suggestions for Scaling the CCS

The following chart (Fig. 21) has been designed to allow the prospective missionary or his sponsor to rank the differences between the missionary's own moral standard (as he understands it) and the moral standard of the country to which he is going, as revealed in four specific areas, i.e., dishonesty, prejudice, sexual laxity, and cruelty.

Numerical Value	1	2	3	4	5
Dishonesty	No	Little	Some	Much	Extreme
Prejudice					
Sexual Laxity					
Cruelty					

Place the proper numerical value in one of the small squares at the lower right of the appropriate measure for each of the four items (dishonesty, prejudice, sexual laxity, and cruelty). Add the four numbers, divide by 4 and place the answer in the space provided at the right of the chart. The CCS can then be scaled as follows:

```
        Identical---------------0
        Very Similar------------1
        Similar-----------------2
        Different---------------3
        Very Different----------4
        Exotic------------------5
```

Figure 21. Social Mores and Moral Standard Scoring Chart.

TECHNOLOGY

"If language is the human attribute that makes culture
possible, technology is the characteristic of culture that
makes it advantageous to man," records Walter Goldschmidt
(Goldschmidt 1960:116). Certainly, technology serves man or,
to put it more accurately, provides the means of serving man.
Technology provides man with comfort, task simplification,
efficiency, and opportunity.

American technological advances are frequently illustrated
by NASA's space program with its record of impressive firsts,
and although space technology has made some impact on our
everyday living habits, that impact is very small when compared
to the sum total of all influences produced by American (and
foreign) technology.

Millions of Americans eat, work, and sleep in buildings with
constant comfortable temperatures. Even the energy crisis has
not caused the average American more than minor discomfort.
Also, the American not only takes these *comforts* for granted
but also his many *conveniences*. For example, when he wants to
talk to someone a considerable distance away, he picks up a
telephone and takes several things for granted, i.e., (1) the
person to whom he wishes to speak has a telephone, (2) if he
dials the correct sequence of numbers, he will reach the
phone he wants, and (3) if the person he is calling is available, they will be able to hear each other. These things are
not taken for granted in other nations especially developing
ones.

Although the energy crisis may have caused Americans to give
some thought to things that were previously taken for granted,
the fact remains that they still live in a highly mechanized
society and, without much conscious awareness, are greatly
dependent upon advanced technology. At no time is this dependence more forcefully revealed than when an American steps into
a society where such technological advances have not yet been
perfected.

In countries where the temperatures are very cold in the
winter, one may have to live and work without ever being
"really warm." In extremely hot climates there may be no air
conditioning, screens, or dehumidifiers. In both cases the
body can adapt to the climate, but it calls for varying degrees
of sacrifice and endurance on the part of the newcomer.

Of course, technology and technological advances are generally means of facilitating more effective and efficient
performance. Thus, where technology is lacking, tasks must be

accomplished by different means. A five minute telephone call may become a three hour trip by car or foot. A comfortable and sound sleep as a placative for yesterday's frustrations may become a fitful slumber due to an excess of heat, cold, or insects. Concentration on a particularly knotty problem may be more easily achieved in comfortable surroundings than when fingers and toes are numb from the cold; fumes from a poorly ventilated heater result in headaches; or where malfunctioning equipment of any type interrupts thought processes and demands attention.

As with other factors previously discussed, the technological development of a nation may be difficult to accurately measure, and there may be vast differences between the urban and rural sections of the country. Also, reports by the government or chamber of commerce may overemphasize technological advances because of their importance and visibility in today's world. Finally, the ideas of comfort and convenience of some people in a developing nation may differ greatly from similar ideas on the part of someone from a technologically advanced nation.

A few years ago, the visitor to a hot spring resort in one Asian country could stay in any one of a dozen inns built in the traditional manner. Simple floor-heated rooms opened onto a covered porch of highly polished hardwood that encircled a patio garden. Beautifully designed doors and windows of paper stretched over light wooden frames dominated each room and slid open to reveal the cool shade (in summer) or snowy whiteness (in winter) of attractive landscaping. A word to the hostess and in moments a guest could be bathing in one of the many steaming mineral water baths.

Today, technology has made its mark and the traditional inns are almost completely gone. In their place are crude replicas of Western hotels (without the plush, clean, immaculate look that Western hotels usually have). The indoor-outdoor carpet is loose in many places and does not fit properly in the hallways. Vacuum sweepers are not available and carpets are difficult to keep clean. There is a private bath in each room, but the hot natural mineral water that is used in all the plumbing has corroded the pipes and stained all the fixtures. Dampness peels paint from the walls, valves clog, pipes are eaten away, floors mold and rusting steel window sashes open to reveal the concrete wall of an adjoining building.

This illustration suggests the potential frustration of semi-developed technology. Indoor plumbing, private baths, and carpeted floors are nice where they have been quite perfectly developed, but where they are still in the developing stage,

they can be more frustrating and distasteful than the primitive
facilities of the past. For this reason, technological development and personal appreciation and comfort do not follow any
simple continuum from low to high or primitive to advanced.
Judging from his own experiences, the author feels that Americans are so spoiled that they enjoy technology only when it
functions smoothly and efficiently.

Technology is recognized as advantageous to many because it
saves man labor, but in Twentieth Century America, the saving
of labor may not be as significant as the saving of time.
Lewis Mumford declares that, "the clock, not the steam-engine,
is the key machine of the modern industrial age" (Mumford 1960:
154).

Although people in other cultures may be governed closely
by the phases of the moon or the movement of the tides, they
are not as completely ruled by seconds and minutes as many
Westerners are. They understand that the seasons must be right
for the planting of seed or the harvest of crops, but they can
hardly comprehend the American business man's preoccupation
with minute by minute scheduling.

For this reason, the lack of specific technological advances
may not cause the missionary as much concern as the lack of
orientation to time as Americans are apt to view it.

> Even the five minute period has its significant sub-
> divisions. When equals meet, one will generally be
> aware of being two minutes early or late but will say
> nothing, since the time in this case is not significant.
> At three minutes a person will still not apologize or
> feel that it is necessary to say anything . . . ; at
> five minutes there is usually a short apology; and at
> four minutes . . . the person will mutter something,
> although he will seldom complete the muttered sentence.
> The importance of making detailed observations on these
> aspects of informal culture is driven home if one
> pictures an actual situation. An American ambassador
> in an unnamed country interpreted incorrectly the signi-
> ficance of time as it was used in visits by local
> diplomats. An hour's tardiness in their system is
> equivalent to five minutes by ours, fifty to fifty-five
> minutes to four minutes, forty-five minutes to three
> minutes, and so on for day time official visits. By
> their standards, the local diplomats felt they couldn't
> arrive exactly on time; this punctuality might be inter-
> preted locally as an act relinguishing their freedom
> of action to the United States. But they didn't want
> to be insulting--an hour late would be too late--so

> they arrived fifty minutes late . . . in American
> time, fifty to fifty-five minutes late is the insult
> period, at the extreme end of the duration scale; yet
> in the country we are speaking of it's just right
> (Hall 1959:175,176).

The subtle differences in time consciousness between the
missionary and the people to whom he has been sent can cause
him no end of frustration and confusion. This is particularly
true if the missionary tries to plan his hours, days, and
weeks on the field in the same manner that he plans them at
home.

Suggestions for Scaling the CCS

In filling out the *Technology* section of the CCS, it may be
reasonable to first establish a simple continuum running from
ultra-primitive to *super-technical*. On the primitive end would
be the tribal village without plumbing, electricity, or transportation; in the middle would be the rural or urban setting
where all of these things are in evidence but where none are
adequate or dependable; and the technical end would be the
typical American city with all of these in perfect working
order. (It is probably safe to assume that the problem of
time will correlate with the presence or absence of these technical advances, i.e., differences in the time consciousness of
the missionary and his hosts will be greater in the primitive
situation.)

Thus the primitive extreme would be *exotic* and the technical
extreme *identical*; however, remembering the suggestion that
people from highly technical areas are sometimes extremely
frustrated by developing technologies where things never quite
work properly, it might be in order to extend the *different*
measure well toward the technology side of the continuum (see
Fig. 22).

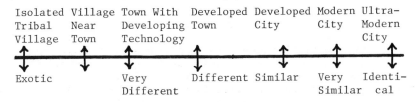

Isolated Tribal Village	Village Near Town	Town With Developing Technology	Developed Town	Developed City	Modern City	Ultra- Modern City
Exotic		Very Different	Different	Similar	Very Similar	Identi- cal

Figure 22. Technology Scale Suggestions.

SUMMARY

The Culture Contrast Scale (CCS) on page 54 has been designed to provide the prospective missionary and his sponsoring organization with a capsuled view of the overall cultural disparity between the missionary and his chosen field. It is assumed that there is a positive correlation between this difference and the adjustment difficulty (culture shock) the missionary will face as he moves into the new culture.

The CCS provides the missionary and the sponsoring organization with three important things. First, it is a very specific reminder of the complex nature of culture and the multitude of elements that comprise the cultural milieu in which the missionary has been raised and into which he will soon be going. Second, the completed scale gives a profile of the relative difficulty or similarity to be expected in each of ten selected categories. Finally, it provides information for a comprehensive of the overall adjustment difficulty that can be expected when a given subject plans to go into a given field.

Thus the CCS serves three important purposes. It helps to create within the mind of the prospective missionary and within the minds of the members of the sponsoring organization an awareness of the need for prayer, planning and preparation as the missionary enterprise is initiated. Second, it helps to focus attention on relatively similar or different cultural categories so that the missionary will be aware of the areas where he needs special help as well as the areas that will provide him with potential re-enforcement. Finally, the comprehensive measure provides a crude means for comparing the potential degree of culture shock to be expected by different individuals going into the same area or the same individual going into different areas.

There are, of course, some obvious cautions that should be exercised in using the CCS. (1) A low total score of 10% to 20% does not indicate that the culture of the field is somehow bad or inferior. It merely means that the missionary will face a culture quite different from the one in which he was raised. (2) Global score differences in scales calculated by different individuals would hardly be comparable because the means of evaluating the difference for many of the categories is highly subjective. (3) Small differences in the global score (1% to 15% differences) are probably not statistically significant. That is, such differences could easily be the result of measurement error rather than a real potential difference in expected culture shock. (4) Since the use of this chart at this time has been very limited, there has been no attempt to standardize results. One could not conclude that a missionary

with a score of 25% is going to have three times the culture
shock of a missionary with a score of 75%. At best, it can
only be safely said that the missionary with the low score
faces more potential culture shock.

One last caution involves the general assumption around
which the CCS was developed, i.e., culture shock will increase
in direct proportion to the degree of difference between the
missionary's home culture and the culture to which he is going.
It has already been stated that a score of 25% (much difference)
would indicate greater potential for culture shock than a score
of 75% (similarity); however, it may not be valid to conclude
that scores of 85%, 90%, 95%, etc., are indicative of less and
less potential for culture shock. In other words, it may not
be correct to assume that where the target culture is *very
similar* or almost *identical* to the missionary's home culture
there will be virtually no potential for culture shock. Quite
the contrary, *the mission to a very similar culture may be
extremely difficult* as far as cultural adjustment is concerned.

The culprit in this case is similarity itself. The missionary going into an exotic culture knows that the change is going
to be great. He is aware of the strange new language, exotic
dress, and unusual customs, but the missionary who goes into
a very similar culture may be unaware of the subtle differences
that are there. The lack of awareness can be a stumbling block
to an otherwise successful ministry.

A drawl may tend to alienate a Southern preacher from the
people of Maine far more than it would the people of Asia or
Africa. The attitudes and mannerisms of the Bostonian may
cause New Mexicans to pay much more attention to these superficials than to the message he might have to share.

Perhaps, for the United States citizen, the best example
would involve a mission into some English speaking section of
Canada.* As suggested on pages 79ff, the English language
itself can be a source of confusion and frustration. The
Canadians will need to hear only a sentence or two to determine
that the missionary is from the United States, and language is
not the only problem that the visitor from the South may face.

Lynn Anderson, a Canadian who has become a successful
preacher in the United States, tells the following story: The

---

*Canada would be considered similar by most of her Southern
neighbors; however, one could plan to go into the French speaking Eastern provinces, to the Ukranians in the West, or the
Indians in the North where the cultural differences would be
more extreme.

outgoing United States Bible Belt preacher seeking to win
friends among the Western Canadians went around slapping people
on the back, shaking hands vigorously, and trying to set people
at ease by making small talk. On one occasion, he sought to
arouse some mirth by comparing the Elizabeth on a Canadian
dollar bill with Hollywood's Elizabeth Taylor. It might have
been humorous or at least inoffensive to many of his country-
men, but to the Canadians it was, to say the least, in very
poor taste (Anderson 1965).

Since similar cultures may present the prospective missionary with some very subtle challenges, it may be well to consider
a modification of the basic assumption underlying the CCS,
i.e., the positive correlation between cultural differences and
the potential for culture shock may be reversed as the identical end of the scale is approached (see Fig. 23).

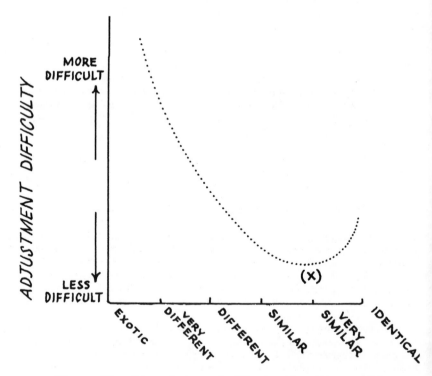

Figure 23.   Suggested graph illustrating the possible
              reversing of a direct and positive relation-
              ship between Difficulty and Difference at a
              point near the identical section of the
              difference scale.

Reflecting Paul's desire to lay a foundation rather than build
upon someone else's work (Rom. 15:20,21), this missionary
wanted to preach Christ in a virgin field. Today, he is quite
enthusiastic about the wonderful things the Lord has done
through him. There are others, however, who have gone into
new fields with just as much joy and enthusiasm but who have
faced such frustrations and problems that their work has been
anything but encouraging. In some cases they left the field
prematurely, while in other cases they stuck it out but only
by virtue of prayer, determination, and an unfailing trust in
God.

The Christian may expect that his life will not always be
joyful and pleasant because God has clearly communicated the
fact that His followers will suffer various trials (Phil. 1:29);
however, an examination of the lives and activities of the
missionaries mentioned above reveals that there was *no significant difference* in the persecution, cultural challenges, resistance, or other factors faced by all of these missionaries.
One element that offers some explanation for these conflicting
feelings was the fact that one seemed, somehow, to fit his
chosen field while the others did not.

It is precisely this idea of *fit* that is the central theme
of this chapter. In chapter III elements in the personality
of the missionary were discussed and in this chapter a frequently ignored element of the field environment is examined
with a view to revealing that certain missionaries may be best
suited to certain fields. The following assumptions are
critical to the development of this theme: (1) The level of
development of missionary activity in a given field is a
significant factor which may contribute to the success or
failure of a new missionary. (2) It is possible to match
prospective missionaries who have particular traits of personality with appropriate levels of mission field development.
(3) Mission field development can be conveniently broken down
into three levels: (a) undeveloped,* (b) newly developed, and
(c) old developed.

UNDEVELOPED FIELDS

With the current emphasis on reaching the unreached people
of the world (Pentecost 1974) more and more missionaries are
going into primitive tribal areas where missionaries have never
gone before or where their impact is little more than a dim
memory. Also when one considers the countries that are

---

*"Undeveloped," in this situation, refers to the presence of
a particular "Christian" religious group in a country and not to
the country itself.

presently closed to full scale missionary activity (Communist nations, the Islamic nations of the Middle East and Northern Africa, etc.), there may be many virgin fields opening up to the preaching of the Gospel in the future.

Although, in the latter case, the virgin field of the future might be highly developed technologically, the unreached field of the 20th century will likely be a technologically underdeveloped or somewhat primitive area. In spite of our anthropological sophistication and understanding of third world and tribal people, the primitive aspect plays a part in the overall aura that surrounds the unreached. Where adventure, romance, and sacrifice have somewhat ceased to be viable elements in some of the older mission fields, these concepts are still factors influencing those who plan to go into certain unreached areas. This is not to insinuate that one's motive for mission is purely quixotic but to honestly admit that the exotic tends to hold a degree of fascination for the Western mind. Deeply involved with his Lord and sensitive to the needs of those without Christ, the prospective missionary may have a very valid motive for mission, but he may also be somewhat moved by the call of the frontier.

The Apostle Paul had a desire to plant the church where no man had ever planted it before and that very attitude is also a part of the attraction held by the unreached field. It is in this total context of feelings and spiritual directives that the desire to be a pioneer missionary is born.

Americans, in particular, have a very special feeling for the pioneer whether it be an American frontiersman like Daniel Boone, an African missionary like David Livingstone, or a combination of both as illustrated by the statue of the pioneer woman in the city park of Ponca City, Oklahoma.* This fascination for the frontier has been fed by legends, books, and films until people have forgotten that for every famous pioneer whose name and story graces the history books of the world there have been untold thousands who died of disease, arrows, wild beasts, or exposure. Then there were the thousands more who discovered that adventure meant little more than hard work, frustration, and ultimate obscurity.

Now and then one still hears reports of missionaries who have been killed by revolutionaries or struck down by disease,

---

*The statue of the pioneer woman, with her Bible in one hand and her son held by the other, was referred to at the 1930 dedication ceremony as a monument to those unknown soldiers of the great battle of civilization.

but the real danger to today's missionary comes in the form of
culture shock, interpersonal conflict, and in general, a magni-
fication of the stresses that seem to accompany advanced forms
of modern civilization. In spite of God's admonition that man
should not be anxious (Matt. 6:25), the missionary is more
likely to suffer from ulcers than from amoebic dysentery.

Church leaders must consider prayerfully the man or family
they plan to send into an undeveloped* field. Once the newness
and mystery wears off, the undeveloped field can become a
source of new and compounded frustrations for the pioneer
missionary. Following World War II and the Korean Conflict
the peninsula of South Korea was left in pretty dire circumstances. Fuel, food, and virtually all raw materials were in
short supply and the economy was resting on rock bottom.
The amazing development of South Korea is now a matter of
record and the casual visitor of today can hardly imagine the
changes that have taken place since those early post war years.
Yet, to the missionaries of various religious groups, those
days are still remembered quite vividly and to many they are
the memories of pioneer missionaries.**

One man tells of survival during those lean years. Getting
sufficient food for his family took a large portion of his time
each day. Fuel for stoves and vehicles was likewise a problem
because it was not only scarce but usually mixed with rusty
water. Thus carburetors were frequently clogged, lines had to
be cleaned, and all mechanical things serviced continually.
Added to these problems was the need for daily trips to and
from school for his children, continual trips to government
offices to satisfy the changing demands of a developing government, and a host of other problems arising out of the confusion
of trying to live in a land that had recently been devastated
by war.

Worn to the very bone by his struggle to survive, ashamed of
how little he was able to accomplish as far as gospel proclamation was concerned, and angry at a local mechanic who did more

---

*In this chapter an undeveloped field refers not to an un-
developed nation but to a place where missionary activity has
not yet been developed. To avoid confusion undeveloped nations
(technologically) are referred to as primitive.

**To the ecumenicist this may seem a contradiction because
missionary work was begun in Korea as early as 1884. However,
the terms *undeveloped* and *pioneer* may refer to individual religious groups initiating the establishment of their own unique
beliefs. To them, the previous existence of another christian
group is relatively insignificant.

harm than good to a faulty water pump, this missionary declared
that it was impossible to be a Christian and a missionary at
the same time. To the uninitiated, this may seem like a very
strange statement for a man of God to make but on the mission
fields of the world one may hear similar ideas expressed all
too frequently.

It would be unjust to pass judgment upon this missionary
without knowing more of the circumstances surrounding his life.
It is possible that he may have been trying to create a little
America for himself and his family and was thus saddling himself with an unnecessary and impossible task. On the other
hand, it may have been a time when survival was, in itself, a
full time job, and he was justified in utilizing his time in
this fashion.

The point here is not to pass judgment or suggest any simple
scale to determine how much time a missionary should spend
taking care of his family but to emphasize the fact that the
pioneer missionary in an undeveloped field will likely have to
face the culture shock common to all missionary activity plus
a host of other problems based upon the fact that he is *alone*
in a strange environment.

The undeveloped mission field makes several demands upon the
pioneer missionary: (1) He must be able to meet emergency
conditions on a daily basis and make decisions quickly and
effectively. (2) He must be a resourceful jack-of-all-trades
who can survive under adverse conditions or be capable of controlling his environment to the extent that he can locate and
coordinate the efforts of local people who can aid him in his
survival. (3) He must be able to respond effectively to
continual challenges without suffering undue physical, mental,
or spiritual damage. (4) He must have the vision and creative
insight necessary to guide the work through the early stages
of frustration and discouragement and the patience to stick
with every plan until he is sure of its value.

Obviously, the self-sufficient (see page 34) missionary has
several of the qualifications needed for a pioneer effort.
He has enough self confidence to make decisions quickly without
over burdening his mind with doubts and second guesses. Also,
the self-sufficient individual is usually able to cope with
contingencies and thus survive in almost any set of circumstances. Finally, he will likely have the vision to see ahead
to that point at which present frustrations begin to be resolved and the main goal of his mission can have his undivided
attention.

Although the self-sufficient missionary may have several
of the qualities necessary for meeting the challenges of an
undeveloped mission field, this is no guarantee that he will
automatically succeed. Sometimes the man with great vision
lacks the patience and skill to carry his projects through to
a successful end, or if his training, methodology, or philosophy of mission is not in harmony with the needs of the field,
he could envision, create, and perpetuate unnecessary institutions, programs, or policies (see pages 201 ff).

The self-sufficient missionary's greatest weakness may prove
to be a lack of intellectual curiosity and patience. With his
eyes focused on the future he may find it difficult if not
impossible to deal effectively with the present. The dull
routine of language study may demand too much immediate concentration and thus be neglected in favor of more exciting plans
and dreams. If this is the case, the danger of missionary
failure will be increased although it may not become obvious
until several years have passed. At a time when the missionary
should be well integrated into the culture, fluent in the language, and well along the way to achieving his mission goals,
he may be alienated from the culture, unable to communicate
except through an interpreter, and frustrated in his attempts
to achieve his goals.

Must it be assumed, then, that a successful missionary to
an undeveloped field must have so many outstanding personal
qualities that such men are virtually impossible to find? Not
at all . . . a group-dependent individual with few of the
qualifications suggested for an undeveloped field, a self-
sufficient individual with little interest in language study
and day to day preparation, or any individual anywhere on the
synergistic variable continuum (see page 34) can, with God's
help and with a healthy relationship to his sponsoring church,
succeed! The point is that unless the individual and the
sponsoring agency are aware of the potential dangers they may
not lean heavily enough upon God and each other to overcome
them.

Secondly, if the prospective missionary or the sponsor has a
choice in the matter of field selection (or of the missionary
selection in the case of the sponsor), they would do well to
consider matching the right personality with the right field.
The missionary enterprise, especially in undeveloped fields,
is frought with sufficient difficulties without adding to them
through negligence and unconcern.

NEWLY DEVELOPED FIELDS

As the world shrinks in size through communication and transportation more and more unreached fields will be reached and new missionaries will find themselves joining colleagues who came into the work a year or so earlier. The presence of someone already on the field is significant because a new dimension thereby is added to the environment. In the first place many problems will have already been solved and many questions answered, and secondly, an informal seniority will have been established.*

Those who have carefully analyzed organizations have discovered that when individuals work together they all begin with a vaguely defined element of natural equality; however, as time passes, one worker may face a problem that he cannot easily solve so he seeks help from his fellow worker. Once this happens that element of natural equality is disturbed and an inequality results. When A has to ask B for help, he automatically sacrifices a portion of his status or self respect and elevates B ever so slightly. If this process continues over a period of time with A doing all the asking and B being continually elevated, the resultant inequality can become so pronounced that B cannot help but harbor feelings of superiority over A and A cannot help but feel inferior to B.

If A and B do not mind this feeling of inequality, they can work together quite effectively with little concern for reversing the direction of the inequality; however, where A feels uncomfortable when B is elevated, A will have to limit his dependence upon B or develop his own area of expertise so that he and B can share advice and thus keep a satisfactory balance.**

Thus when a missionary comes into a newly developed field he will naturally ask many questions and seek advice from his colleagues who preceded him. This is expected behavior, however, and merely confirms the accepted view that the early

---

*The actual impact of this informal seniority concept will depend largely upon the organizational structure of the church involved (in groups recognizing no clerical hierarchy one missionary may have absolutely no control over another except in cases where cooperation leads to a voluntary submission for the sake of accomplishing specific goals).

**For a full discussion of this phenomenon, see Blau and Scott 1962:128-134.

arrivals know a little more and are thus cast in the role of
experts; however, if continued, this very process of learning
from others will establish their increased seniority or superiority and perhaps cause the newcomer to feel somewhat uncomfortable and perhaps even make him reluctant to continue
asking questions and seeking advice. He may counter this
feeling by offering advice to them, perhaps in the area of
mission methods or some other study that he has made, or as
time passes, he may seek to learn things about the field that
the others do not know so that he can bring a better balance
into their interpersonal relationships. At this point another
problem can arise. If the early comers have enjoyed the prestige of being the experts who guide the new missionary, they
may resent his attempts to offer them advice especially if they
have not asked for it.

It should be understood that the potential interpersonal
conflict suggested here may not be consciously recognized by
the missionaries themselves. All of these feelings concerning
equality and inequality will probably be experienced at the
subconscious level; however, this makes them none the less
real, and the missionary must be aware of these feelings if he
is going to satisfactorily cope with them.

At a recent seminar in missions a group of enthusiastic
students was advised to remain silent on the subject of missionary methods until they had been on the field at least six
months or a year. This advice was given in reaction to criticism that had come from fields where freshly trained student
missionaries had gone in and immediately begun to criticize
the resident missionaries and parade their own expertise. One
reason that this behavior had displeased the resident missionaries was that their seniority, experience, and prestige was
ignored and an attempt made by the newcomers (quite unconsciously perhaps) to elevate themselves at the expense of their
older more experienced colleagues.

The need for sensitivity to one's fellow missionaries cannot
be over emphasized and especially when missionary activity is
still at the newly established level. Colleagues must be able
to freely communicate with each other so that their activities
are mutually supportive. Getting off on the wrong foot can
cause friction that can never be completely overcome; therefore, the missionary going into a newly established field is
encouraged to go in cautiously, courteously, and lovingly.

Once communications between missionaries break down several
problems are likely to surface. (1) Duplication of effort
becomes more probable, (2) Unilateral planning can result in
conflicting activities, and (3) increased division of the
missionary force by local persons is facilitated.

(1) Duplication of effort is a serious problem when the amount of time, talent, and money available for mission work is compared with the need for Christ in a world dying in sin. Everything is in critically short supply and the conscientious steward of God's message must not be guilty of wasting anything. Yet, where missionaries fail to work together and keep one another informed of their efforts duplication is frequent.

Some years ago a meeting of several church elderships was held. Each of the elderships represented were sponsors of missionaries in a single Asian nation. During the progress of this meeting, they discovered that one of the men being supported by one of the elderships was operating a printing press for religious literature while one of the missionaries supported by another of the elderships was printing similar literature (some of it identical) in his own print shop. Finally, a third eldership reported that a missionary they were supporting was having literature printed by commercial shops in that country.

These elders were shocked to learn that three missionaries belonging to the same religious group were wasting hundreds of dollars per month simply because they were not working together. Of course, each missionary had his personal reasons for going it alone. One wanted a higher quality of printing than the church sponsored press was capable of producing, another thought his material should be printed first and was not willing to wait for anyone else, and the third had given up trying to cooperate with the others. It took a firm guiding hand from the elderships at home to pull the missionaries into line and bring a halt to the duplication of effort on the field.

(2) Unilateral planning is especially dangerous due to the fact that some mission methods do not complement other methods; therefore, when one group of missionaries develops a program of missionary activity, it can wipe out another program being developed by another group. In one nation the missionaries had worked for months to try and nationalize the local congregations as far as support was concerned. The churches had all been subsidized for many years and the missionaries in consultations with prominent local leaders had approved a plan for cutting foreign support gradually over a period of about eighteen months.

Things went well although there were some bad feelings on the part of some local church members who did not want to see the foreign aid stopped. Then a new wave of missionaries came onto the field, spoke to these dissatisfied local people through interpreters, were immediately sympathetic, and, without consultation with their colleagues already in the field, began arranging for new avenues of foreign support. Within less

than three months the whole program of self-support was de-
molished, the older missionaries were cast into the role of
villains, and the new missionaries were saddled with a burden
of foreign involvement already proven faulty.

(3) Finally, a lack of communication and cooperation between
missionaries can pave the way for greater and greater division.
Local people of questionable character will frequently try to
infiltrate a missionary program. They may be after money,
position, or influence, but whatever their motive,* they are
quick to note weaknesses in the missionary organization. For
example, one of the most common weaknesses they can find is that
of insecurity, and when one has a feeling of insecurity, it is
natural to try and overcome it by placing blame for problems on
others and accepting credit for success whether it is deserved
or not. Sensing this the local worker can reenforce the
missionary's feelings by criticizing one missionary while heap-
ing praise on the other. Some of the more clever ones will go
back and forth telling each missionary exactly what he wants
to hear until he has driven them so far apart that there is
little chance of their coming together and discovering the
deception.

Of course, communication is a two way street and the older
missionaries should do their part to make the way easier for
those who come after them. They can do this by offering help
freely in those areas where the new missionary is trying to
adjust to the new environment while, at the same time, keeping
the proper equality of relationship by asking questions and
seeking to learn from the newcomer. This latter ploy may
actually do more than ease tension and build better interpersonal relationships; it may also result in some new insights. The new missionary may have some good ideas, his
insights may be fresh and objective, and he may provide a
good lens through which to examine the ongoing program.

The positive value of warm brotherly relationships between
missionaries cannot be over emphasized yet there are those who
enter the field without having given any serious thought to
the problem of developing healthy interpersonal relationships

---

*The tendency to play one missionary against another is not
limited to people with bad motives but is also present in otherwise sound church members who merely want to be informative.
The latter situation is bad enough but most experienced preachers are familiar with this problem and know how to handle it.
However, in the situation under discussion here the person has
deliberately set out to cause division and the missionary may
not expect such behavior.

with fellow missionaries. Still, year after year missionaries
report that the most serious problems they see on the mission
field stem from poor interpersonal relationships between
missionaries. One author of a missions book even titled his
chapter on interpersonal relationships, "The Missionary's
Greatest Problem" (Cannon 1969:34).

At a recent missions seminar* attended by this writer the
students all participated in a program of group dynamics as an
integral part of the seminar experience. It was enlightening,
to say the least, to observe how long it took these prospective
and returned missionaries to begin developing meaningful relationships. Even with expert group leadership it usually took
a week of daily sessions for the members to *begin* peeling back
the superficial layers of their personalities in an attempt to
communicate frankly and honestly.

Without some experience of this type or at least some study
in the area of human sensitivity, most people will never be
able to accept the risk and open up to others in a manner that
is necessary if a sound relationship is going to develop.
Every prospective missionary would do well to prepare himself
by participating in a group dynamic experience, by studying
literature appropriate to the subject, and by making a conscious
effort to pay close attention to others so that he can be sensitive to their needs.

One word of caution may be in order, physical proximity
should not be relied upon as the only means of creating good
interpersonal relationships. Although it is true that when two
or more missionaries are on the field together, they can offer
each other mutual support, it is also true that too much personal contact can contribute to friction and ultimately
alienation.**

OLD DEVELOPED FIELDS

The older developed fields are usually marked by the presence of rather sophisticated institutions (hospitals, clinics,
feeding stations, mission stations, schools, seminaries and
orphanages) which reflect the confidence missionaries have
placed in these methods during the past century. The missionary entering a field like this will face missionary traditions,

---

*Seminar in Missions, Abilene Christian College, Abilene,
Texas, 1975.

**For a fuller discussion of this concept, see the discussion
on *scope* on page 157 .

attitudes, and methods that have been handed down from generation to generation.*

Going into an old developed field the new missionary should
have his philosophy of mission clearly in mind, the firm
support of his sponsoring church, and know precisely how he is
going to fit into the ongoing program. Most of the difficulties encountered in a newly established field are also present
in an older field plus some unique problems related to the
pervasive influence of the long established work itself.

There may be compounds where missionaries live together,
numerous institutions, as well as set patterns for doing things
that are visible in the traditions that have been handed down
over the years. Thus the new missionary, if he is going to
work harmoniously with his colleagues, must be prepared to
fit smoothly into one of the ongoing programs or have the sensitivity and finesse to be innovative without being a threat.

Obviously, the old developed fields will have frequent needs
for specialists to fill gaps in established programs. Seminaries need teachers and administrators, hospitals need doctors
and nurses, and mission stations need all sorts of specialists
including mechanics, electricians, dairymen, and agricultural
experts. Due to the rising cost of supporting large families
over long periods of time, some agencies are sending younger
single missionaries for shorter periods of time.

The old developed field may offer temporary work for individuals who have a special skill and who may not want to spend
the time learning the language and becoming an effective evangelist. For example, a school may need a business manager to
come in and set up a system of finance or a hospital may
need a lab technician to help oversee the training of local
personnel. Such jobs may last for a month, six months, or a
year and provide an avenue for temporary but necessary service.

Of course, there are always demands for full time missionaries who will be expected to learn the language and stay on the
field for lengthy periods of time; however, whether going for
a short or long tour, the new missionary in an old developed
field will generally be more comfortable if he fits somewhere
near the *group dependent* end of the synergistic variable continuum (see page 38). If he feels comfortable as a part of a
cooperative effort and appreciates the security and effective-
ness of the group process he will be able to adjust much more

---

*There are sons and grandsons of earlier missionaries on
many mission fields today.

easily than a self sufficient individual who has been accustomed
to making his own decisions and following his own ideas.

The missionary entering an established program without
knowing exactly what his role is going to be should exercise
due caution and evaluate the programs carefully before commit-
ting himself. This is necessary if one is to avoid involvement
in what might turn out to be a less than satisfying ministry.
Where missionary activity has been in existence for a long time
there are sometimes programs in operation that have displaced
original and legitimate goals. Such programs have either
assumed new and perhaps meaningless goals or have merely become
ends in themselves.

The eager new missionary may be fascinated by the smooth
flowing operation with secretaries, paper work, neat files,
and impressive wall charts. Later, totally involved with fund
raising to keep the operation going, a staggering amount of
paper work, and a full schedule of meetings with disgruntled
employees, he may realize that nothing is being accomplished
and that he never comes into personal contact with the people
he came so far to teach and serve.*

Since old developed fields may have rather large numbers of
missionaries in residence at any given time and due to the
past tendency for missionaries to build and live in compounds
the new missionary should be aware of the potential danger of
unusually close contact with his fellow workers. Dissension
among missionaries is more of a problem than most missionaries
are willing to admit. The hesitancy to face up to this problem
is mainly due to the feeling that Christians, of all people,
should be able to solve interpersonal problems; however, it
must be remembered that even the Apostle Paul and Barnabas had
a rather serious dispute over Mark and each went his own way
(Acts 15:39). Today's church workers are not immune to similar
conflicts and should give some attention to finding reasons for
and solutions to such problems.** Missionaries, like musicians,
printers, military personnel and prison inmates, tend to be
thrown together with their colleagues and separated from the
rest of society in a very unique manner.

Musicians, printers, and others whose working hours do not
correspond with the working hours of the majority of persons

---

*For a more complete discussion of this and similar problems,
see page 210 ff.

**The writer has discussed this problem rather fully in an
article entitled, "The Missionary and the Concept of Scope,"
(Hardin 1971:222-226).

tend to be drawn together in their own groups. Prisoners and
other institutionalized persons are forced to be together due
to the nature of their confinement. Military personnel have
an exceptionally close relationship with each other because
they live on compounds and work together, especially when on
overseas tours.

Missionaries tend to have an unusually close relationship
because of their common religious beliefs and because they are
foreigners or outsiders in a strange culture. They often live
close to each other, borrow from each other, attend the same
meetings, work together, and even engage in the same recreational activities.

Although it has previously been suggested that inter-
missionary contact can be supportive, there is significant
evidence to support the idea that too much contact can lead to
problems. This should not be surprising because even Solomon
has told us not to be too often in our neighbor's house lest
he come to hate us (Prov. 25:17).

The term *scope* has been applied to the number of activities
carried out jointly by the same set of participants. It has
also been demonstrated that broad scope (i.e., many joint
activities) is dysfunctional (Etzioni 1965:669-674). Joint
participation in too many activities tends to compound tensions
and conflicts. Petty annoyances, personality conflicts, and
differences of opinion can be minimized if persons leave one
group and meet different persons in another group. But where
the same persons are thrown together continually, seemingly
insignificant factors can become almost unbearable.

Thus the missionary would be well advised to seek significant
other group contacts. This advice may seem easy enough to
accept until considered more deeply. When a Christian seeks
and finds enjoyment in contacts with those outside the fellowship of his missionary colleagues, he may find himself faced
with guilt feelings, and since guilt can be a serious problem
itself, he may be solving one problem by plunging into another.

To assuage the feeling of guilt and actually profit from his
contacts with significant *others*, the missionary must be certain
that he is not compromising his Christian morals or giving in
to the temptations of the world. Christ ate and drank with
sinners, not because he took this as an opportunity to glut
himself, get drunk, or consort with evil men but because he had
come into the world to minister to sinful men and to lead them
into righteousness.

The missionary, like his master, must seek every opportunity for showing his love to the people of the world. He need not be tarnished by their sin but rather should help them escape from the slavery of sin, and if these contacts can also contribute to the adjustment of the missionary to his fellow missionaries, then they are even more to be prized.

Of course, all extra missionary contacts cannot be construed as contact with tax collectors and sinners but this extreme has been used here for the sake of emphasis. Outside contacts with local Christians can also serve the same purpose as far as narrowing missionary scope is concerned and without so many feelings of guilt. In general, scope can be narrowed and interpersonal relationships helped as the new missionary gets more and more deeply involved in the life and culture of the field to which he has been sent.

SUMMARY

Field selection is an extremely important part of overall mission strategy and one seldom considered element in field selection that can make the difference between a joyful ministry and a frustrating ministry is the *level of missionary development* in a given field. Three significant levels include the *undeveloped* field where no mission work (at least by one's own religious group) is being done, the *newly developed* field where mission work has been going on for only a limited period, and the *old developed* field where missionary activity is well established.

The *undeveloped field* presents an aura of romance that must be countered with an objective evaluation of the realities that face the newcomer. The attraction of the exotic wears off quickly, especially in areas where living conditions are somewhat primitive. The self sufficient missionary would likely be the best choice for a worker in an undeveloped field especially if he has the patience to learn the language and sees his plans through.

The *newly developed field* confronts the new missionary with colleagues who have preceeded him and challenges him to develop healthy interpersonal relationships. Unhealthy relationships interfere with the free flow of communication and the dangers of duplication of effort, unilateral planning, and increased missionary division are facilitated.

Old developed fields offer security and structure and are especially appropriate for group dependent missionaries; however, the incoming missionary should know exactly how he is going to fit into the ongoing programs or be capable of finding his place without upsetting the status quo. While determining his area of ministry, he should avoid any programs that may have outlived their usefulness.

6

Missionary
Control Structure

> But how are men to call upon him in whom they have not
> believed? And how are they to believe in him of whom
> they have never heard? And how can men preach unless
> they are sent? (Romans 10:14-15)

The sending forth of preachers into the world carries with
it implications of control and support. Even the sending off
of the Apostle Paul by members of the church at Antioch was in
response to the Holy Spirit who had a specific work for Paul
to accomplish (Acts 13:3). Later in his ministry Paul wrote to
the church of Philippi and thanked them for their partnership
in the gospel from the first day until the time of his writing
(Philippians 1:5). From these scriptures it can be understood
that even the Apostle Paul was sent on a specific journey
(though his plans continually developed under the guidance of
the Holy Spirit) and was partially dependent upon churches,
in Philippi and perhaps other places, for his support.

Today, missionaries continue to be sent out and supported
and the nature of that sending and support varies from group.
to group and missionary to missionary. On one hand there are
the vocational missionaries* who travel here and there (as
employees of secular companies) preaching Christ to the unsaved
and attempting to establish churches. These may be soldiers,

---

*A vocational missionary is any Christian who, while suppor-
ted by a secular job, serves the interests of the church in
areas where the church is relatively weak (Hardin 1974:29-36).

private business men, or State Department personnel who carry
the message of Christ with them wherever they go. On the other
extreme are those missionaries who have submitted their appli-
cations to an eldership or, in the case of some groups, to a
national or international board of missions and accepted an
appointment to a field selected, organized, and controlled by
the eldership or board.

To help classify and indicate the relationships of possible
control structures for missionary activity the control structure
continuum (Fig. 24) was developed. The division between one
classification and another cannot be established with any degree
of precision; therefore, the areas are certainly subject to
considerable overlap.

INDEPENDENT   ENDORSED   PARTNERSHIP   SUPERVISED   CONTROLLED

Figure 24.   Missionary Control Structure.

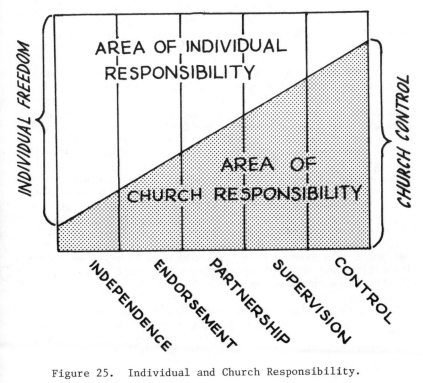

Figure 25.   Individual and Church Responsibility.

As the five divisions of the missionary control continuum
are discussed, one especially important aspect of control
structure will be given rather careful treatment. This is the
area of *responsibility*. It will be pointed out that independence and responsibility go hand in hand and that the missionary
who has maximum independence also has maximum responsibility.
Figure 25 illustrates this point and the following discussion
gives some of the pros and cons with regard to independence
and responsibility and the need for balance between the two.

THE INDEPENDENT MISSIONARY

The independent missionaries are those who support themselves
by engaging in fulltime work with some company or agency. They
draw no church support and, for the most part, are free from
church control. Of course, as Christians they are not free
from Christ or free from the responsibilities of all Christians
but as far as local church control or missionary society control is concerned, they are on their own. (To this group could
also be added the independently wealthy individual who can
support himself without church help and also without the responsibilities of a job.) The independent missionary is sent out
by the church in that he accepts God's challenge to use himself
for the kingdom. He also assumes that wherever he goes and
wherever he is stationed, God has a work for him to do.

It is not uncommon to hear prospective missionaries express
their desire to be fully self supported. This desire, of
course, comes from a somewhat naive view of independence and
responsibility; however, it is a view also shared by some of
those who have already been on the field. For example, one
may hear missionaries, who are dependent upon church support,
express their desire to be financially independent so that they
can fulfill their mission without the interference or control
of any church or religious agency. Such a desire can be
appreciated by anyone who has had to take orders, file reports,
and in any manner be subject to the whims of superiors who may
seem, at times, unrealistic, arbitrary, or even antagonistic.
Although it is not the purpose in this discussion to either
persuade nor disuade a missionary from seeking a particular
approach to his mission work, it would be well if every prospective missionary and every sponsoring group would weigh carefully the pros and cons involved.

There is an attraction in the concept of freedom, and there
may be times when such freedom might help one take advantage of
an opportunity that would ordinarily slip away before a traditional system of authority could ever get into gear and bring
forth any positive action. Even the Apostle Paul supported
himself by making tents in Corinth (Acts 18:3); however, this

same Apostle also received support from the church in Philippi
while he was in Rome (Phil. 4:15-18). On one occasion he refused to set out on a mission with Mark and Barnabas
(Acts 15:37-39) but later called for Mark when he felt that
they could work together effectively (II Tim. 4:11). Evidently Paul did not think that independence and "going it
alone" were the final answers to a successful ministry but
rather was willing to meet each new challenge with whatever
method seemed most appropriate.

Hopefully each missionary will continually subject his work
to as objective a scrutiny as possible and then be flexible
enough to use whatever honorable methods are best suited to
each particular phase of his work. There may well be a time
and place for the self supported missionary, but self-support
should not be looked upon as a cure-all for a missionary's
problems.

In spite of the fact that businessmen, nurses, or soldiers
may qualify as missionaries according to the author's definition they should understand that those who do not consider
them *real* missionaries are not being discriminatory without
some justification. Since the independent missionary must
support himself, a major portion of his time and talents must
be directed toward his area of employment.

Most employers demand not only a full day's work but also
certain social responsibilities that may require a considerable amount of time and attention; thus, there may be a very
limited amount of time available for active participation in
preaching, teaching, and benevolent activities. Of course,
much depends on the exact nature of the job and the attitude of
superiors, but the responsibilities of making a living can
seriously limit the time a person can contribute to his mission.
Likewise, a person working for a private or government organization may have to move on to a new location at a very inopportune time as far as his missionary activities are concerned.

On the positive side, the independent missionary, because
he is a full time employee of some non religious organization,
may be able to enter countries where full time missionaries
would not be permitted. An independent missionary working
with the U.S. State Department entered one African country and
discovered that no missionaries were allowed into the nation
without the formal invitation of a church already established
within the country. In a few weeks this new vocational
missionary, during his free time, located some Christians,
organized a congregation, and received the recognition of the
local government. From that point it was an easy matter to
get full time missionaries into the country. That vocational

missionary did not have much time for personal evangelism,
although he did teach and baptize a few, but his greatest contribution came from his ability to get a job done that no one
else could do and thus open the way for full time missionaries
through an otherwise closed door.

Perhaps the independent missionary's greatest potential
problem hinges around the subject of personal responsibility.
Although governments and large private corporations provide
many things for their workers and consider all of their
physical needs, they will not, generally, have any specific
interest in an employee's religious views.

The self-supported missionary must make *all* religious
decisions himself and although this might seem refreshing and
desirable to some, it may actually become an unbearable burden.
Especially during times of trial and frustration it can be a
great relief to be able to look to others for help in the form
of advice, counsel, sympathy, and physical and moral support.

It is distressing to see every new missionary re-invent
the wheel, so to speak, when if his efforts were somehow coordinated with others, he could learn from their experiences,
profit from their mistakes, and cooperate with them in a
broader, more far reaching program. The independent missionary
may be able to work in close harmony with others but he,
alone, must assume the responsibility for making it happen.

Since an independent missionary must make his own decisions
the breadth of his responsibilities is extremely important.
A single man or woman responsible only for his or her welfare
might find it much easier to make all the decisions and earn
all the support needed than a person with a large family.
Housing, schooling, health, sanitation, and diet, become increasingly more critical as a spouse and children are added
to the list of one's responsibilities.

The number and nature of personal responsibilities are so
important that the prospective missionary considering self
support as a means of doing mission work should consider these
areas very carefully. Freedom is a grand word and carries many
good implications, but it can also be synonymous with being
alone and all that can be associated with loneliness.

THE ENDORSED MISSIONARY

Moving down the scale from independent to controlled missionaries, the next category is the endorsed missionary. To those
who do not consider self supported church members as true
missionaries, the endorsed missionary would be, to them, the

extreme example of an independent missionary. He has a church
sponsor, he receives church support, and he even sends a few
reports to his sponsor from time to time, but other than this
his freedom is virtually unlimited.

Persons associated with highly organized missionary societies may be unfamiliar with this system of endorsement, but to
those associated with churches that practice complete congregational autonomy the endorsed missionary is quite common. He
raises most of his own support, chooses his own field, makes
his own preparation (if, indeed he does prepare), and proceeds,
on the field, according to his own ideas of what should be
done. Endorsement is necessary because most religious groups
demand that each missionary work within some type of structural framework. It is due to this demand that endorsement has
become very popular.

In 1956 the author decided that he wanted to be a missionary.
Korea was selected as a field and then various congregations
were visited in an attempt to gather support. One congregation
pledged $50.00 per month and several others tentatively
pledged $10.00 to $25.00 each on the condition that some
responsible eldership would oversee or sponsor this mission
to Korea. Finally, a small congregation in Albuquerque,
New Mexico, agreed to act as sponsor.

This sponsoring church's sole responsibility was to receive
and transmit funds and keep in contact with Korea so that they
would know what their missionary was doing and thus be able
to vouch for his orthodoxy and competence. As a sponsor they
served to legitimize a program of missions already planned and
initiated.*

The missionary who works within this type of arrangement has
a responsibility to his sponsoring church but that responsibility may be very limited or perhaps extremely vague. There
is usually no written contract but merely an ill defined verbal
agreement between the missionary and one member of the sponsoring church's leadership. The missionary in this situation
is generally the initiator of the program who raised his own
support and will be responsible for keeping the funds coming
even after the endorsing church begins handling the transfer
of funds.

---

*Over the years this sponsor took a very personal interest
in their missionary and a warm relationship still exists, but
when an opportunity came to switch the responsibilities of
sponsorship to another congregation they were happy to be un-
burdened.

The endorsed missionary works within a framework of delegated authority but actually enjoys a position of almost complete independence. As in the case of the self supported missionary, this missionary must also shoulder the major burden of all responsibility. From fund raising to policy making he is definitely the decision maker and active participant. Whether he comes or goes, uses one method or another, stays or gives up, the endorsed missionary has only a nominal responsibility to his sponsoring church.

Also, in times of difficulty the endorsed missionary must generally carry on alone. Although he may have an avenue of communication with his sponsoring organization, the very nature of the arrangement precludes the possibility that the sponsor will feel any great responsibility for the missionary's mistakes or frustrations. This does not mean that they will not sympathize and feel sorry for anyone in trouble, but it does mean that they will feel no obligation to repay debts, borrow large sums of money, or greatly increase their own normal participation in the program just because the man they have endorsed is in a bind.

Under arrangements of this nature a sponsor has been known to drop support and withdraw sponsorship during a man's mission tour and thus leave him in a foreign country without adequate support. Likewise, missionaries working under this type of arrangement feel very little responsibility to heed the demands or suggestions of their sponsors. If a sponsor becomes too demanding, the missionary may sever his relationship with that congregation and seek endorsement elsewhere.

The missionary or the sponsoring group operating under this type of arrangement would do well to clarify the detailed aspects of their relationship from the very beginning. If mutual trust is strong and both missionary and sponsor are mature, wise, and dedicated to a common goal, such an arrangement can be very practical; however, all too frequently these arrangements end in less than satisfactory circumstances.

The following hypothetical example is given to show exactly how the endorsed missionary could find himself in a very uncomfortable situation. Consider the endorsed missionary who decides to develop a program of printing on the field. He finds a nice hand press to use while getting started and then orders a new off-set from the United States when the program gets underway. Facilities are rented, printers hired, translators set to work preparing material from English texts, and the missionary is thrilled and excited about his new project. When the elders of his sponsoring church ask him how he is going to pay for the off-set and all the new employees, he explains that he can sell his car to pay for the press and that income from some commercial printing jobs will more than pay for the hired help.

A month later the commercial accounts quit coming in (because the quality of printing is substandard), his car is being held by the department of justice because it was unknow-ingly sold without the proper tax payments (tax payments amount-ing to 2/3 the price of the car), and the missionary is in serious financial trouble both at home and abroad. At this time he writes, in desperation, to his sponsors asking them for help.

It is at this point that the tenuous thread of endorsement may be strained to the breaking point. The sponsors knew nothing about the whole printing project until it was well underway. They had, among the elders, men who knew business and who could have foretold the dangers of the project, but they were neither asked or even informed. Who would blame them if they abandoned the whole project?

From another viewpoint consider the endorsed missionary who, after five years on the field, receives a letter from his sponsoring church informing him that they are concluding both their sponsorship and 50% support.* This may seem a bit cruel to the objective observer, but it must be understood that sponsorship is generally offered only after a missionary has assured a congregation that they have absolutely no obliga-tion beyond endorsing him for one or two years. Generally they will renew that endorsement for a few more years and sometimes indefinitely; however, when they come across a pro-ject that they really like or run into financial problems that force them to cut their own budget, they may decide to conclude sponsorship arrangements that they had continued long past the agreed upon period.

Finances are another of the endorsed missionary's most seri-ous problems. Not only must he raise most of his own funds and make up for drop-outs along the way but he must also keep track of the funds he does use. Since the sponsoring church is merely acting as a banker for the missionary they endorse, they usually forward to him whatever comes in regardless of the amount. Also, the missionary who raises his own support

---

*Most sponsors also contribute some portion of their missionary's support. This is necessary if they are to be used in promoting fund raising. No church has much interest in supporting a program that the sponsor is not willing to support.

will likely make many personal acquaintances around the world
and will receive direct contributions from time to time. The
dangers inherent in this type situation are not difficult to
guess.

First, unless the missionary keeps accurate books he may
leave himself open to all sorts of negative speculations and
criticism. Anyone who lives by a carefully planned budget
knows how easy it is to misjudge where funds have been used
if accurate records are not kept. Surely everyone has had
the experience of going on a vacation or shopping spree with a
specified amount of cash on hand. At the end of the day the
funds are running a little short and one sits down to try and
account for every dollar. Generally there will be a significant number of dollars that cannot be accounted for. The
person knows that he has spent the money during that very day
but simply cannot recall where it has all gone. This simple
everyday event illustrates how a missionary over a longer
period of time can spend hundreds of dollars and not be able
to account for them unless he keeps *absolutely complete* records.

In a brief conversation that the writer had with a total
stranger some very disturbing information came to light. The
stranger, a U.S. government worker in the South Pacific,
discovering that he was in the presence of a missionary,
engaged him in conversation. In the course of the conversation he mentioned some missionaries who worked in a town near
his duty station. He had met these missionaries on various
occasions and was deeply disturbed because they were continually receiving large sums of money from the United States but
kept no records and had nothing to show as to how they were
using the money.

This un-believer had a very negative attitude toward
missionaries because he really doubted the honesty and inte-
grity of those who made so little effort to keep track of funds.
Whether these missionaries were honest or dishonest is not
really the question. The fact is that they were handling funds
in a very sloppy manner and were thus not above suspicion.

Secondly, the missionary may become so emotionally involved
with his ministry that he will put his own money into it to
the point that he causes himself financial disaster. This is
not the "giving beyond their means" of the people of Macedonia
(II Cor. 8) but the giving away of money that one does not
possess. More than one missionary has given in this manner
to the extent that he has had to call upon his sponsor or some
other source for help to clear him of his indebtedness. This,
too, can cause a sponsor to consider severing a relationship

with an endorsed missionary. Again, the burden of responsibility for remaining above reproach, handling himself honorably
in the sight of all, and keeping his house in order rests with
the endorsed missionary himself. He has maximum freedom but
must accept, along with that freedom, considerable responsibility.

Obviously, the self-sufficient missionary (see page 34) will
be attracted to the idea of endorsement. He will likely want
maximum freedom so that he can make his own decisions and do
things without too much interference from others. If he has
good judgment and the patience to get the job done effectively,
he is an ideal missionary for the church that wants to do
mission work but has no desire to have any close supervision
over the details of the field activity.

Also, endorsement fits in quite well with undeveloped
fields if the pioneer missionary is as patient and dependable
as he is self-sufficient. Of course, if the missionary is not
self sufficient or does not have what it takes to do the work
effectively, endorsement becomes an avenue for failure because
there is no modifying element (strong sponsor support) to make
up for his weaknesses.

THE PARTNERSHIP

As originally developed, there were only four divisions on
the missionary control structure continuum (Fig. 24); however,
when Mitchell Greer (returned missionary from Sweden) used the
continuum in a mission seminar he added a fifth intermediate
category which he called *partnership*. At first it seemed that
such a category would demand equal control and equal responsibility on the part of the missionary and his sponsor. Such a
relationship would be impractical because, in the event of a
disagreement where someone must break the stalemate, there
would be no way to break the deadlock. On the continuum,
however, the intermediate category takes in more than just a
single midpoint, i.e., it includes 1/10 of the area to the
left of the mid-point (where individual freedom slightly
overreaches church control) and 1/10 of the area to the right
of the mid-point where church control slightly overreaches
individual freedom.

Whether or not this relationship was in the mind of Paul
when he spoke of the partnership he had with the church in
Philippi (Phil. 1:5), it is difficult to say; however, for
many missionaries it offers an escape from the full burden of
responsibility they see in the endorsed category and yet protects them from the complete domination of an eldership or
presbytery in which they have not yet developed full confidence.

Quite likely those churches who began their mission work by endorsing some missionary will want to move toward a partnership as they become more deeply involved and feel a growing sense of interest and confidence. They may realize that their missionary, especially if he is self-sufficient, will be reluctant to give up his freedom and independence; thus, they may assert themselves cautiously in an effort to avoid a confrontation or dispute with the man they have been sponsoring.

Sometimes a church will develop an interest in a given field and then search for a prospective missionary to send; at other times a prospective missionary will become interested in a field and begin searching for a sponsoring church; however, to have a truly successful partnership both ultimately must have a vital interest in the mission work in which they become involved. Just as missionaries should be prepared before they go to the mission field, sponsoring churches who wish to play an active role in their missionary work must also be prepared.

Of course, preparation for the eldership of a local congregation need not be identical to the preparation of a missionary Although it might be good if elders could make an in depth study of missiology, it is doubtful that the typical eldership would ever find the time to attend as many classes and read as many books as the average student of mission. This book, a selective list of mission books* and various mission seminars held at local congregations can help give the leaders of a local congregation enough insight into mission work that they can oversee a mission program properly.**

It is especially important that the active sponsors be aware of the missionary's need for special training, aware of the problems he will face on the field, and knowledgeable of the resources that are available to him and themselves. They, along with their missionary, should develop a clear-cut mission policy, determine what they want to accomplish, develop a plan for field selection, select an appropriate field, plan a strategy for evangelization, send their missionary, and constantly monitor and evaluate the program.

Perhaps the most critical element of the partnership is communication. The sponsor and missionary can hardly be expected to function effectively and harmoniously unless they

---

*See Allen, Gurganus, Hodges, Lindsell, and McGavran, in the Bibliography.

**For a more complete discussion see Daniel Hardin 1976:1-3.

are in close contact with each other. Letters, telephone calls,
and tapes should provide a continual link between field and
home; however, these alone will not be enough. The sponsors
should plan periodic visits to the field so that they can
truly get the feel of what is taking place there.

Successful businesses or industries with branch offices or
assembly plants in foreign countries usually send people from
the home office several times a year. This may seem rather
expensive but to the administrator it is just good business.
Frequently, elders will not visit a field until serious
problems develop. It would be much more effective if they could
visit more frequently and perhaps resolve problems before they
happen.

Also sponsoring church elders, not preachers and deacons,
should be the first choice for such visits. Although the
younger preacher or deacon may have more free time than the
elder whose responsibilities at home may be very demanding,
the elder should, if at all possible, be the one to visit the
field. In spite of their good intentions the younger preacher
or deacon seldom sees the mission field as objectively as the
older and wiser elder.

This writer's impression of the younger visitors is of
rather starry eyed tourists who are absolutely fascinated by
the strange customs, clothing, and behavior of the local people.
They come with camera loaded and return home a few days later
with pictures, souvenirs, and local color, but with little
insight into the problems facing the local evangelist.

The elder, on the other hand, seems less inclined to be
caught up in the whirl of tourist excitement and much more
alert to the down to earth problems of the work itself. Not
to say that visitors should not have some fun and see some of
the interesting sights but only that such superficials should
not blind them to their real mission.

One group of visiting deacons stayed in a missionary home
which was shattered by a divorce shortly after the visitors
left. The situation was extremely serious and the air in that
home was charged with tension, but the visitors were so ena-
moured with being in a foreign country that they were completely
oblivious to the impending disaster. No one knows for sure if
their understanding of the situation could have helped or not
but at least they could have tried to do something if they had
been aware that a problem existed.

Partnership may be about the closest thing to supervision
or control to which the self-sufficient missionary will be

willing to submit. It is, however, advantageous to the
missionary. For example, he has the advice and counsel of
other interested persons, decisions are made by the sponsor
and the missionary rather than unilaterally by either one,
responsibility is shared and the missionary need never find
himself dropped or forgotten.

For the church, partnership demands a missionary in whom
the elders have the utmost confidence. After all, he is
their prime resource person and co-laborer. He cannot be so
thoroughly self sufficient that he resists cooperation nor so
group dependent that he exercises no initiative. An ideal
partner will likely be somewhere midway along the synergistic
variable continuum (see page 35).

THE SUPERVISED MISSIONARY

This category includes, not only those missionaries from
religious bodies that have no other method of doing mission
work but also those potentially independent or endorsed
missionaries who choose to surrender a measure of freedom for
the sake of working in a supervised capacity. Independent,
endorsed, and partnership missionaries or prospective missionaries contemplating going into the field under one or the
other of these structures would do well to give serious consideration to this fourth option.

Generally, the church which intends to supervise a missionary
has enough interest in mission to become fairly expert in the
missionary enterprise. They will form a mission committee and
expect the members to become familiar with the literature on
mission, to attend lectures or seminars on mission work, and
to develop a mission policy for the congregation. Not all
committees will achieve the same level of sophistication or
expertise, but they will have some clearly defined ideas about
mission work.

A supervising church will want to lead in the selection of
the field, the selection of the missionary, and the determination of the methodology to be used on the field. One immediate
criticism of this structure will come from missionaries who do
not feel that a sponsor thousands of miles from a field can
adequately supervise a field program.

Of course, elderships, congregations, mission committees,
and missionary societies may vary considerably in their
ability to satisfactorally supervise any kind of program be it
at home or abroad. No doubt there are sponsors of missionary
activity who are ill prepared as far as missionary supervision

is concerned; however, the same can be said for those who
supervise local preachers at home or any of the activities of
the church anywhere.

The point is that nothing hinders any sponsor from becoming
well informed and well prepared in this day of mass communication and easy travel. There are good books to read, excellent
seminars to attend, college courses to take, and unlimited
opportunities for first hand visits with experts in all mission
related fields. Today, America has thousands of companies
doing business outside the United States. Assembly plants,
component factories, refineries, and a host of other highly
organized activities are being carried on by American based
businesses. Sometimes they fail and they naver have it easy
but in spite of the distance and difficulty the majority continue to make profits.

These business enterprises are operated by the same kind of
intelligent persons one would expect to find in the leadership
of the church. In fact it would not be unreasonable to expect
a little more from the church leader because of his contact
with God and his reliance and trust in God. Therefore, how
can we say that the church leader cannot supervise a program
in another country?

An investigation of those who are most adamant against
sponsor supervision might reveal personalities that do not
appreciate any kind of supervision anywhere. No doubt there
are a few (hopefully very few) missionaries who have chosen
mission work for the reason that it gives them freedom to
function without the critical eye of anyone in a supervising
capacity.

A supervised missionary is not a robot that has become
completely passive. The sponsor may have some basic ideas
about missionary work but will likely not make too many
specific plans until a missionary has been selected. The
prospective missionary may become one of the most active and
forceful members of the sponsoring committee or group. He
will likely be involved in field selection, strategy, fund
raising, and all aspects of the planning and preparation that
must take place before he actually arrives on the field.

Once he is on the field the missionary becomes the main
resource person from that field because he is there. Decisions
are not made without his advice, and he may have more influence
over policy making and modification than anyone else in the
group (elders, mission committee, etc.), but throughout the
program he is definitely a part of a group and closely scrutinized by those who hold ultimate authority.

There are various advantages to the *supervised structure*.
First, there is greater stability to a mission program when the
sponsor is vitally interested in the program itself. Sponsors
who merely endorse are frequently uninterested in the field
where their missionary is working. This is one reason that it
is so easy for them to sever their relationship under any sort
of pressure. Likewise, when the missionary they endorse leaves
a field, the sponsor also forsakes that field because the
interest was in the missionary more than in the field.

Second, two heads are better than one and group decisions
over time are superior to individual decisions. An interested
sponsor can bring together literature, expertise, and all
manner of resources that would be out of the reach of the
independent missionary. The endorsed missionary may go into
the field unprepared, fail to study the language, and use
second rate methods, but the supervised missionary will have
the several members of the committee to satisfy and will likely
be encouraged to prepare himself before going, encouraged to
study language and culture on the field, and provided with the
latest information on methods so that he stands a good chance
of succeeding in his missionary effort.

Third, the supervised missionary, as a part of a larger
group is freed from full responsibility in all phases of his
work (see Fig. 25). Everything is shared including fund
raising, reporting and planning. He need not face the problems
of housing, sanitation, health, education, and travel by himself. The sponsor is also interested in these factors and
will see to it that these present no insurmountable obstacles
to the missionary.

Fourth, the supervised missionary is less likely to involve
himself in legal or financial problems. Emotionally carried
away by some fascinating idea the supervised missionary feels
a sense of responsibility to his sponsor that compels him to
write or call them before jumping into anything new. This
gives the missionary a few hours for personal reflection (which
can, in itself, save him from some foolish moves) and also
brings sage advice from more objective sources.

Fifth, the supervised missionary knows that if problems do
develop on the field, his sponsors will respond with funds,
troubleshooters, or whatever is necessary to solve the problems.
Since everything the supervised missionary does is the result
of a group effort he knows that all responsibility is shared.
If the group makes a mistake, the group will rally to make
amends. This can mean a great deal to a foreigner far away
from home.

Although an extremely self-sufficient missionary might find
the restraints of group work and close supervision too con-
fining, those near or in the intermediate category and those in
the group dependent (see the synergistic variable scale on
page 35) category would seem to be well suited to the controls
of the supervised structure. Of course, the exact nature of
the supervising control structure might determine more precisely where the best fit would occur.

THE CONTROLLED MISSIONARY

Complete missionary control may not be considered a real
possibility by some who would claim that no human being can
be *completely* controlled; however, the use of the term *control*
in the present context is merely a modification or intensifi-
cation of the idea of supervision discussed above. There is
no measurable point at which supervision becomes control, but
the use of the two terms serves to locate relative points or
areas on a continuum.

An example of control would be any one of a number of missionary societies which handle the missionary activities of their
particular religious group; however, this discussion is not
limited to those groups but may also be applied to autonomous
congregational situations where a single congregation assumes
complete control over the missionaries it sponsors. Control is
quite common in missionary apprentice programs where student
missionaries are sent into mission fields for a few months or a
year or so. Although there may be considerable variety as to
specific plans and policies, a controlling agency will usually
present the prospective missionary with the following structure.

He or she will be required to file an application with the
elders or mission committee listing personal information,
references, motivation for wanting to be a missionary, etc.
The sponsor will have firmly established policies regarding
such things as family size, education level, age, experience,
and background. Once these requirements are met the applicant
may be granted an interview, tested, and perhaps classified.

If fully qualified, an applicant may be offered a position
somewhere in the missionary enterprise being overseen by that
sponsor or even another church. Salary will be carefully calculated and fixed, housing will be provided, language training
will be required, and teachers will be supplied. According to
a standard, although not inflexible, schedule the new missionary will move from student to intern to full fledged missionary
over a period of months or years.

On the positive side this highly dependent missionary has many advantages. First, he need not worry about raising his own support.* He may be required to assist in some programs that are an integral part of the church's mission fund raising procedure but he will likely serve as a participant with very little responsibility for the overall successes or failure of the effort.

Second, there will usually be a rather complete package of side benefits such as a retirement plan, or social security and withholding tax procedure, an annuity, an education allowance for children, insurance, and scheduled vacations.

Third, control indicates what organizational theorists call *close supervision*. That is, the missionary will be so closely supervised by some super-ordinate that there is little chance in his making many serious mistakes. Therefore, his work as a missionary need not be plagued with problems and difficult decisions.

Fourth, if the controlled missionary does have a problem, he can rest assured that his super-ordinate will soon be on hand to help solve it. He will always have ample advice, physical and moral support, spiritual guidance, and expertise based, hopefully, upon a long history of missionary involvement.

On the negative side the controlled missionary by definition has almost no freedom or independence. For example, his personal life may not be his own. He and his wife may decide to adopt a local orphan only to discover that the church frowns on international adoptions.** Second, he may feel that it is important for his children to attend a different school than the one recommended by the church, and he may not be given permission to make that change. These are but two examples of a host of personal decisions that a controlled missionary may not be permitted to make. Finally, he may be absolutely helpless as far as a program modification is concerned. Any deviation from a prescribed course of action could result in his being sent home. Obviously, the self-sufficient missionary would be least likely to function satisfactorily in a controlled program unless he were given a high priority leadership role. The group dependent missionary, on the other hand, would likely fit very well into a program of this type.

---

*In apprentice programs students frequently have to raise their own support but churches sending fulltime missionaries, under this category, usually provide the support.

**In some of the denominations with missionary societies, adoptions, etc., may be absolutely forbidden.

Also, the controlled structure is going to be much more realistic in an old developed field. A sponsor wishing to exercise close supervision will have to modify its wishes somewhat if a typical pioneer effort is to be launched. There may be a need for them to drop back into a supervising capacity and allow the pioneer missionary greater latitude in making decisions.

SUMMARY

Missionary control structure refers to the amount of control that a church or arm thereof exercises over a missionary who functions formally or informally as an agent of that church. This control may vary from virtually no control to complete control and has been classified according to relative positions along a continuum (See Fig. 24, page 161). Five categories have been suggested, (1) the independent missionary, (2) the endorsed missionary, (3) the partnership, (4) the supervised missionary, and (5) the controlled missionary.

The independent missionary is best represented by the employee of a secular firm (with an international outreach) who teaches Christ in his free time wherever he is sent. Although not always considered a true missionary by some, he does represent an evangelistic force that is not dependent upon the church for support and thus is not strongly controlled by the church.

The independent missionary has the advantage of complete personal freedom within the parameters of his employment responsibilities. Also, he sometimes is able to enter countries where full time missionaries would not be permitted; however, since his first responsibility is to his employer his time for evangelism is often limited, and he may have to leave an area at an inopportune time as far as his religious activities are concerned. Finally, he must bear, along with his freedom, the full responsibility for his actions.

The endorsed missionary is one who is dependent upon church support but is in almost every other respect independent of church control. To meet the demands of legitimacy and to have a physical contact with a church at home, the missionary may request that a church become his sponsor.

The endorsed missionary has the freedom which allows him to take advantage of all field opportunities and to approach his work as he thinks best; however, this lack of real supervision places on the missionary the full burden of responsibility for the actions he does take. In times of crisis, especially when the problems are due to his own errors, he may discover that his sponsor will not come to his rescue. Likewise, if the sponsor of an endorsed missionary wishes to make a special demand of the missionary (ask him to return home or change his approach), they may find that the missionary will resign from their sponsorship and seek a new endorsement from another congregation.

Finances must be handled carefully by the endorsed missionary because he generally has not only sole responsibility for handling funds that come to him through the sponsoring church, but he also receives funds directly from various sources. If he does not keep accurate financial records, he can easily become subject to suspicion and doubt. Also, he must take care lest he confuse his personal funds with working funds and in his enthusiasm for some project spend more than he has.

Endorsement fits in quite well where sponsors want only limited responsibility, where self-sufficient missionaries are involved, and where the target area is an undeveloped field. Assuming that the self-sufficient missionary is also capable of enough self discipline and persistence that he does not fall into any serious pitfalls, the endorsed relationship can be quite satisfactory; otherwise, it can be disastrous.

The partnership is the intermediate category where control and freedom are most closely balanced. Either the church or the missionary might have the final say under this arrangement and they will generally work very closely together.

Perhaps an extreme for the self-sufficient or the group-dependent missionary, this category would be quite natural for those in-between. In any case both missionary and sponsor need training to prepare them for their active roles in the mission enterprise. Although the local church leaders might not be expected to become as expert as the missionary himself, they will need to know how to oversee a good mission program.

The supervised missionary has some personal freedom and a voice in the decision making process but works as a group member and thus shares in every respect with all the members of the group.* This arrangement demands increased interest on the part of the church. It gives the program the benefit of broad interest and careful planning, removes a load of responsibility from the missionary, helps keep the missionary from

---

*Group here refers to the church, mission committee, eldership, and missionary as they work together in the total missionary enterprise.

making thoughtless snap decisions, and assures him of concern and help if, at any time, problems develop.

The controlled missionary must fit into a highly organized process of selection, training, and service. His freedom to make field decisions is limited and he may have various restraints imposed on his personal life (in the area of adoptions, family size, life style, etc.); however, he is virtually relieved of all concerns for support, housing, education, health, retirement, and other extras that are generally included in controlled programs. Obviously group dependent individuals would fit most easily into this structure. Also, it seems most advantageous where older fields already have on-going programs and there is little room for new programs.

7

Goals and Methods

For so the Lord has commanded us, saying, "I have set
you to be a light for the Gentiles, that you may bring
salvation to the uttermost parts of the earth."
Acts 13:7.

When they had preached the gospel to that city and had
made many disciples, they returned to Lystra and to
Iconium and to Antioch, strengthening the souls of the
disciples, exhorting them to continue in the faith, and
saying that through many tribulations we must enter the
Kingdom of God. And when they had appointed elders for
them in every church, with prayers and fasting, they
committed them to the Lord in whom they believed.
Acts 14:21-23.

Once a sponsor has brought the right man and right field
together under an appropriate and mutually beneficial control
structure; once the man has learned the language, made a satisfactory cultural adjustment, and found his place among fellow
workers; the next critical step is for him to use the proper
method to accomplish his mission goals. In a sense, this
chapter should have preceeded some of the others because mission
goals are so closely allied with mission philosophy and policy.
Goals should be established early in mission strategy because
they are the real guides to all else that takes place. Field
selection, the choosing and training of a missionary, and even
the determination of the control to be exercised over him are
all influenced by the goals of the total missionary enterprise;
however, after considering all the pros and cons it was decided

that the section on goals and methods might be more meaningful following the other chapters.

The subject of mission methods has been a popular one among missionaries and mission writers for many years. The purpose of this discussion is not primarily to defend one method as superior to another but to indicate the strengths and weaknesses of various methods and the need for exercising caution lest one be drawn into a method that does not suit his personality, his philosophy of mission, or the plans that he has made with his sponsors. Undoubtedly there are many satisfactory ways of categorizing methods and the one used here is not upheld as superior but merely as one that offers a proper vehicle for the suggestions that will follow.

One basic assumption is that the formal goals of all missionary activities are related to the three main philsophies of mission presented in chapter V. This would include *presence, church growth,* and *social reform.* In the model accompanying this discussion (See Fig. 26) the presence philosophy is illustrated by the term *gospel dissemination;* church growth encompasses four types of church establishment: (1) *indigenous,* (2) *nationalized,* (3) *national front,* and (4) *mission directed;* and Social Reform is represented by the term *social services.*

Methods have been divided into three main categories: (1) *itinerant preaching,* (2) *mission station development,* and (3) *institution establishment,* which includes radio broadcasting, Bible correspondence courses, reading rooms, evangelistic leagues, seminaries, hospitals, clinics, relief clothing distribution centers, and schools.

A model of this nature does not exhaust all possible relationships between method and method or goal and method; however, it is an attempt to illustrate the more obvious relationships and thus clarify understanding concerning what expectations a sponsor can have for success as a particular method is used to bring about a specific result. One dimension not included in the model involves constraints that might be imposed by nature, governments, personnel, or any number of factors.

For example, one's philosophy of mission might be *church growth* but if there should occur an opportunity to establish a small clinic in a hitherto unreached Islamic stronghold, the need for a Christian presence (in the form of a benevolent program) might demand that a clinic be supplied and supported. In this situation the clinic, a benevolent program, would be the nearest possible thing to *church growth.* Under the circumstances it would be the expedient method to employ. Thus,

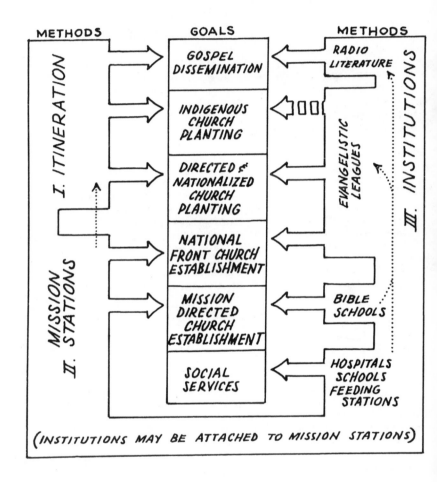

Figure 26. Mission Methods Model.

the model should not be viewed as an inflexible statement of absolute relationships but as a general guideline indicating probable relationships between methods and results.

MISSION GOALS

In the discussion of philosophies it was indicated that once a person determined his philosophy of mission he would be in a position to formulate a policy statement. Such a policy statement should make it very easy to determine mission goals and once the goals are stated, the next step, selection of an appropriate method, is necessary. Below are some general mission goals that, in turn, will guide the way to the selection of specific methods.

Gospel Dissemination

If one holds a presence philosophy of mission, he will likely be satisfied with any activity or program that disseminates the gospel, regardless of the response. In some resistant areas there is little more that the Christian can do than be there with the gospel and present it through word and deed whenever and wherever the opportunity presents itself.

The holder of a presence philosophy might pray and wish for the salvation of many souls and the establishment of many churches, but he would not consider this result a significant criterion in his selection of nor persistence in a given field. Regardless of response he would feel that his job and his responsibility would be fulfilled in the offering of the gospel, which could, in the sense of responsibility fulfillment, be an end or goal in itself.

Gospel dissemination may also be an initial step in a plan to plant churches. In fact, any of the mission philosophies might call for gospel dissemination as a part of a more comprehensive goal; however, as a goal or end in itself, it would have to stem from a presence philosophy.

The Indigenous Church

This term has become so popular with missionaries and students of missions that it can hardly be avoided; however, it is not only a much used word but also a much abused one. Missionaries (the writer included) use the term as though they and all others understand exactly what it means in spite of the fact that probably no two missionaries would define an indigenous church in exactly the same way.

There might be some unanimity over the definition given by Melvin Hodges when he said that an indigenous church is a national church, produced by a missionary effort, which shares the life of the country in which it is planted and finds within itself the ability to govern itself, support itself, and reproduce itself (Hodges 1971:9); however, even this popular concept has too many critics for it to be considered the last word in determining the nature of an indigenous church. Some feel that it is not comprehensive enough and needs additional dimensions such as self edification, self sacrifice, and self awareness (Mathews 1975).

Still others question the three basic selves (self support, self government, and self propagation) on the basis of their reliability as indicants of indigenousness. Smalley points out that a church can copy a foreign pattern completely and support itself, govern itself, and reproduce itself all in the borrowed, non-indigenous mode of another culture. Likewise, churches can benefit from outside support (loans, grants and gifts) without losing their indigenous character (Smalley 1958:51-65).

With due credit to the thinking of these and others who have struggled with the concept of an indigenous church a more satisfactory definition might be: *An indigenous church is a church in which God, Christ, and the Holy Spirit, in contact with people of a particular cultural setting, give rise to a Christian body that is outwardly and uniquely molded by that culture over a fixed framework of fundamental scriptural doctrine.*

This basically Christian, uniquely cultural church remains extremely vague and ill-defined until one can specifically determine the extent of the underlying doctrinal substructure and thus the limitations imposed upon the overlying cultural superstructure. Obviously, the more comprehensive and detailed the doctrinal substructure the less variation and uniqueness possible through cultural modification; thus, the definition of an indigenous church will vary with each variation in the balance between these two structural elements. The more limited the substructure the greater the freedom for cultural diversification, and the more complete the substructure the more limited the cultural modifications.

To aid in determining the extent of the doctrinal substructure and thereby fixing the limits imposed upon the cultural

superstructure, the following exercise is recommended:*
Read the list of thirty** items below and then place an "X"
in the space provided (at the left of each number) that represents an element of *fundamental scriptural doctrine*. This
would mean items that include the absolute, unchanging, permanent will of God for all men of every culture throughout the
ages. The items left blank would be the cultural elements or
items referring to the relative, changing, temporary will of
God during a specific period in history.***

_____1. A man must believe in Jesus Christ to be saved.
         (John 3:16)
_____2. A man must repent to be saved. (Luke 13:3,5)
_____3. A man must confess Jesus Christ to be saved.
         (Rom. 10:9,10)
_____4. A man must be baptized to be saved. (I Peter 3:21)
_____5. A man must be buried in water to be saved.
         (Rom. 6:4)
_____6. Christians must partake of communion.
         (I Cor. 11:23-26)
_____7. Christians must partake of communion each first
         day of the week. (Acts 20:7)
_____8. Christians must meet on the first day of the
         week. (Acts 20:7)
_____9. Churches must have elders to be complete.
         (Acts 14:23)
____10. Elders must be qualified. (Titus 1:5-9)
____11. Christians must take up collections.
         (I Cor. 16:1,2)
____12. Christians must sing as part of their worship
         service. (Colossians 3:16)

---

*The basic idea for this exercise was borrowed from a modi-
fied copy of an unpublished manuscript written by Mont Smith
at Fuller Theological Seminary.

**This list could be much longer but these 30 items should
call attention to the range of possible sub-structural elements
in the development of a church.

***For some, this list may be a source of frustration, espe-
cially if they try to use the exact same criteria for evaluating
each item, i.e., avoiding pre-conceived ideas and relying
solely on a clearly stated rationale. Try it! On a piece of
paper complete this sentence: The items I have checked represent the absolute, unchanging, permanent will of God because:

_____

_____ .

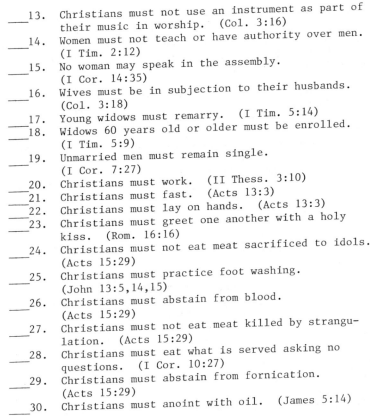

_____ 13. Christians must not use an instrument as part of their music in worship. (Col. 3:16)

_____ 14. Women must not teach or have authority over men. (I Tim. 2:12)

_____ 15. No woman may speak in the assembly. (I Cor. 14:35)

_____ 16. Wives must be in subjection to their husbands. (Col. 3:18)

_____ 17. Young widows must remarry. (I Tim. 5:14)

_____ 18. Widows 60 years old or older must be enrolled. (I Tim. 5:9)

_____ 19. Unmarried men must remain single. (I Cor. 7:27)

_____ 20. Christians must work. (II Thess. 3:10)

_____ 21. Christians must fast. (Acts 13:3)

_____ 22. Christians must lay on hands. (Acts 13:3)

_____ 23. Christians must greet one another with a holy kiss. (Rom. 16:16)

_____ 24. Christians must not eat meat sacrificed to idols. (Acts 15:29)

_____ 25. Christians must practice foot washing. (John 13:5,14,15)

_____ 26. Christians must abstain from blood. (Acts 15:29)

_____ 27. Christians must not eat meat killed by strangulation. (Acts 15:29)

_____ 28. Christians must eat what is served asking no questions. (I Cor. 10:27)

_____ 29. Christians must abstain from fornication. (Acts 15:29)

_____ 30. Christians must anoint with oil. (James 5:14)

Filling out the above list should draw one's attention to the fact that not all Christians feel the same way about substructural doctrine. Thus disagreement can be expected concerning methods for planting indigenous churches.

For example, consider two hypothetical missionaries, one who checked only item number 1 and another who checked items 1 through 5 inclusive. As they evaluate each other's work, the first one will likely criticize the second because he spends so much time talking about cultural things like repentance, confession, and baptism while the second will criticize the first because he allows too much freedom and does not teach necessary truth. Obviously their real differences do not center around indigenousness but, rather, around theology.

Reading the literature on the indigenous church, church growth, and missionary work in general, it is quite clear that the demarcation line between the doctrinal sub-structure and the cultural superstructure is critical to many ideas concerning successful and unsuccessful missionary activity. The missionary and his sponsors should know where they stand with regard to this important factor and then enter their work with an appropriate goal in mind.

Any factor that tends to upset the balance between the doctrinal and the cultural or which in any way interferes with the natural development of either may be viewed with suspicion as being detrimental to the proper development of the church. Most methods in mission work have their place if used properly and prayerfully; however, at some time most methods will need to be questioned and some methods need to be questioned most of the time. In other words the missionary and his sponsor need to be constantly aware of the need for critical evaluation of any work and be ever alert for any danger signals that might focus a little special attention on a field or method.

After the theological question has been resolved there is still one more condition which must be determined before practical plans for indigenous church planting can be considered. The field itself should be receptive. In other words, indigenous churches can best be planted in areas where many people are accepting Christ and the church is growing rapidly.

Some have wondered how the Apostle Paul could preach, lead people to Christ, establish churches and then in a very short time appoint elders in those churches. The answer must rest, in part, on the receptivity of the people. Men who were already leaders among the people must have been among those converts. In the cities of Lystra, Iconium, and Antioch, the impact of the gospel had been profound and many people accepted Christ (Acts 13:48; 14:1). There was evidently no need to develop qualified leaders over a long period of time.

Sensitive to the fact that not all areas are receptive, Donald McGavran has warned against making a new idol out of indigenous principles. He notes that indigenous principles work best in receptive areas where church growth is rapid, and he cautions the missionary to resistant areas not to depend too completely on them. The goal of mission work, he asserts, is not to use methods just because they are popular and Biblical, but to save souls and plant churches (McGavran 1974:345).

Finally, with our theological framework clearly understood and a receptive population with which to work how does one plant indigenous churches? One of the earliest answers comes from John Nevius, who feared the use of mission funds to pay local workers. Thus many of his suggestions are closely

related to the problem of subsidy. Here are his six suggestions written over three quarters of a century ago:

1. Allow converts to abide in their old calling.
    a. Let each man abide in the calling wherein he was
        called (I Cor. 7:20).
    b. At a future time those who have the call may leave
        their former occupations and become full time evan-
        gelists.
    c. The local church is the best developing ground for
        future evangelists. Thus they should be allowed to
        stay and develop naturally.
    d. "Be not many teachers, my brethren" (James 3:1) and,
        "lay hands hastily on no man . . ." (I Tim. 5:22)
        are warnings that should be considered before em-
        ploying new converts to preach.
2. Be cautious of setting precedents.
    a. If early converts are employed in one area, all men
        in all areas will expect employment.
    b. Early leaders, like Paul, should not give the im-
        pression that they are working for money, i.e., they
        can work with their hands.
    c. Missionaries could follow this advice if it were
        practical but for them to compete for local jobs
        would diminish their influence.
    d. Voluntary unpaid workers must be trusted. Also,
        they must be encouraged to destroy the idea that an
        effort to lead a Christian life will interfere with
        temporal responsibilities.
    e. This may be asking for more zeal than the home church
        has but it is Biblical and practical.
    f. Not giving employment to new converts may retard
        growth temporarily but not for long.
3. A certain amount of care, and especially the right kind
    is necessary; too much or injudicious care is injurious
    and may be fatal.
4. Young converts should be proved before they are employed
    and advanced to responsible public positions.
5. Young converts should be trained.
    a. The processes of training and proving are carried on
        simultaneously.
    b. Practical training in their local environment is
        best.
6. Converts should be committed to the Lord (Nevius 1958:
    19-29).

Roland Allen gave Biblical support for these basic ideas
(Allen 1972) and Melvin Hodges has explained in detail just
how they can be put into practice (Hodges 1971).

Even though one accepts as valid the generalization that foreign subsidy destroys local initiative, it does not necessarily follow that the absence of foreign subsidy will guarantee local initiative. The same thing could be said about self government and self propagation, i.e., the absence of a paternalistic missionary will not guarantee the development of indigenous leadership, nor will the absence of other forms of foreign help guarantee that a church will grow and plant other churches.

The indigenous church is an ideal that can challenge the most astute missiologist, tantalize the most enthusiastic sponsor, and frustrate the most experienced missionary. Like most ideals it may seldom be achieved to the satisfaction of the more discriminating critic. Nonetheless, it is a valuable guide to those who would see the spontaneous growth of the Lord's church throughout the world.

The Directed and Nationalized Church

Although Nida (Nida 1961:97) and Smalley (Smalley 1963:51-65) wrote about indigenized churches and McGavran, nationalized churches (McGavran 1974:335), all seem to be referring to about the same situation. These are churches that were originally established and controlled by missionaries but later were allowed to revert into the hands of the local people. Foreign support is usually withdrawn systematically, the missionary quits attending business meetings, and the church is forced or allowed to make its own way. Thus, hopefully, the local church becomes indigenized or, perhaps more accurately, nationalized; however, it is difficult to adequately indicate the full range of possible forces that could still be at work during this period of nationalization. The missionary might still hold title to the church property and thus be in a position to consciously exert control over the church. Or, the mission could relinquish control over the property only after the church selected *mission approved* (and perhaps even mission trained) elders. Such leaders would be expected to echo the feelings of the missionaries for years to come.

It is not difficult to imagine all manner of hidden mission controls over seemingly nationalized churches and this seems to have been the original idea of those who wrote about indigenizing or nationalizing churches. However, in the present discussion, the nationalized church as a goal of mission will be viewed as a church that begins with a considerable amount

of mission control* and then is freed from that control until
it is as completely indigenous as possible.**

There is an obvious need for a category of this type because,
on many fields, missionaries are trying to undo what was done
in the past and transform mission dependent churches into independent national churches. Also, some missionaries feel
strongly that, due to the broad range of doctrinal elements
necessary in the development of a new church, the missionary
must be quite closely involved with the church he establishes
during its early growth. Later when he is satisfied that the
sub-structure is complete, he can disengage himself and bring
about the full nationalizing of the church.

Present day examples of attempts to nationalize churches
reveal at least two basic motivations. Some missionaries feel
that missionary control, frequently enforced by the use of
subsidy, may have been detrimental to their past efforts. To
remedy the situation, they have devised plans whereby funds
and, obviously, direct missionary influence are to be decreased
month by month with a view to forcing the local churches to
assume their own financial and leadership responsibilities. In
other cases missionaries have entered a field with the idea of
planting churches first around themselves as leaders and
teachers with a view to relinquishing control and withdrawing
support as soon as local members have had sufficient training
to enable them to function in leadership roles.

In the former case, the nationalizing process has been initiated to remedy a mistake made in the past but in the latter
case the nationalized church approach is the conscious goal of
a mission effort, i.e., to start with considerable involvement
and then withdraw at a later time. For this reason, the third

----

*The term *considerable* is important because no missionary
planted church can be entirely free from some form of missionary control. The missionary's force of personality, message,
and methodology will all have some influence on the planted
church. However, in the present case, the mission control goes
far beyond subtle or incidental influences to actual control,
i.e., where the missionary is a member of the congregation and
assumes a leadership role or where he functions as a hierar-
chically superior administrator.

**The extent to which a mission directed church can actually
become indigenous is open to debate but, as a goal, it would
be assumed that in the *ideal* situation, complete indigenousness
could be possible.

goal on the chart in figure 26 is labeled, *establishing, directing, and nationalizing local churches*.

The National Front Churches

As the name implies, the national front church is a church with national figure-head leadership which is controlled by the missionaries. Churches of this nature frequently appear on mission stations or very near to them. They may be frequented by missionaries and their dependents, used as training grounds for seminary students, and as showplaces for visitors from home.

National front churches are not uncommon and to their advocates offer the best means of transplanting a church from one culture to another. Since the mission has absolute control, there is little chance for unorthodox behavior or embarrassing heresy to manifest itself. It seems to offer a safe effective way of demonstrating just exactly how a church can and should function, or at least how a church functions in the missionaries' home culture.

This plan has been violently opposed by those advocating indigenous church planting because the missionary presence is so dominant that the chance for local cultural modification is almost nil; however, it is an option and has its advocates. Some of the strongest proponents for this mission goal are sponsoring churches who fear that the far away mission field church may become heretical.

As the author was travelling through Southeast Asia, he became aware of several American sponsors who were sending large sums of money for the construction of church buildings, schools, and housing; and who were demanding control over their *investments*. Missionaries were spending much of their time trying to understand complicated local legal requirements, figure ways of maintaining foreign control over local properties, or fighting legal entanglements in local courts.

The word *investment* was used in the above paragraph because it best illustrates the attitude of those who use the national front approach. They are willing to use money but only as a kind of endowment that is designed to bring about the Christian behavior that the donor feels is correct. This method suffers from two weaknesses; first, there is no adequate method of determining the sincerity of the behavior of the recipients of such funds and, second, the motive for their Christian behavior may be material rather than spiritual.

The Mission Directed Church

The mission directed church may be found on almost any
mission field in the world. Here the missionaries form the
nucleus of a congregation that may have many members from the
local community or they may form a congregation made up predominately of fellow foreigners. Around American military
bases overseas, there are frequently American congregations and
these often include American missionaries and military personnel as well as English speaking local people.

On the mission compound, the missionaries may establish such
a church and do all or most of the preaching. As in the case
of the national front church, this missionary directed church
is safe from heresy and can stand as an example of how a church
should operate. Here again the aim is to transplant both the
sub- and super-structural elements of the church from one culture into another. There is little or no room for the unique
nature of the local culture to modify the church.

Sometimes the cultural conflict between the borrowed and
local can result in some unique modifications that leave everyone frustrated. Such frustrations were quite obvious in a
mission directed church in Seoul, Korea, in the late 1950's.
The church building was located on the mission compound and the
membership was composed of missionaries, United States military
personnel, and local Korean residents. The missionaries and
a Korean preacher shared the pulpit.

Upon entering the building the Americans, as a compromise to
local custom, pulled baggy denim shoe covers over their shoes
while the Koreans simply removed their footwear and left them
at the door.* Inside, the Korean men all sat on the left hand
pews while the Korean women occupied the right hand pews.
The servicemen, however, having no such custom, sat at random
anywhere in the building, and the American missionaries sat
with their families, some on the left side and some on the
right. Before the formal opening of the service, the Koreans
sat with bowed heads muttering semi-private prayers to God or
burst into the spontaneous singing of hymns while the Americans
walked about slapping each other on the back, shaking hands,
and talking over the events of the past week.

To the uninitiated, be he American or Korean, pagan or
believer, the spectacle of those Mickey-Mouse footed Americans

---

*Traditionally Koreans always remove their shoes when enter-
ing a dwelling. Although the custom is changing where modern
public buildings are concerned, it is still observed in homes
and smaller church buildings.

dotting and dominating the larger but quieter Korean audience, could never be forgotten and the impression created could not do justice to either an American or Korean congregation. How can such an aberration be an example of anything other than the cultural confusion it represents!

Social Services

Since social services are often begun as a means of attracting attention to the presence of Christians on a mission field and since the initial idea behind the development of many social service projects is to attract people to Christ and open the door for the preaching of the gospel, there would be some justification for placing this goal alongside of gospel dissemination. Nevertheless, in spite of the gospel spreading intentions of many social service projects, the results indicate that such projects are not generally efficient in spreading the gospel. There are successes here and there or isolated examples that seem to be encouraging but on the whole, social service is much more easily justified on its own merits (God's love extended to mankind) than for its contribution to gospel dissemination. On the chart (Fig. 26), there is a line drawn from the social service institutions (IIIc) to the gospel dissemination goal. Also, there is a line drawn from these institutions (IIId) to the evangelistic league section because evangelistic leagues frequently involve doctors, nurses, teachers, and other social service personnel.

The most significant contribution of social service institutions is to social service itself. Hospitals offer medical care to the sick, feeding stations aid the starving, schools give education to those who would otherwise remain in ignorance, and the poor are clothed through relief clothing centers. Projects like these are usually welcome in any developing nation and doubtless much good is accomplished through them; however, although social services may lend credibility to the gospel message it cannot replace the need for the persuasive proclamation of that good news.

MISSION METHODS

The following discussion covers three mission methods, i.e., (1) Itineration, (2) Mission Stations, and (3) Institutions. Itineration and Mission Stations are touched only lightly while Institutions are discussed at length. This is due to the wealth of material that is already available with regard to these first two and the lack of specific information with regard to the latter. In any case we are dealing with broad generalizations and there can be considerable overlap. Someone connected with a Mission Station could itinerate or develop an institution so the distinctions may, at times, be more analytical than actual; however, these divisions do provide a means of determining just how one might wish to proceed in the attainment of a given goal.

Method I (Itineration)

Method I involves the itinerant missionary who moves among the people and contacts them on a highly individual basis. He may be a full time preacher who does nothing but teach the gospel or he may be a vocational missionary who offers a social service as well as the gospel. He may spend time disseminating the gospel or may become involved in planting churches which he directs prior to turning them over to local persons but most significant he is the key to the dream of planting indigenous churches. He has no funds to give, no institutions to build, and is free to move into the most receptive areas. Why then do all too few missionaries itinerate? Because it is one of those ideas rather easy to write on paper, simple to include in planning, predictable when analyzed logically, but extremely difficult to realize in actual field experience. Perhaps the reason is that one of the most significant elements in indigenous church planting is the *adequately trained* missionary himself. Beginning with a fully qualified itinerant missionary, it should be no great problem to plant churches if the population is receptive; however, if that missionary has not progressed satisfactorily through language learning, cultural understanding and identification, he may find that planting indigenous churches is almost impossible.

Language Study: Language learning is probably the single most difficult task facing any missionary (Smalley 1963:49-56 and Larson and Smalley 1972:1-52). There are no short cuts, no easy methods; it just takes time and lots of self discipline. Yet, language learning is a must if the planting of indigenous churches is the goal. Preaching the gospel and converting men from their traditional religion to Christianity requires communication at the *heart* level and thus the heart language must be mastered.

Many missionaries never learn the language of the people they try to convert. For this reason a real understanding is difficult if not impossible to develop. The tongue-tied missionary becomes the target of many unsavory persons who happen to know a little English. Teaching cannot be done except through an interpreter, and this method is always suspect because the missionary never really knows what his translator has said. Even though he may record a sermon and then have it re-interpreted later, he cannot get the feeling, emotion, or general impact that is so important when one is trying to communicate deeply with others.

All too often the missionary who teaches through an interpreter soon becomes involved in the subsidizing of his interpreter, the congregations they establish, or the preachers they contact.* One recent report from a missionary indicates that he, alone, distributes $4,000.00 per month to some four score preachers who work for a like number of congregations. This total program may be quite effective and efficient but the fact that the missionary does not speak the local language makes him a less than satisfactory witness of what is really taking place in that area.

Another missionary who failed in his attempts to establish successful churches by direct evangelism has formed a group or a league of local evangelists who preach, establish churches, and edify them until they can stand on their own. Again, the missionary has only an elementary command of the language and handles a monthly budget in excess of $7,000.00. In time the fruits of this ministry will be clearly revealed, but at the present the value of the program is subject to serious doubt because there is no one there who really knows what the motives of the preachers are, what they are teaching, or what manner of churches are being established. The use of subsidy violates one basic condition of the indigenous approach and should make sponsor and missionary alike take a very close look at the overall situation if, indeed, they planned to use indigenous principles.

A second involvement that may overtake the person who is not successful in language study is busy work. Since language study is difficult the student may begin finding other things that demand his time. There are always letters and reports to be written, errands to run, churches to visit, and innumerable administrative details to consider. Little by little language study time is consumed by these real but lower priority activities until language improvement grinds to a halt (Smalley 1963:34,35).

Whatever the reason, the missionary should beware of any conscious or unconscious attempts to escape from the responsibility of language study. Language ability is the master key

---

*It may not be possible to support with evidence, an absolute cause and effect relationship between lack of language skill and the using of subsidies but the fact that the two seem to go together so frequently lends support to the probability of such a relationship.

to cultural understanding which is the next step along the road
to indigenous church planting.

Cultural Understanding: Anthropologists have demonstrated
that students of culture can enter a given area, use interpreters to communicate with the local population, gather information from selected informants, analyze the culture on the basis
of their observations, and arrive at a good understanding of
the culture without ever having learned the language of the
people. Of course, such persons are highly trained so that
they know what to look for and how to go about gathering data.
Also, such anthropologists have no interest in being agents of
change, but are satisfied to observe and record.

The missionary, if especially sensitive or carefully
trained, may be able to understand a new culture quite completely without having a knowledge of the local language, but
it is doubtful that the average missionary could function as
expertly as a trained anthropologist. Also, the missionary
wants to understand the culture because he wants to identify
with the people and lead them to Christ. His interest goes
beyond knowing that family kinship has certain well defined
parameters. He wants to know individuals and their kin in a
very personal way.

It is during a missionary's language study on the field
that he will have an opportunity to develop a deep understanding of and appreciation for the culture of the people he hopes
to convert. Of course, he must learn to discipline himself
and subdue his natural egocentrism. It will be quite natural
for the new missionary to feel that his own way of doing things
is superior to the way local people do them. It is only by
the exercise of sufficient strength of will that a missionary
can begin to see local customs objectively or, more significantly, through the subjectivity of the local population.

When the writer first arrived in Korea, he was a bit uncomfortable when he had to remove his shoes upon entering a house.
It seemed not only strange and offensive but at times absolutely
ridiculous. U.S. military personnel visiting local churches or
homes had so much trouble unlacing their high topped boots that
the Koreans prepared denim shoe covers for any American who did
not want to remove his shoes; however, after leaving the
Westernized mission compound house and moving into a typical
Korean home with its delicate straw mats and varnished paper
floors, the removing of shoes became a necessity. One sat,
reclined, and scooted about the floor continually and any dust
or dirt would naturally spoil clothing. Thus to protect the
delicate floor coverings, keep them spotlessly clean, and derive
the most benefit from the warm floors (Koreans have been

heating their floors for centuries), shoes were left at the entry way.

The custom of removing ones shoes is no longer strange, repulsive, nor ridiculous. Upon entering his home in the United States today, the writer will remove his shoes before stepping on the living room carpet and when he walks into the homes of others he feels that it is strange, repulsive, and, yes, ridiculous to step with filthy street shoes onto their plush living room carpets; however, neither by look nor word should he betray this reverse cultural bias. Rather, with a true missionary's determination to appreciate the culture in which he is living he should seek to understand and honestly accept the Westerner's custom of tracking street grime into the intimacy of his home.

Identification: An ability to communicate in the local language plus an understanding of the local culture gives the missionary the tools for developing a genuine person to person identification with the local people; however, identification is not automatic when the missionary reaches this point in his relationship with people because identification is much more than just knowing and doing. There are several reasons why it is important that the missionary understand that there is more to identification than merely a degree of physical and social conformity to the life style of the local people.

First of all, it is virtually impossible for individuals from one culture to become completely conformed to another culture. Except in the case of some new world nations where modern international and inter-ethnic cultures are being developed* one must be born into the culture in order to ever be considered a part of it (Reyburn 1960:6). A six foot six inch, blue eyed, blonde Scandinavian can officially become a citizen of some Asian country, but there is no way that he can become one of the short, dark complexioned, black haired people.

Secondly, identification does not necessarily demand complete absorption into the target culture even if such were possible. After all, the missionary goes to the field with a specific message to deliver and not just to become one with

---

*In the United States, Canada, Brazil, etc., people from many nations are trying to join together to form new and unique societies and cultures. Certainly success has not been achieved because the subcultures in these nations are still antagonistic toward one another and each strives to elevate to the norm his own native culture but, at least, an attempt is being made.

the local people. It is quite possible that a missionary's attempt to make a complete change of culture could damage his influence on the people in the culture itself.

Some missionaries do not have the best motives for wanting to make a complete identification. One missionary wife who was quite frustrated in her marriage and family life, and even her relationship with colleagues, tried to escape these pressures and frustrations by melting into the local society. She adopted the traditional mode of dress even though most local women of her age were wearing modified western clothing. She began cooking only local foods and even lowered her standards of sanitation to the level of the uneducated lower classes.

Although she had a good education and was well read, she tried to adopt the vocabulary, coarseness, and interests of the uneducated and unrefined women in the market. The result of all this effort was polite but almost total rejection by the community because her behavior in the eyes of the market women was irrational. She was trying to escape the realities of her own frustrated life and this fact was recognized very quickly by the local people. They pitied her and treated her kindly, but were never once deceived by her behavior because they were well aware of her motives.

Third, identification is not even a matter of the degree of similarity a missionary is able to develop toward a given culture. Wearing local clothing may be very helpful as far as identification is concerned but it can be very harmful (Joyce Hardin 1973:64). If the missionary can wear the local clothing and feel very natural about it, if the local people seem pleased but not overly conscious of it, and if the clothing seems functional and practical, it may be of some benefit to wear it. On the other hand if the missionary feels like he is in a costume; if local people stare, point, snicker, and show undue attention; and if the clothing is merely exotic without being practical, it will probably not help much in the process of identification. Physical conformity may be an aid to identification, but it is no guarantee that identification has taken place (Muldrew 1971:210,211).*

Identification has taken place when the missionary can look into the eyes of local residents and discern their thoughts and attitudes almost as well as another local person can. Identification is revealed through the smiles, frowns, gestures and other forms of communication that imply mutual understanding and acceptance in spite of outward differences.

---

*This is a good case history approach to complete physical identification and the problems to expect.

The missionary who has successfully identified with the local
people may be aware of his achievement by being treated more
like everyone else. The politeness, reserved for guests or
foreigners, may be replaced by jokes, casual indifference,
criticism, or any number of natural person to person responses.
The astute missionary may consider it a true mark of progress
when he becomes the target for a painful practical joke, is
told to shut up because he is talking out of turn, is ignored
as he walks through the market, or is asked to participate in
a discussion of serious local problems.

Identification takes place when two or more individuals
accept each other as authentic, significant, mutually relevant
persons. It goes beyond physical and social conformity or
personal likes and dislikes, and cannot be successfully feigned.
But once it is achieved the missionary's chances of successfully leading people to Jesus Christ are greatly improved.

To summarize, several factors are extremely important in the
preparation of the itinerant missionary: (1) He must be fluent
in the language of the people among whom he intends to work.
(2) He should be sensitive to cultural differences and able to
understand the customs, values, mores, and attitudes of the
people. (3) He should be able to meet people on a one to one
basis and win their confidence and respect.

The above factors are not only individually important but
are also listed in a rather significant order. For most missionaries, a knowledge of language is essential if one is to truly
understand another culture. Then, when one has a sufficient
understanding of the values and customs of a culture, he can
make a serious and intelligent attempt to fit into that culture
and, be in a position to influence people for Christ. Thus,
the full realization of step three is dependent upon a degree
of success in steps one and two.

Method II (Mission Station)

The mission station is one of the oldest establishments of
contemporary mission work. When the first missionaries came
to the new world they built their church buildings in or near
the stockades or fortresses erected by the invading armies.
Later as missionaries went out to Africa, Asia, India, and
South America, they faced hostile populations, disease, and
the terrifying dangers of the unknown. For the sake of self
preservation, sanitation, and mutual support they built and
maintained compounds where they could live together in

reasonable safety.* This idea continues to be employed as the great majority of overseas agencies, the military, and business concerns continue to build compounds for their workers.

The compound makes it possible for its dwellers to help one another, share scarce and expensive equipment, and cope with culture shock. Cooperation is facilitated and institutional development is simplified. As works are carried on within the walls** of the compound, the missionaries who live there need waste little time on transportation to and from work.

There are disadvantages which include isolation from the mainstream of local community life, immobility, and broad scope (see page 156). Especially today as even the smallest and weakest nations are coming to realize that they have a significant role to play in international politics, nationalism is growing stronger everywhere. People who might have been quite content to kowtow to the white or at least foreign missionary in days gone by now openly demand equal respect and equal treatment. Thus the mission compound, perhaps never honestly appreciated, is at best merely tolerated today.

Most people of the world are intelligent and reasonably gracious and do not mind if a missionary modifies the local standard of living slightly to make it more adaptable to his own needs; however, they do resent it when the missionary obviously ignores, excludes or rejects their culture, and it is the mission compound that stands as the single most visible element of contempt for the local community. At least this is how it is viewed by an increasing number of people around the world.

----

*A current missionary who has studied anthropology and has been living in a village hut for three years might feel critical of these early pioneers who built their compounds and lived somewhat to themselves; however, it should be remembered that they could not drive into a modern city spending one week out of every four getting refreshed. They could not return home on a furlough every summer or every four or five years. Air mail letters, telephone calls, and one day jet service to anywhere in the world was not awaiting them over the way in a nearby town. They had cut almost all ties with home and were at the mercy of the culture they had chosen. For many of these pioneers the trip to their mission field was one-way and they did what they could to enhance their chances for survival and service.

**A compound does not necessarily have to have a wall around it but quite often they do. In many countries all houses have walls around them.

It is the immobility factor that makes many mission stations questionable, to say the least. Land and housing soon amount to sizeable investments, and if school buildings, church buildings, printing presses, and similar facilities are constructed, the station becomes much too large to ever imagine abandoning. Thus, the station or compound quite naturally turns in its emphasis from out-reach to pull-in. Students, trainees, patients, or church members come to the station where the missionaries administer the institutions that draw them.

Method III (Institutions)

In the model, *institutions* are given a prominent place among methods because of their place of importance on most mission fields. The institutional approach to mission work is probably the single most popular approach to missions in the world today. Closely tied to the mission station approach and frequently an integral part of the mission station, institutionalism seems to have overwhelmed the majority of mission enterprises during the past twenty-five years.

Many specific programs can be subsumed under the institutional heading. In fact, it could almost be said that everything outside of itinerant preaching will likely fall under the umbrella of institutional work. However, by way of identification, *an institution is any goal oriented project that involves a formal organizational structure, the several components of which function in coordination, and a formal or informal power structure involving at least one superordinate and one subordinate.*

This definition can easily be divided into four components and the following discussion illuminates these and gives a basis for evaluating the strengths and weaknesses of the organizational approach to mission as well as determining what an institution is.

(1) An institution must have stated or implied goals even though the actual success in achieving goals is not a necessary qualification. Missionary goals could involve any of those listed in figure 26 or any number of modifications of those goals.

(2) A formal organizational structure is necessary and involves clearly defined patterns of activity which are related to the purposes of the organization (Merton 1961:48). Two or more missionaries might work in close proximity each conscious of and sensitive toward the other's activities, yet without any stated or even clearly implied policies. A kind of sympathetic awareness and natural coordination could result but this does

not qualify as an institutional approach to the work because an institution demands clearly defined roles.

(3) Coordination is a key element in any organization because it is only when coordination has at least been attempted that the idea of an organization can be suggested. Again, two or more missionaries could agree on specific goals, clearly define roles, and then each go his own way doing his own thing and an institution would not exist. Such an organization might exist on paper but unless there is at least an attempt to coordinate efforts to achieve common goals according to specific roles there can be no formal organization.

(4) A power structure is sometimes implied in the use of the term *coordination* (Selznick 1961:21), but to avoid any doubts or confusion in this definition of an institution, it is clearly stated that there must be at least one superordinate and one subordinate. Thus in a situation where all other qualifications are met but where no one member of the group has control whatsoever over any other member the group does not qualify as a formal organization or institution; however, the likelihood of all the qualifications being met except the fourth one is extremely remote. This is especially true when the necessary power structure may be either formal or informal. For example, if any of the group forming the organization is older, has field seniority, controls finances, is especially charismatic, or can by any means command the allegiance of the others, he must accept the fact that he does, indeed, exercise control over the others. Typical hospitals, clinics, relief clothing distribution centers, schools,* feeding stations and seminaries** easily fit the definition of institutions. Reading rooms, Bible correspondence courses, and radio work may be institutional if they meet the requirements of the definition (see page 201), but one man on his own can preach over the radio, send out Bible correspondence material or stock a reading room. Frequently two or more persons are involved, the other criteria are met and such projects become institutionalized.

Schools include those institutions offering general education, special training programs for the deaf, blind, mute, etc., and vocational or technical schools.

Seminaries include all schools where religion is the core of the curriculum, i.e., preacher training schools, Bible schools, etc.

Team evangelism could involve relatively independent*
missionaries working together cooperatively for the sake of a
common goal. One missionary could convert a local man, train
him to preach, and then encourage him to become a local evangelist without developing an institution; however, when the
missionary supports the local evangelist (giving the missionary
economic power over the local preacher), he satisfies another
qualification of an institution. If the preacher is free to
go about his own business preaching where he wishes, then the
arrangement has still not become institutionalized; however, if
the missionary and the preacher work together cooperatively to
achieve a common goal, an institution has come into being.

In this case the institution is a very simple one with one
superordinate and one subordinate cooperating within the framework of an informal economic control system. Nonetheless, it
would meet the minimum qualifications for an institution
through which the missionary would hope to accomplish a specific goal. The term evangelistic league is used to identify
this institution. The term evangelistic team was reserved for
teams of missionaries supervised by a sponsoring church in
America or some other home base. Such teams are not considered institutions because they are formed abroad rather than
on the field. Otherwise, even the itinerant preacher would be
a member of an institution because his sponsors are super-
ordinates.

Advantages of Institutions: Institutions are potentially
superior to individuals for the very reason that they involve
individuals working together. Two heads are not only better
than one but they can function more efficiently together than
they can independently. The basic appeals of the institutional
approach are efficiency and productivity. Whatever one's
ideas of mission activity might include, it is not unreasonable
to assume that a cooperative and coordinated effort will save
time, talent, and money as well as produce the greatest possible results in the shortest time.

For example, each of five individual missionaries might expect to teach what he knows to one or two contacts during a
given period of time. Thus, during a one year period five

---

*Institutionalism as a method does not include the organi-
zation that sends the missionaries in the first place. That
is, the sponsoring church or agency may meet the qualifications
of an institution with the missionaries being a part of the
institution. However, field institutions include only those
institutions formed on the field. They would include at least
one missionary and any number of local persons.

missionaries might teach portions of the word of God to five, ten, or even fifteen people; however, if these five teachers could coordinate their efforts at some central location, then thirty or forty people could meet regularly and learn from all five (thus increasing the number of students and giving each one more information). In this manner, at the end of the year there would be more people (increased productivity) who would . have learned more (increased efficiency).

Another motive for the institutional approach is service, either as an end in itself or as an example of active Christianity to stimulate interest in Christianity. For example, a missionary may adopt an orphan, pay someone's hospital bill, or provide clothing for some poor family. In this manner one missionary can help several people and set a good example of Christian love.

There are limitations, however, to the amount of personal service a few individuals can render. With a little vision, cooperation and finance these same individuals can organize orphanages, hospitals and feeding stations capable of bringing relief to hundreds.

If production and efficiency are the best two reasons for forming organizations on the mission field, the third and fourth reasons are not far behind, i.e., visibility and publicity. Even in a resistant area five missionaries working independently might contact and directly influence two dozen or so people over a year's time, but those same missionaries through the development of an institution can satisfy a government's desire for better education, benevolence, or health services and have such high visibility that thousands of people become aware of the missionary presence.

When one hundred head of dairy cattle were shipped to Korea in the 1960's, there were so few cattle in Korea that nearly everyone who read a newspaper was made aware that Christians were involved in helping the Korean cattle industry and thus the health and well being of the society at large. For several months after that shipment of cows arrived in Korea the missionaries had an informal "most favored relationship" with the Korean government. Ordinary red tape was mysteriously absent, officials were especially friendly, and the total program benefited in many ways from the good publicity that the cow project created.

A fifth advantage may be the introduction of structure, cooperation and authority into an otherwise fragmented collection of independent missionaries. Institutions have been known to solve interpersonal conflicts and bring somewhat hostile elements together for the sake of a common goal.

In a relatively old mission field a school served as a catalyst to bring several factions together. The school board was composed of American missionaries who were somewhat united as a group, local preachers who were hostile to the missionaries, and local church members who were not involved in the hostility between the other two groups. Although they did not always agree on everything, the obvious needs of the school dominated the thinking of the board and decisions which involved the good of the school tended to draw all parties together. From this point a more cordial atmosphere was developed during the board meetings and this was in turn carried into all of their interpersonal relationships.

It is difficult to visualize the complete range of possible institutions and their potential advantages in every circumstance. The important thing is to keep long range goals clearly in mind and continually evaluate the institution to determine how well it is fulfilling these goals. If the goal of an institution is directly related to the basic thrust of the institution itself, then goals will likely be reached if the institution functions in a normal manner. For example, a feeding station that does in fact feed people, an elementary school that provides a reasonable education for the students, or a hospital that successfully treats disease can be said to be fulfilling the goals that are inherent in the very thrust of the institution itself.

This point should be noted very carefully. Most of the institutions found on mission fields are patterned after secular institutions but have been modified to meet religious goals. For example, a Christian college is first of all an educational institution with an imposed religious goal.

History and reason both confirm the fact that from the very beginning the primary or inherent institutional goals tend to conflict with the imposed secondary religious goals. Every religious institution administrator is aware of the tension that is caused by this conflict. In the case of the Christian college one need only trace the history of any existing example to confirm the truth of this concept. Traditionally, a college or university is a place where teachers are free to teach and students free to learn. In a Christian college or university the original goals usually include a narrow defense of the faith. This struggle between broad freedoms and narrow restrictions generally results in an increased secularization as the primary thrust of the institution slowly erodes the secondary religious goal orientation.

The ultimate danger is that the secondary but more important religious goals of an institution will be completely displaced and the institution settle into the secular pattern for
which it was originally designed. This form of goal displacement can only be avoided by being sure that board, administration, staff, and clients are all vitally interested in the
religious goals. Once this standard begins to be compromised
the institution will naturally begin to secularize.

Disadvantages of Institutions: Although increased production and efficiency are the basic aims of any production
oriented institution, there are certain sacrifices that the
missionary may have to make if he uses an institution as a
method of spreading the gospel, planting churches or perfecting the saints. The beginning missionary should be especially
careful lest he thoughtlessly entangle himself in the administration of programs that may prove to be not only dissatisfying
but so demanding that he cannot easily extract himself at a
future time. Let this point be doubly emphasized . . . *The
prospective missionary should be extremely cautious about
involving himself in institutional projects especially on the
administrative level.*

(1) One problem involves the tendency of administrative
activities to pull the missionary away from the work he really
likes. Many prospective missionaries go on the field with a
strong motivation to meet people and share with them both in
physical and spiritual ways. There is a special thrill that
comes to some missionaries as they minister to someone who is
ill, homeless, or hungry. They draw great encouragement and
a source of fulfillment when someone says, "I believe and want
to have my sins washed away in baptism" (Acts 22:16). This
sense of fulfillment and the thrill of ministry can be severely
hampered when institutions have been established and the
missionary finds himself spending most of his time behind a
desk doing administrative work.

The change from a person to person ministry to the receiving
and shoving of sheets of paper can be very slow and subtle.
The unwary missionary may not realize what has happened until
one day he finds that his time is completely consumed with fund
raising to keep an institution alive, personnel problems as he
attempts to coordinate and cooperate with the employees of the
institution, and paper work as he tries to unravel the red
tape of local bureaucracies and meet the demands of government
officials.

As an orphanage director, he no longer has any personal contact with orphans; as a hospital director, he has no time to

spend with patients; as an evangelistic league director (see page 216), he has no time for personal contact with the lost; and as a Bible college administrator, he does not have the time to do an effective job of teaching the Bible. This is the loss of that personal touch that means so much to many missionaries, and this can be a high price to pay for the potential efficiency of an institutional approach.

(2) A second problem involves the very basic elements that should prompt the use of the institutional approach in the first place . . . these are productivity and efficiency. In his attempt to maximize efficiency man has developed the organizational form called *bureaucracy*. In its ideal form it is a superior organizational model; however, the very word *bureaucracy* has come to mean just the opposite, i.e., inefficiency, red tape, waste and frustration.

A bureaucracy on paper should function effectively, efficiently, honestly, and smoothly. In reality the human element becomes involved and all manner of problems can and do develop. Also, for the newcomer to administration there are things involved in organizations that go far beyond direct goal oriented action. There must be thorough planning, policy making, and fund raising followed by the development of facilities and the hiring of personnel. During this time it is usually necessary to contact local or even national government offices to secure the proper permits and licenses.

(3) A third problem results when the missionary lacks experience and expertise in administration. The actual bringing together of teacher and student, doctor and patient, or case worker and client, involves rather sophisticated administrative procedures. Strangely enough the size of an organization has little to do with the complexities of administration. One superordinate dealing with six subordinates will face most of the problems and challenges of a department head in a large organization. All institutions are composed of complex arrangements of formal or informal rules and regulations; two or more unique human beings with specific need orientations; prescribed organizational roles; hidden, implied, or stated goals; and a power structure.

Unless an administrator is capable an organization can cease to be efficient and actually destroy efficiency. Missionaries are especially susceptible to hard luck stories, helping those who are down and out, and in various ways staffing organizations with workers of questionable ability. If for the sake of poorly qualified personnel the goals of the organization are forsaken, the administrator has some serious problems on his hands.

The missionary as an administrator will frequently overstaff an institution. It is not unusual to find seminaries or Bible colleges with as many staff members as students. One reason for overstaffing is the missionary's fear of hurting someone's feelings by firing them. The missionary may not realize that adding personnel does not always result in increasing productivity because the workers themselves know the production limits. They will tend to underproduce to maintain general job security rather than overproduce and threaten anyone with a possible cut back in personnel.

(4) A fourth problem that faces every institution is finance. As newspaper accounts of government projects continually indicate even the experts seldom adequately plan for all the money necessary to support a given project. The missionary turned administrator is generally no more perfect in this respect than the full time businessman. In fact, the missionary may play down the cost factor and underestimate costs for the simple reason that, if he is trying to sell the institutional idea to his sponsors, he wants to make it sound as good as he possibly can.

Local individuals will sometimes play the lead role in getting a missionary involved in establishing some sort of institution. For them, it may give promise of future employment, prestige and security. Thus, their interest may not be completely objective and they, too, may tend to understate costs.

Institutions also tend to grow and the missionary administrator may find that the task of supporting a growing institution may become unbearable. This brings up the knotty problem of fund raising itself. Stated briefly, fund raising activities are only as successful as the ratio between money raised and money spent on raising it indicates. A friend of the author spent one year raising funds in the United States. At the end of that year he had raised a total of $23,000.00; however, he had driven 60,000 miles which, at 15¢ per mile, would cost $9,000.00, leaving only $14,000.00. Then, at $1,000.00 per month living expences, this man actually raised only $2,000.00.

Specific financial headaches too numerous to discuss in detail can frustrate the administrator of an institution. (1) Employees who were willing to work for almost nothing during the time when they were selling the missionary on the idea of establishing an institution become more demanding as time goes on. (2) Insurance and retirement requirements may be overlooked during the early stages of development but become more important later on. (3) Legal suits can develop as

employees are fired, injured, or not given what they consider
proper remuneration and this calls for legal fees and court
costs. (4) As land prices are inflated an institution might
discover that its basic real estate holdings are worth many
times their original cost. Then when re-registration time
comes the registration tax may be so high that the missionary
cannot pay without going into debt. (5) As an institution
increases in size it will not only increase in real estate
holdings but also visibility and prestige. These factors may
then begin drawing the attention of greedy businessmen, entre-
preneurs of questionable repute, and out and out criminals.
Such persons, many of them financially powerful, can give the
missionary all manner of serious concerns.

These five financial problems are not in any sense unusual
or extreme. They have been experienced by many missionaries,
are presently frustrating various missionaries, and will likely
continue to be a major source of difficulty on mission fields.
Nor are these the only financial problems; the list could go
on and on, but these should alert the prospective missionary
and his sponsor and prepare them to exercise due caution when
entering any institutional project.

(5) A fifth problem has to do with an institution's appeal
to the missionary's desire to escape. An institution can
easily be abused by an administrator who consciously or unconsciously uses it as a means of escaping from his primary responsibilities. Escape can be stimulated by at least four
significant factors: (a) failure to learn the language,
(b) failure to gain converts through conventional means,
(c) a desire to make a favorable impression, and (d) a search
for a sense of fulfillment.

(a) *Failure in language study* is possibly the missionary's
greatest stumbling block. The missionary who cannot seem to
stick it out through those months or even years of language
study will soon realize that he cannot be very effective as an
evangelist; however, rather than return home and admit failure,
he may turn to any number of alternative courses of action,
most of which will involve the establishment of some kind of
institution.

He may found a seminary where local church members who
speak English can gather to study the Bible, hire a translator
and publish correspondence course material, or begin caring for
widows and orphans. Such programs may be quite legitimate but
a sponsor should be suspicious if a new missionary's goals
suddenly change after he arrives on the field and gets into
language study. An institutional effort based upon anything

less than clear forthright planning and confidence in the institution to fulfill an important mission objective should be
scrutinized very carefully.

(b) *Failure in preaching* may seem, to the missionary, the
utmost insult to himself and his mission. When he communicates
the gospel but gets no response he may be at a loss. It is
quite clear in the New Testament that the gospel was spread
through face to face preaching and teaching. Men and women
went out from Jerusalem carrying with them the saving gospel
of Jesus Christ. Today the serious missionary learns the language of a target area, makes contact with the people, and does
his best to communicate to them that same saving gospel.
Sometimes the response is immediate and numerically great and
sometimes the only response is a negative one.

When the response is negative, the missionary may do well
to evaluate his preparation, methodology, and presentation for
the sake of locating the source of the problem. After modifying his own part in the communication process, if there is
still no response, he may assume that the people are just
resistant. At that point he may decide to remain in the area
for the sake of keeping a gospel presence before the people,
remain in the area but search for a more receptive sub-culture,
or move on to another place. To keep a presence and perhaps
prepare for a future time of receptivity he may establish some
form of institution; however, if he establishes an institution
on the basis that it will have better results in making converts than his evangelistic approach he is likely deceiving
himself.

Institutions may augment evangelistic outreaches in receptive areas and complement evangelism in many ways, but there is
very little evidence to support the thesis that institutions
will make converts and plant churches where more direct evangelism has failed. Hospitals make contacts and create good
will, orphanages encompass a small captive audience, radio
broadcasts attract attention and give some instruction,
seminaries are designed to train those who are already converted, and other institutions likewise are designed primarily
to do something other than lead people to an acceptance of
Jesus Christ.

In spite of this it is very common for those who have had
limited success in making converts to turn their energies into
institutional channels with the hope that the institution will
be the key to more successful evangelism. Such hopes are, for
the most part, unrealistic and the institutions created seldom
truly fulfill their original goals.

(c) *A desire to make a favorable impression* can completely
blind a missionary to what he is doing. Too many missionaries
become involved in institutional work because it offers easy
access to an outward show of success. By its very nature an
institution is impressive with its rules, regimentation, paper
work and images of activity. In no time at all an enthusiastic
director can have a massive volume of paper work being pro-
cessed each day. Maps with beautiful pins, charts with colorful geometric figures, and graphs with encouraging upward
swings can grace walls and impress visitors.

Every capable administrator understands the *administrative
fallacy*, i.e., the mistaken idea that a smoothly running organization is in great shape. The truth is that such an organization is likely almost dead! The dynamic living institution is blazing new trails, innovating, and in other ways
interfering with the status quo. This in turn sends out waves,
rocks the boat, gets people upset, and in various ways shows
the telltale signs of progress; however, unless the observer
is aware of organizational structure and theory he can be
fooled into thinking that a cycle of meaningless activity is
really accomplishing something. Perhaps the impression should
not be left that a missionary would consciously develop a busy
work organization as a cover for his own failure as an evangelist. The situation can develop very naturally and honestly
because it is in the nature of an institution to protect
itself. Thus the unwary administrator can become tied to a
massive bureaucratic machine that does little more than perpetuate itself and give the impression of efficient operation.

(d) *The search for fulfillment* can put the most sincere
missionary under tremendous strain. There may be some overlap
in these four escape patterns yet each is in its own way distinctive. In his search for fulfillment the missionary may
become involved in an institutional activity that is actually
accomplishing something but is not accomplishing what he would
really like. He may be directing a radio program that reaches
into homes of thousands of people. To someone with a presence
philosophy, this might be very rewarding and satisfying, but
if this missionary is church growth oriented and no church
growth is forth coming from the broadcasts, his initial response must be one of disappointment; however, if his need for
personal success or fulfillment is especially strong, he may
rationalize and overlook the discrepancy between what is being
accomplished and what he really wants to accomplish. This self
deception will prove harmful to the missionary who falls prey
to it as well to the mission field where it all takes place.

The idea of false fulfillment must not be taken lightly,
nor should the guilty missionary be held in undue contempt by

his critics because so many Christians are guilty of the same
basic escape though perhaps disguised in different ways. The
building of ornamental buildings of worship here at home can
be a similar kind of false fulfillment. Instead of communicating the gospel we launch into massive building programs where
the end result is tangible and visible even though it might
not contribute to any church growth.

Institutional Goal Displacement: Goals are the beginning
and end of all institutions. Desired goals are expected outcomes that determine the shape and form of the institution.
Sometimes goals are written down and afford clear guidelines
for those who would organize and develop an institution capable
of achieving those goals. At other times stated goals may not
guide the development of the institution, but this is only
because the stated goals are not the actual goals of those who
are involved in the institutional development or because those
developers are unable or unwilling to respond accordingly to
the stated goals.

In spite of the importance of clearly defined goals they are
often obscure, unrealistic, or ignored. Whatever the reason
goals are continually subject to the threat of displacement.
Etzioni states that:

> Organizations are social units oriented toward the
> pursuit of specific goals. In this sense they can be
> conceived as tools which gain their meaning and direc-
> tion from their function. But one of the most impor-
> tant observations of students of organizations is that
> often "the tools" in part determine the goals to which
> they are applied. This process takes several forms:
> initial goals may prove to be "utopian" and organiza-
> tional personnel may adjust these goals by making them
> more "realistic." The organization's original goals
> may be neglected without being changed officially;
> the organization may develop alternative or competing
> goals which are more in line with the interests of its
> staff. Or the organization may see its predominant
> task in maintaining and expanding itself (Etzioni 1961:
> 143).

Mission field institutions are especially susceptible to
goal displacement, because as mentioned previously, the more
obvious goals of the institution may be secondary to indirect
goals established by the sponsor or missionary. A Bible
college may be established to develop church leaders for local
congregations, but local staff members and students may exert
a tremendous pressure to make prestige, job opportunities, and

education itself the goal of the institution. To them, the church leadership goal is too unrealistic and unusual whereas the earning of a degree with all the privileges pertaining thereto is very realistic and practical.

It may be assumed that any institution, regardless of stated goals, will tend to orient itself to traditional goals of similar institutions in the society and culture. The missionary who plans to establish an institution with unique goals may as well accept the fact that he will have to wage a continual battle to keep that institution directed toward those original and unusual goals.

Another form of goal displacement that may be especially frustrating to the missionary involves the change of the institution from a means to an end. Blau and Scott assert that:

> As long as an organization's very survival is threatened by a hostile environment, its officers will seek to strengthen the organization by building up its administrative machinery and searching for external sources of support. This process is often accompanied by a retreat from the original goal to more modest objectives (Blau and Scott 1962:231).

An institution may be a mere tool in the mind of a sponsor or missionary, but to the personnel who staff and operate it, it becomes something more. Alliances are formed, personal loyalties cultivated, and a vibrant living entity is formed as the work of the institution is carried on. It can no longer be treated as an impersonal tool but as a dynamic reservoir of personalities and feelings. At no time is this more evident than when an institution has achieved its goals and no longer has reason to exist or when it has obviously failed to achieve its goals and thus should be eliminated.

The missionary involved in closing down an institution may soon feel like a combination of Simon Legree, Scrooge, and Madame DeFarge. The very unpleasantness of the task in terms of interpersonal relationships may be very traumatic. Add to this the possibility of outside and inside forces at work trying to gain control of real estate, facilities, or other assets that will somehow have to be liquidated. Finally, consider government regulations that forbid the sale of basic assets, limit the use of funds obtained through liquidation, or otherwise complicate the closing down process.

There are institutions operating on mission fields today for the simple reason that they are too expensive to close down

or because no one has the expertise to close them down. Consider the hypothetical but realistic example of a school with
ten professors, five administrators, fifteen staff members, and
one hundred students. This school can operate on a monthly
budget of four thousand dollars per month; however, to close
the school would involve retiring all of the employees at the
approximate rate of one month's salary for every year of service with the institution. Assuming that half the people have
been with the school for ten years and the other half for five
years the total retirement fee might be $16,875.00. Needless
to say, this expense alone, could prohibit many schools from
closing and is just one of the many closing out expenses for
an institution that has been in existence for a few years.

In some cases the whole problem of closing is so complex
that no satisfactory solution seems possible. In such cases
a frustrated missionary may decide that it is better to keep
things as they are and not upset the status quo. This is piti-
fully inadequate motive for supporting and operating a mission
field institution and serves to illustrate the stranglehold an
institution can have on an unsuspecting missionary.

The Profit Motive: Generally there is never enough money
to do all the things that missionaries and their sponsors wish
to do. For this reason, fund raising can become a very important part of a missionary's life. Somewhere along the line
some have decided to sidestep the distasteful task of raising
funds by establishing a profit making institution on the
mission field. This may be a printing press for religious
literature that is supposed to support itself by taking in
commercial jobs on the side; a hotel or apartment house that
should earn funds for a seminary; or perhaps a farm that is
intended to be the money making asset of an orphanage.

There are several factors that should give a sponsor or
missionary reason to reconsider a decision to establish a
profit making institution on the mission field. First, there
are few missionaries who have had the training and experience
to properly prepare them to enter successfully into the competitive world of business. Given adequate capital and opportunity, the average missionary would not be likely to succeed
in business right in his own home town, let alone in a strange
culture.

Second, administrators of schools, hospitals, and welfare
agencies are not generally recognized as examples of managerial
efficiency and financial wizardry. Colleges, both private and
public, in the United States are well known for their lack of
economy and efficiency. Hospitals that are successfully
operated for profit are the exception rather than the rule,

and they generally involve several hospitals tightly controlled
by a capable central administrative committee.

Even in the United States where all colleges have been
feeling a financial pinch for the past few years, there are
few colleges that earn more than 12% to 20% of their income by
engaging in any form of business. A private business is too
demanding and most colleges do not have the proper organization,
personnel or expertise to successfully operate a money making
asset.

Third, unless the profit making asset is quite large it
probably will not make enough to do more than adequately
support those who tend to its operation. Especially where an
expert manager is hired he will expect a salary commensurate
with his ability. For this reason a small business might make
enough profit to pay the manager and employees their salaries
but not enough beyond that to justify its establishment and
operation by a college that already has enough work to keep
everyone busy.

Types of Institutions: With the above discussion of institutions in mind it might be well to look briefly at the various
types of institutions frequently found on mission fields.
These institutions all appear on the Methods-Goals model and
it should be remembered that that is an evangelism model and
each institution will be viewed as a means of evangelism.
If an institution is serving some other purpose it does not
really belong on this model.

(1) Radio broadcasting, Bible correspondence courses, various forms of printed literature, and even some social services
can do an outstanding job of gospel dissemination. If this
is the goal of a mission venture, then these methods are not
only effective but also quite economical when one considers
the relationship between time, talent, and money expended with
the potential portion of the population that can be touched.

The radio can reach into virtually inaccessible areas of a
nation while simultaneously saturating a major metropolitan
center. Correspondence can be sent wherever the mail is
delivered and gives the teacher a type of personal contact
with the students. As questions are asked and then graded,
comments and ideas can be exchanged. Books, tracts, and other
forms of printed material allow readers to study privately
wherever and whenever they please. Printed materials can also
be reviewed, analyzed and passed on.

Radio and to some extent each of these other methods have
outstanding potential for initiating contact with a wide range

of people in any given population. The late Dr. Lowell Perry, missionary and communications professor, asserted that radio has five basic potentials: (a) to inform, (b) to entertain, (c) to create awareness, (d) to create interest, and (e) to reinforce (Perry 1975). When this potential is exercised with messages that are culturally relevant and offered in the language and idiom of the people, it can be an extremely effective and efficient mission method.

Although there are some cases on record where this type of institution has been responsible for the establishment of churches without the benefit of any face to face contact, such cases are not the rule. When church growth results from the extensive use of radio broadcasting and printed material, these are used in conjunction with some form of personal evangelism. For this reason, on the model (Fig. 26) these methods by themselves are limited to the goal of gospel dissemination.

(2) Evangelistic Leagues. The evangelistic league as an institution is more than a cooperative effort of two or more evangelists. Several evangelists could divide a given area and each be responsible for preaching in certain villages or certain sections of a metropolitan area. They could even travel together and share in presenting the gospel to the same individuals and groups while maintaining a non-institutional posture.

An institution involves clearly defined roles and some form of power structure that formally or informally gives at least one member of the league a superordinate position over the others (see page 205). If a missionary works with one or more local preachers in a cooperative effort to evangelize and has control over their salaries (or any other form of power), then the resultant evangelistic league qualifies as an institution.

Institutionalized evangelistic leagues are quite common on the mission field but are organized and controlled in different ways, depending upon the nature of the sponsoring group involved. Those religious groups with a definite organizational hierarchy might use the church as a means of control. The missionary in charge would be named the supervisor, and the rest of the team members would be subordinate to him.

Missionaries of churches not recognizing any hierarchy of control beyond the local congregational level cannot have any official superiority over their fellow workers, including locals, but can exercise power over the latter by controlling the funds for their support. This control can be direct, in that the missionary receives and distributes funds, or indirect in which case he merely has the power to influence where the funds will be sent.

Where church growth and indigenousness are concerned, methodology is generally evaluated from a rather pragmatic viewpoint. If, indeed, any honorable method results in indigenous church growth, it must be considered a good or acceptable method. This is true because results are primary and means must always be secondary where mission work is concerned.

The line on the Mission Methods Model on page 182 (Fig. 26) which connects league evangelism to goal 2 is a broken rather than a solid line. This is because the institutionalized league approach has not yet been demonstrated to be an effective method for establishing indigenous churches. The fact that a missionary (or missionaries) performs a paternalistic function as they control the subordinate local evangelists who work for them and with them in the league seems to weaken the possibility of the establishment of indigenous churches. Frequently the churches eatablished by the league are directed by one or more of the league members during the early stages of development; thus, they tend to be indirectly controlled by the missionary during this period. Of course, the extent of the impact of the missionary upon the local church will vary from league to league but it seems very unlikely that a league leader who controls a group of evangelists will succeed in establishing churches without communicating to them his *superior* position.

The sponsor of a missionary who proposes the establishment of an evangelistic league after he has arrived on the field is initiating a red flag situation. He or his sponsors should consider the situation very carefully and ask several significant questions: (1) Has the missionary been able to learn the local language? (2) Has he been able to successfully identify with the local culture? (3) Is his desire to form a league the result of failure in some aspect of his plans for planting indigenous churches? (4) Is the league method superior to other methods? (5) Does the league method involve subsidy to local evangelists and/or churches?

A more realistic goal for an evangelistic league would be to establish, direct, and then nationalize churches. This would definitely be the case when the newly established church is given some form of subsidy (land, a building, funds for a preacher, etc.). This control might continue for a period of months or years before any attempt would be made to turn everything over to the local members.

It might seem unlikely that a foreign evangelistic league leader working through local evangelists would have a greater *paternal* image among newly established churches than an itinerant preacher who establishes churches by direct contact. The answer lies in the word *image*. The itinerant preacher who visits a village, preaches the gospel, baptizes, converts, and helps them organize themselves into a functioning congregation can do so without leaving the impression that he is anything other than a messenger delivering a message from God. The league leader, on the other hand, with his financial control over local evangelists has firmly established the fact of superiority in the minds of the local people.

Also, the evangelists who are controlled by a missionary will very likely behave in a manner expected of subordinates in an institutional setting. When questioned by the local population as to why they teach and require certain responses (repentance, faith, baptism, etc.), they will probably find it easier to explain that it is the missionary's wish rather than explain that it is God's will. This response is natural under the circumstances and may reflect the paid evangelists' attitude as well as his desire to answer the question in the simplest way possible.

If the league method involves subsidy for the churches as well as for the traveling league evangelists, then it is likely that the results will be national front churches. Here the missionary control extends to the congregation or to the local preacher in the congregation. Thus controlled by the league director, the preacher or the congregation is forced to conform to the director's wishes or else risk losing the outside support.

The missionary in charge of a league like this will often exercise his powers in a very dramatic manner. He may shuffle local preachers around from church to church, demand absolute allegiance from evangelists and church members alike, and demonstrate his power by cutting the support of any who defy him.

Such a leader will generally feel that he is justified in what he is doing because, after all, he does know what is orthodox and acceptable. Also, he is handling funds from foreign church members who look to him to see that their funds are used correctly. He will also feel that once the churches get the feel of doing things the way he tells them they will realize the wisdom of his manner of worship, his doctrine, and his opinions.

(3) Religious Schools. Seminaries, Bible Colleges, Church Leadership Schools, and Preacher Schools are a few of the names

used to refer to those institutions, frequently found on
mission fields, which are supposed to educate the local
Christians especially with regard to church doctrine and leadership. Religious schools are given special emphasis at this
point because of a natural tendency for graduates of such
schools, who wish to teach others, to turn to their own familiar
alma mater as a pattern. Most missionaries have studied in
religious schools of one kind or another and there seems to be
a persistant force directing them toward the fulfilling their
own ministry through a similar institution. In some cases the
establishment of a school on the mission field may reflect
wisdom and insight but all too often it reflects little more
than a desperate attempt to find a short cut to successful
evangelism. Stan Shewmaker illustrates this as he discusses
the establishment of a school which was intended to be a re-
placement for itinerant preaching. The proclamation of the
gospel had not been sufficient to plant strong churches so the
missionaries turned to schools as a means of evangelizing
(Shewmaker 1970:54-57).

Generally, the field school is a carbon copy of a religious
school in the missionary's home country; therefore, the exact
nature of a seminary or Bible college on the field will depend
largely on the religious group which established it and the
kind of schools they have on their home ground. For example,
if the majority of preachers for a given church in the United
States have received their training in schools for preachers,
then on the field the missionaries of that church will be
likely to establish schools for the training of local preachers.
On the other hand when the missionary is more familiar with
leadership training in church sponsored liberal arts colleges,
he will tend to favor a liberal arts curriculum for the field
school.

There are at least five basic reasons why schools for religious training are established on the mission field. First,
there are times when church growth is relatively rapid and the
members of the local congregations feel a pressing need for
educational institutions to which they can send their children.
Second, during a time of rapid growth the missionaries may feel
that there is a need for training the emerging leadership of
the churches. Third, when a new church is having difficulty
grasping the significant doctrines being taught by the
missionaries, the missionaries may feel that it is necessary to
train a core of dedicated and indoctrinated followers who will
in turn, function as guides to the churches. Fourth, when a
field is resistant and no one seems to be interested in
Christianity, some missionaries hope that a school will draw
local people who would then be subjected to intensive teaching,

converted, and developed into a significant church movement.
Finally, there are those fields where there are not many church
members and only a few potential leaders. These few leaders
sometimes request the establishing of a school so that they can
be taught and, in turn, bring others to be taught.

Reasons for establishing schools do not always conform to
the services that schools are designed to render. Since most
seminaries are designed either to train young men for the
ministry or to give a Christian liberal arts education to the
children of church members, only the first two of the above
reasons seem to warrant the establishment of schools similar
to those found in the United States or other Western nations.
Even then it cannot be assumed that the training of leaders
or the general education of the children of church members can
be satisfactorally accomplished through the establishment of
carbon copy Western schools. With these thoughts in mind,
consider each of the five reasons for establishing schools in
mission fields.

First: To Provide Education for Members' Children. Before
seeking to establish an educational institution on a mission
field to meet the needs of a fast growing church, the missionary and his sponsor should consider several significant factors.
First, if the local church members want a general education for
their children are they capable of supplying, each year, the
necessary youths needed to comprise the student body? To
function efficiently, a four year college must have four complete classes.*   It may take four years to arrive at this
full student body, but after that it is possible to maintain
an adequate enrollment provided there are students available
who want the education offered.

Second, will the general education patterns of the Western
school satisfy the needs of the local youth? In America the
liberal arts education comes from ancient Greece and Rome via
Europe. It is a traditional education that exposes the students

---

*In some countries permission is given for a certain number
of students in each class, i.e., Freshmen, Sophomores, Juniors,
and Seniors. In other countries it is a matter of space and
faculty, but there is a minimum enrollment below which efficiency is severed. The local draft, marriage, employment, and
a host of factors can rob a school of upperclassmen. The gaps
in attendance left by dropouts must be filled by an increased
number of new Freshmen (sometimes not permitted by the government) or transfers from other colleges (sometimes impractical
due to the Bible curriculum of the church related college).

to the classics of Western civilization. Even in the United
States there are critics of the liberal arts education who
stress the practical need for a vocational or technical education in 20th century America. In many third world nations the
government is making every effort to stop the establishment of
traditional colleges and universities and is stressing the need
for technical education.

   Third, if a school is needed and there are enough church
members to supply a full student body, why do they not establish and operate the school themselves? If their needs for
help are only temporary, how soon will they be able to assume
the financial burden of the school? Most private colleges in
the United States receive approximately 60% of their operational budget from student tuition and fees. The other 40%
must come primarily from gifts. Religious schools established
in other countries are generally even more dependent upon the
mission for the major portion of their support. However,
foreign support should not be expected to continue forever and
some realistic financial planning should be involved right
from the beginning.

   Second: Training For Emerging Leadership. If a school for
the training of church leaders is needed, will a carbon copy
of an American preacher training program meet the needs of the
local leaders? Stateside seminaries and Bible colleges are
designed to prepare leaders for an old established American
church and may not be suited to another culture. Also are
there adequate natural leaders coming out of the local churches
to comprise a full student body over a long period of time?
A seminary like any other school must have enough students to
operate efficiently. There are presently numerous seminaries
in operation with only a small portion of the student body they
are capable of handling. Thus the cost per student becomes
astronomical.

   Third: Indoctrination for Core Personnel. When a missionary is considering the establishment of a religious school to
meet the needs of a church having doctrinal difficulties, he
should pay special attention to the following factors. A
mission school is not necessarily the best means of changing
the doctrinal thinking of church members. For one thing, when
church members discover that the school is being used by the
missionary to change the thinking of the students, they will
likely quit attending and quit sending their children. Once
the members of the church quit supporting the enrollment of a
Bible college, the college must seek enrollment elsewhere.
Thus, the student body is no longer made up of church members
who want what the school has to offer but strangers who may

have all kinds of motives for attending a religious college.*
A religious college with a student body of this type must
change its goals slightly and seek to convert the students as
well as indoctrinate them.

As president of Korea Christian College in Seoul, Korea, the
writer found himself in just such a situation. Eighty percent
of the freshmen students were not particularly interested in
the church. Thus the curriculum and extra-curricular activities were designed to first convert the new students then train
them to be church leaders who could properly influence the
local churches.

Over a sixteen year period the faculty was successful in
baptizing all but one or two of the non-Christian students but
was not always successful in making church leaders out of them.
Since they were very young (not emerging church leaders before
they enrolled) and perhaps not potential leaders at all, it
was a real challenge to try and meet the leadership training
goals of the school. The school had actually become an evangelistic arm of the church, a task not ideally suited to an
institution of higher education and one not originally considered when the school was established.

Fourth: To Draw Potential Converts. Where the school is
established for the purpose of drawing otherwise uninterested
persons into a situation where they can be taught, the missionary should consider the plan very carefully and critically.
Is a college classroom really the place for evangelism to take
place? Are the typical stateside seminaries and Bible colleges
designed to convert unbelievers or to train believers? How
honest can the mission be when luring unbelievers into this
kind of program? These questions are not necessarily rhetori-
cal but should be studied and answered prayerfully and honestly.

Fifth: To Train a Few Local Leaders. When a few local
leaders request the establishment of a college where they can
learn and pass on training to others, the missionary should be
very critical in his search for motives. In many countries an
education carries a great deal of prestige and one who works
for an educational institution has high status in the community;
therefore, many ambitious young men are quite anxious to see an
educational institution developed. They will typically start

---

*Frequently such students are marginal members of society
who are not able to attend national schools and who are attending the religious school as a last resort.

out with a one room training session where the Bible is the text book but will soon opt for better facilities and an expanded curriculum. The unwary missionary may soon find himself operating a full fledged college that tends to pull more towards typical secular education than religious training.

The writer once stood at a window of the graduate Bible Department of Yonsae University in Seoul, Korea, looking out over the sprawling campus of what was originally a Bible training program. A student of a small seminary pointed out to the massive buildings of this large university and remarked that some day his seminary might be as big and impressive. He looked forward to such growth without stopping to realize that the Bible department he was visiting was located on the second floor of a tiny obsolete building at the edge of the campus. A great university had grown up but the original religious goal had long since been abandoned and religion nudged over to a rather insignificant portion of the campus.

(4) Health and Benevolent Agencies. Hospitals, clinics, relief clothing distribution points, schools, and feeding stations have all been used by missionaries and their sponsors as means of paving the way for evangelism. Except in some very unique cases the establishment and operation of institutions of this sort has not resulted in any significant amount of church growth. These programs are basically service programs and are more likely to succeed in fulfilling a service goal than an evangelistic goal.

To some extent these institutions may help create an awareness of Christianity, but they are generally much more expensive and much less effective than other gospel dissemination methods. Also, on occasion churches have been established as the direct result of a program of this type; however, there are not sufficient reports of such events to generalize via the model that these institutions do much more than provide social services.

SUMMARY

Goals and methods are the beginning, middle, and end of any enterprise. Without goals to guide policy making, determine methodology, and evaluate progress, even good ideas can be lost and wholesome dreams frustrated. Six mission goals, i.e., gospel dissemination, indigenous church planting, directed and nationalized church planting, national front church establishment, mission directed church establishment, and social services, were determined by various philosophies of mission. Then three methods of achieving these goals were presented, i.e., itineration, the mission station, and institutions.

Itineration and the mission station were discussed briefly and a rather lengthy discussion of institutions followed. Institutions were studied with emphasis on their advantages, disadvantages, susceptibility to goal displacement and lure as substitutes for fund raising. Various types of institutions were then discussed with an emphasis on their relationship to successful evangelization.

Finally, the value of the Mission Methods Model as a guide to mission strategy was discussed. One hypothetical example was given to show how a sponsor can use the model to analyze an on-going program and make intelligent decisions concerning modifications.

8

Synthesis

The information in the previous seven chapters has been presented as a practical guide to those who would sponsor mission
programs or accept the challenge to become missionaries. Each
variable has not only been identified but also accompanied by
a suggested means of measurement. Hopefully, the sponsoring
church or prospective missionary can now follow these guidelines and embark on a program of mission work with a high degree of confidence.

Perhaps the best way to pull all of the above material together and illustrate the practical value of the total approach
will be to consider a hypothetical situation including a sponsoring church, a prospective missionary, and a program of
mission work. It should be noted that each element selected
for this hypothetical situation was selected for illustrative
purposes and *not necessarily as the best or only way to do
mission work.*

Ideally, congregations or the elderships of congregations
should have the vision to plan and initiate the evangelistic
outreach of the Lord's church. As suggested in chapter II,
each eldership would be advised to first determine their own
philosophy of mission and/or that of the total congregation so
that they might be able to form a clear policy for evangelism.
In the present hypothetical situation let us assume that the
congregation is *Church Growth* oriented and has written a policy

statement that places a priority on the planting of indigenous churches in receptive fields.*

Assuming that the elders or a mission committee has selected what seems to be a receptive field their next step is to find a missionary capable of carrying out the mission they wish to initiate. To do this they will need to know something of the challenges the field itself will have to offer. In this present hypothetical situation it is assumed that the selected field is a primitive tribal area which will likely be quite exotic to the typical middle class American missionary.

As prospective missionaries are evaluated the sponsors can, as suggested in Chapter III, gain insights into each candidates personality. They can determine whether or not he or his wife need special training, counseling, or guidance before going abroad. By use of the Synergistic Variable they can anticipate the prospective missionary's reaction to the control they wish to exercise, to the field he will be entering, and to the working conditions he will have to face.

Personality variables will be closely associated with the environmental variable as discussed in Chapter IV. Assuming that the missionary selected ranks high on the adaptability variable, this should indicate that he will be able to adjust to the primitive and perhaps exotic culture to which he is going.

Also, on the synergistic variable this missionary has been placed on the self sufficient end of the continuum closer to the midpoint of the continuum than the extreme self-sufficient end. This indicates that he will have enough leadership potential to carry out the sponsor's plans without too much close supervision. This could be extremely significant if, for example, it is also assumed that his will be a pioneer effort in an undeveloped field, as discussed in Chapter V.

Another reason for the selection of this missionary was because his moderate self sufficience, though not ideal for a pioneer effort,** offered a compromise with the missionary control demanded by the sponsor. The sponsor in this situation wants to supervise their mission program or at least share as

---

*It should be born in mind that this is a hypothetical situation and that another philosophy, policy, or methodology could have been chosen.

**A more extremely self sufficient missionary might be more capable of dealing with an exotic pioneer situation.

partners with the missionary they select. As indicated in Chapter VI, the self sufficient missionary may not be suited to close supervision or even a partnership; however, this moderately self sufficient missionary has enough self suffi- ciency to survive in the primitive culture and get enough group dependency to function comfortably under a sponsor that wishes to supervise its missionary effort.

Finally, after all preparation has been made and the missionary faces the challenge of the actual field situation, he must know exactly what results he is going to try and achieve as well as what means he is going to use to bring about those results. Information helpful to this phase of the task is found in Chapter VII. Since the philosophy of the sponsors calls for indigenous church planting by an itinerating mission- ary the plan of approach calls for the missionary to master the language, identify with the local population, persuade people to accept Christ and form themselves into responsible churches.

In this hypothetical situation we may assume that three years were allowed for language mastery and identification. At the end of that time the missionary would be expected to be in a position to devote almost full time to his evangelistic work.

At this point let us assume that 18 months have passed since the missionary departed to the field, and during that time there has been some modification of earlier plans based upon the missionary's last two letters and these letters call for a change in methodology and/or goals. Without going into the details of the missionary's reasoning and justification for this new approach, let us focus upon the sponsoring church and an appropriate response on their part as they evaluate this request in light of their planning and their use of the Mission Methods Model.

It is important that they should not be hasty in making any decision that would alter the method-goal relationship that they have previously determined to be in harmony with their strategy for mission work. They should neither reject the new suggestion because it is different nor accept it because it sounds plausible at first glance. Rather, in prayerful seriousness they should look to the Mission Methods Model and try to understand the possible ramifications of the new pro- posal.

The original plan called for the planting of indigenous churches by an itinerating missionary with three years of preparation and practice in language and identification. Since

only one half of the three year period has elapsed it would be
well for the sponsors to evaluate the missionary's progress to
this point.

Their first question would be, "Is the missionary progress-
ing satisfactorily with the language?" Since language is the
all important first step to successful itineration and since
language study is frequently the new missionary's most difficult challenge, it is quite possible that a failure to learn
the language is at the bottom of the missionary's desire to
change his method or his goal. A few probing questions by mail
or perhaps a visit to the field by an elder can easily determine the missionary's progress in language study.

If, in fact, the missionary is having trouble learning the
language, it is quite likely that his suggested change in
methodology is a reflection of his own fears that he will be
unable to function satisfactorily as an evangelist. Under such
circumstances the sponsoring church has several options:
(a) they can encourage the missionary to get back into language
study and concentrate on his original plans, (b) they can send
him home and select another missionary with a greater propensity for learning language, or (c) they can decide that rather
than send the missionary home they will agree to his new plan.
In this case they consciously move to a second best method due
to a contingency that they are willing to accept.

If, however, their missionary is having no serious difficulties with the language but still wants to change his
method of approach they should evaluate his success in identifying with the local people. Assuming that the approach he is
suggesting demands less face to face contacts with prospective
converts it is quite possible that a failure to identify is
the real reason for the suggested change. Here again the sponsors have several options, they can (1) help the missionary try
to make the proper adjustment, (2) replace him with someone
else, or (3) decide to back him in his new methodology in spite
of the fact that it is not the most direct way to the goal they
espouse.

The elders might, upon evaluation of the situation, decide
that the problem is not with their missionary but with the
field. Perhaps their earlier ideas are now proving false and
a field that they considered highly receptive may actually be
resistant. In this case they might work with the missionary
to replan the strategy for the work.

Ideally, they would want to maintain their original goal or
at least select a similar one. They might decide on Goal III
under these circumstances. Here again, the missionary could

(1) adjust to the new goal, (2) be replaced, (3) or influence the sponsors to opt for another goal of his choosing.

At the very best, this systematic use of the Mission Methods Model will guarantee that mission goals are being approached by the most appropriate methodology. This will in turn, save time, talent, and money. Finally, it tends to keep sponsor, missionary, and local people on the field fully informed as to what is taking place and why.

At the very least, the Mission Methods Model provides those interested in mission work with a guide which should alert them to the strengths and weaknesses of each method as it re-lates to the various goals. Even when a less than ideal relationship is indicated it should be clear to all concerned so that no one is misled, confused, or ignorant as to that relationship. This should open the avenues of communication between sponsors and missionaries because there is no more need for fog or less than candid reports to cover inconsistancies between methods and goals.

It should be obvious that a single hypothetical situation can do no more than suggest a general approach to real life situations which might differ in any number of ways from the example. It is, in fact, difficult in a brief space to de-scribe the total strategy suggested by the above chapters. This is due to the complexity of the possible relationships. For example, the Synergistic Variable, missionary control structure, and field development levels relate to one another in a very significant way. Figure 27 illustrates the most obvious match between these three elements. The solid lines connect the missionaries, sponsorship control levels, and fields which seem to go best together. The dotted lines suggest alternatives which would be almost as natural as the others. From this point one could connect these variables in any number of ways with the danger of mismatching increasing with each added departure from the suggested sample norms.

Philosophies, goals, and methods obviously depend upon one another and thus must always be viewed with stress on their interrelatedness. Finally, the culture contrast scale and the other personality variables have a general relationship to all missionaries regardless of where they go or what they plan to do.

Finally all must be done in and through the power of God, Christ, and the Holy Spirit. After all has been said and man has done all that he can do, it is the Lord's work and He is the one who must guide, instruct, and give the increase.

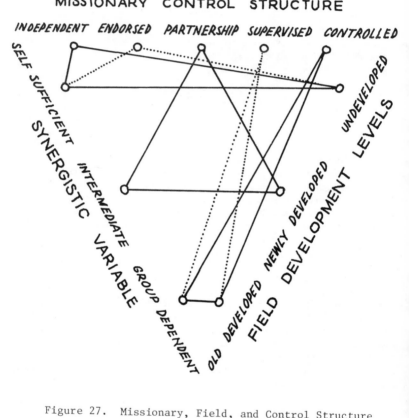

Figure 27. Missionary, Field, and Control Structure
Relationships.

Appendix

A study of the psychology of individual differences can make one very hesitant to attempt the categorizing of human beings according to anything more than their physical measurements. Each individual is so complex and unique that he almost defies any attempt to place him into any accurately delineated classification scheme; however, to effectively deal with man it is necessary to group him in some manner that will facilitate a certain amount of generalization.

The isolation of the synergistic variable is an attempt to group missionaries in a manner that will permit the development of certain generalizations which will, in turn, help sponsors as they attempt to fit prospective missionaries into fulfilling programs of mission work. It appears possible to distinguish, at least in some missionary circles, two distinctive but related personality types. The cooperation model (Fig. 28) indicates the basic elements of this variable, their relationships and the resultant personality types.

Informal Leadership Role   Informal Followership Role

Charisma Ego Persistance	Persistance

Figure 28.   Cooperation Model.

Leadership and Followership Roles: The horizontal axis
(Fig. 28) is divided into two roles, one being for leaders and
the other for followers. Of extreme importance to this model
is the term *informal* because it distinguishes between leaders
or followers who are constrained to fill their roles by some
system of authority, and those who fill them because of their
own determination. A leader, for example, that is given power
to lead in the form of legitimate authority (rank, status, etc.)
is generally referred to as an *official*. However, this person
may or may not be the unofficial leader of the organization. If
he is, then he may be called the *official leader*. If he is not,
then he is still the official but someone else may be the
*unofficial leader.**

Charisma: Leadership, is of course closely associated with
decision making power. The individual who makes the decisions
is the leader because he controls the process that orients the
group or organization to its goals. Whereas the *official* must
be obeyed by reason of his authority, the *unofficial leader*
must exercise coercive (force), utilitarian (rewards) or identative (charisma) power to maintain his leadership role
(Etzioni 1970:650-51).

The prison inmate with mafia connections might be able to
lead due to his coercive power, the rich industrialist using
utilitarian power might be able to control a political party,
and in the context of a church sponsored missionary enterprise
involving several missionaries from different local churches**
it is likely that the only alternative available would be
identative power. Thus *charisma* is an important trait in the
isolation of the synergetic variable.

Charisma is used here in the sense of that quality one has
who is able to command attention and gain recognition. This
is the individual who walks into a room and soon is allowed to
dominate or lead the conversation, not offensively or

---

*Consider a prison where the warden is the *official* (the man
with legal authority) but where the prisoners are also controlled by an inmate who may represent the mafia and be the
unofficial leader of the inmates. Unofficial leadership is a
real factor in any organization but is most obvious in the
prison illustration.

**Missionaries sponsored by individual congregations may
subscribe to no field organizations which would coordinate
their efforts. Each man would be independent except to the
degree that he might relinquish his independence for the sake
of cooperative activity.

impolitely, but because all others tend to defer to him. It
is this ability to be heard and recognized that gives him a
distinct advantage where informal identative power is needed.

Ego: Because of its extremely important place in administration, decision making has been carefully studied by those
interested in administrative theory. One of their important
discoveries is that decision making is so complicated that no
individual or group is capable of pin-pointing every contingency, evaluating every restraint, and predicting all possible
outcomes. Thus man has had to be content not with maximum
efficiency decisions but with *satisfying* decisions (Thompson
1967:8,9). Thus, every important decision any group makes is
naturally subject to doubt and criticism.

For this reason it is important, once a reasonable decision
has been made, to move ahead with optimism and confidence not
paying too much attention to one's critics. Those who never
get away from the drawing board may not make many mistakes but
it is quite certain that they never make any progress.

For the informal identative leader it is as important to
carry out his decisions as it is to make them. And to overcome
the natural criticism and doubt that can easily frustrate any
plan the leader must be able to inspire confidence in his decision. This can best be accomplished when he believes in himself to such an extent that his confidence is contagious. This
confidence in one's own decision is a form of egotism, therefore the second important trait for an effective informal leader
is a strong ego.*

Persistance: Once an informal leader has initiated a course of
action then his ultimate success is dependent upon his ability
to carry the action through to its conclusion or to successfully commission someone else to do it. Failure** to achieve
goals will soon undermine the informal leader's power. He
might move on to new groups and initiate new programs with his
charisma and ego but without persistence he ultimately will
lose his power over the group with which he is working. Therefore, *persistance* is the third trait so important to a successful informal leader.

---

*Terms like egocentric and egotism will hereafter be avoided
due to the negative connotation they have. Ego, as used here is
a positive factor in effective informal leadership and does not
necessarily indicate arrogance or pride.

**Failure due to causes beyond the leader's control are not
considered leadership failure.

Thus far all that has been said has been with reference to the informal leader; however, equally as important as leadership is followership. Followers as used here include all the members of any group or organization who coordinate their efforts to achieve group goals. In a democratic organization the followers may actually make decisions by vote but if they are true followers they will respect the opinion of the majority and cooperatively work to carry out a group policy even though they might have preferred a different one.

Of extreme importance to the informal followership role is persistance because without it nothing would ever be accomplished in an identative organization (where there is no coercive or utilitarian power being exercised). At this point it will be noted that persistance is necessary if either the informal leadership or the informal followership roles are to be effective (see Fig. 28). This then leaves charisma and ego as distinguishing traits between the two roles, i.e., charisma and ego are necessary for effective leadership behavior but have a negative effect on followership behavior.

THE SYNERGISTIC VARIABLE

In the ultimate development of an operational continuum it is obvious that any number of elements could have been used, i.e., leadership, charisma, ego, or cooperation (see Fig. 28); however, in Western society the aura of positive value which surrounds the elements of potential leadership, ego and charisma, is so pervasive that such a continuum would seem to be strong and good on one end and weak and bad on the other. Thus, to counter this subjective value arrangement and free the continuum from undue favoritism for either extreme, the element of cooperation was selected.

Of course, *cooperation* itself is a value laden word but since, in the continuum, it is positively related to the group dependent follower and negatively related to the self sufficient leader, it tends to give balance to the continuum (see Fig. 29). Also, the element of cooperation easily includes all that has been said about the other elements and thus becomes a simple reference for a combination of forces.

The synergistic variable, then, is based upon one's *inclination toward cooperative activity*. At one extreme are those who are so inclined toward cooperative activity that they can scarcely function outside the group and these are called group dependent individuals. On the other extreme are those who function so well on their own that a group tends to represent interference and these are called self sufficient individuals.

Self Sufficient	Intermediate	Group Dependent
(minimal inclination		(maximal inclination
toward cooperative		toward cooperative
activity)		activity)

Figure 29.   The Synergistic Variable.

Self Sufficiency: The term *self sufficient* was selected to identify the minimal inclination extreme of the synergistic variable because it is descriptive of the individual with strong charisma and ego whether or not he has persistence and thus, whether or not he is a successful leader. The self sufficient missionary is the one who has confidence in himself and seemingly, little need for the security and support of others.* Perhaps because of his high degree of self confidence he is often willing to go into difficult fields, blaze new trails, and take on monumental challenges. If he is successful he may become quite famous and respected but if he lacks the persistence to see things through and leaves too many broken dreams behind he may become the Bohemian, outcast, or misfit who comes so very close but never seems to be able to realize his full potential in life.

Group Dependency: At the opposite end of the synergistic variable continuum is group dependency. Having persistence to carry his activities through to the end, the group dependent individual is a doer who finds fulfillment in making his contribution to some task or project. Not having or, at least, not revealing any large measure of charisma or ego, this individual functions most comfortably in group activities where he either follows someone else's lead or determines policy as a part of a group process.

The group dependent missionary does not necessarily lack self confidence. Once a group decision has been made or a recognized leader has shown the way the group dependent individual will put his shoulder to the wheel and move ahead with the utmost confidence. It is only when he is called upon to make those difficult decisions by himself that he feels uncomfortable. His analytical mind sees too many reasons why any course of action might not succeed, and by the time he

_____

*The self sufficient missionary may need the respect, appreciation, or even the adulation of groups but does not feel the need for their help in making decisions, formulating plans and taking care of personal needs.

satisfies himself with a course of action it may be too late
to put it into operation.

During a period of brain storming he may have numerous
suggestions to make but when it comes to selecting a course of
action he will readily accept the best idea even if it is not
his own. He fits very smoothly into on-going programs although
he may try to initiate change if he believes it is necessary.

Group dependency does not indicate weakness or inferiority
but only a personality that is not characterized by that ego
that says, "I am right and others are wrong," nor the charisma
that commands attention and radiates authority.

Intermediate categories: The synergistic variable has been
isolated due to the unique problems associated with the extreme
cases of self sufficiency and group dependency. However, the
less extreme intermediate categories would be expected to
apply to the majority of missionaries and suggest some rather
interesting possibilities.

Here would be those individuals who have sufficient charisma
and ego to provide leadership in situations where no one else
seems inclined to take the lead but who are also dependent
enough to defer to someone whom they respect as a superior
leader. Such individuals successfully move from leadership
roles to followership roles depending upon circumstances.

Here also might be those individuals who would hold secondary or terciary leadership or followership positions. For
example, in a university administration the president would
represent the leadership position, his deans might represent
secondary leaders, and departmental chairmen terciary leaders.
Or, from the followership side, the clerks and secretaries
might represent the followers, student recruiters secondary
followers (having slightly more independence of action), and
departmental chairmen terciary followers.

Bibliography

ALLEN, Roland
    1972   *Missionary Methods: Saint Paul's or Ours?*
                Grand Rapids: Wm. B. Eerdmans Pub. Co.

ANDERSON, Robert Lynn
    1965   *An American Preacher in a Canadian Situation.*
                Unpublished Master's Thesis, Harding College
                of Bible and Religion.

BERNARD, Chester I.
    1964   *The Functions of the Executive.* Cambridge,
                Mass.: Harvard University Press.

BLAU, Peter M. and SCOTT, Richard W.
    1962   *Formal Organizations.* San Francisco: Chandler
                Publishing Co.

BREWSTER, Thomas E. and BREWSTER, Elizabeth S.
    1976   *Language Acquisition Made Practical.* Colorado
                Springs: Lingua House.

BROOM, Wendell
    1976   "Church Growth Principles," *Guidelines for
                World Evangelism.* Abilene, Texas: Biblical
                Research Press.

CANNON, Joseph L.
    1969   *For Missionaries Only.* Grand Rapids: Baker
                Book House.

CATTELL, Everett L.
    1967   "Hinduism," *Religions in a Changing World.*
                Chicago: Moody Press.

CLEVELAND, Harland, et. al.
    1960   *The Overseas American.* New York: McGraw Hill
                Book Co.

COON, et. al.
    1950   *Races: A Study of the Problems of Race Forma-
                tions in Man.* Springfield: Charles C. Thomas.

DEER, Donald S.
    1975   "The Missionary Language-Learning Problem,"
                Missiology, Vol. 3, No. 1, January, pp. 87-91.

DOLGUM, Alexander and WATSON, Patric
    1975   *An American in the Gulag.* New York: Alfred A.
                Knopf.

ETZIONI, Amitai
    1970   "Organizational Control Structure," *Handbook of
                Organizations.* Chicago: Rand McNally and Co.

ETZIONI, Amitai
    1961   "Organizational Goals," *Complex Organizations.*
                New York: Holt, Rinehart, and Winston.

GOBLE, Phillip E.
    1975   *Everything You Need to Grow a Missianic Syna-
                gogue.* South Pasadena, California: William
                Carey Library.

GOLDBURG, Carl
    1970   *Encounter: Group Sensitivity Training Experience.*
                New York: Science House, Inc.

GOLDSCHMIDT, Walter
    1960   "Education," *Exploring the Ways of Mankind.*
                New York: Holt, Rinehart and Winston.

GURGANUS, George (ed.)
    1976   *Guidelines for World Evangelism.* Abilene,
                Texas: Biblical Research Press.

HARDIN, Daniel C.
    1971   "The Missionary and the Concept of Scope,"
                Practical Anthropology, Vol. 18, No. 5, Sept.-
                Oct., pp. 222-226.

HARDIN, Daniel C.
1974   "200,000 Missionaries," *What Lack We Yet?*
            Abilene, Texas: Biblical Research Press.

HARDIN, Joyce F.
1975   "Questions Answered for Women Missionaries,"
            Mission Strategy Bulletin, Vol. 2, Mar.-Apr.,
            pp. 2,3.

HARDIN, Joyce F.
1973   *Sojourners: Women With a Mission.* Inchon,
            Korea: Korean Consolidated Corporation.

HODGES, Melvin L.
1972   *The Indigenous Church.* Springfield: Gospel
            Publishing House.

HOPKINS, Charles H.
1940   *The Rise of the Social Gospel in American
            Protestantism, 1865-1915.* New Haven: Yale
            University Press.

HUME, Robert E.
1959   *The World's Living Religions.* New York: Charles
            Scribner's Sons.

JOHN, Matthew P.
1968   "Evangelism and the Growth of the Church,"
            International Review of Missions, July, p. 283.

KIM, Chin-Wu
1974   "The Making of the Korean Language," *Korea
            Journal,* August, p. 11.

KIYOOKA, Eiichi
1953   *Japanese in Thirty Hours.* Tokyo: Hokuseido
            Press.

KLUCKHOHN, Clyde
1960   "The Educational Process," *Exploring the Ways of
            Mankind.* New York: Holt, Rinehart and Winston.

KROEBER, A. L.
1940   *Anthropology.* New York: Harcourt, Brace and
            World, Inc.

KUZNETSOO, Edward
1975   *Prison Diaries.* New York: Stein and Day.

LARSON, Donald and SMALLEY, William
    1972   *Becoming Bilingual.* South Pasadena, Calif.:
                William Carey Library.

LINDSELL, Harold
                Missionary Principles and Practice. Westwood,
                N. J.: Fleming H. Revell Co.

MATHEWS, Edward
    1975   Lecture on Christian Growth, Abilene Christian
                University, Abilene, Texas.

McGAVRAN, Donald
    1974   *Understanding Church Growth.* Grand Rapids,
                Michigan: Wm. B. Eerdmans.

MERTON, Robert I.
    1961   "Bureaucratic Structure and Personality,"
                Complex Organizations. New York: Holt, Rine-
                hart and Winston.

MULDREW, William F.
    1971   "Identification and the Role of the Missionary,"
                Practical Anthropology, Vol. 18, No. 5, Sept.-
                Oct.

MUMFORD, Lewis
    1960   "The Clock and Technical Development," *Exploring
                the Ways of Mankind.* New York: Holt, Rinehart
                and Winston.

NEVIUS, John L.
    1958   *The Planning and Development of Missionary
                Churches.* Philadelphia: The Reformed and
                Presbyterian Publishing Co.

NIDA, Eugene
    1972   *Message and Mission.* South Pasadena, Calif.:
                William Carey Library.

    1961   "The Indigenous Church in Latin America,"
                Practical Anthropology, Vol. 8, No. 3, May-June.

NIDA, Eugene and SMALLEY, William A.
    1974   *Introducing Animism.* New York: Friendship
                Press.

NOSS, John B.
    1961   *Man's Religions.* New York: The MacMillan Co.

PEI, Mario
    1957   *Language for Everybody*. New York: The Devin-
               Adair Company.

PENTECOST, Edward C.
    1974   *Reaching the Unreached*. South Pasadena, Calif.:
               William Carey Library.

PHENIX, Philip H.
    1964   *Realms of Meaning*. New York: McGraw-Hill
               Book Co.

PIKE, Kenneth L.
    1957   *Tone Languages*. Ann Arbor, Michigan: University
               of Michigan Press.

REYBURN, William D.
    1960   "Identification in the Missionary Task,"
               Practical Anthropology, Vol. 7, No. 1, Jan.-
               Feb., pp. 1-15.

ROGERS, Carl R.
    1970   *Carl Rogers on Encounter Groups*. New York:
               Harper and Row, Pub.

SELZNICK, Philip
    1961   "Foundation of the Theory of Organization,"
               Complex Organizations. New York: Holt, Rinehart
               and Winston.

SHEWMAKER, Stan
    1970   *Tonga Christianity*. South Pasadena, Calif.:
               William Carey Library.

SMALLEY, William A.
    1958   "Cultural Implications of an Indigenous Church,"
               Practical Anthropology, Vol. 5, No. 2, April-
               May, pp. 51-65.

    1963   "Culture Shock, Language Shock and the Shock of
               Self Discovery," *Practical Anthropology*, Vol. 10,
               No. 2, March-April, pp. 49-56.

SMITH, Ebbie C.
    1976   *A Manual for Church Growth Surveys*. South
               Pasadena, Calif.: William Carey Library

SOBEL, B. Z.
    1974   *Hebrew Christianity: The Thirteenth Tribe*.
               New York: John Wiley and Sons, Inc.

SOLZHENITSYN, Aleksander I.
    1974   *The Gulag Archipelago*. New York: Harper and
                Row, Publishers.

SWEET, Henry
    1964   *The Practical Study of Language*. London:
                Oxford University Press.

THOMPSON, James D.
    1967   *Organizations in Action*. New York: McGraw-
                Hill Book Co.

TIPPETT, A. R.
    1973   *Verdict Theology in Missionary Theory*. South
                Pasadena, Calif.: William Carey Library.

VAN RHEENEN, Gailyn
    1976   *Church Planting in Uganda*. South Pasadena,
                Calif.: William Carey Library.

VOSS, Howard F.
    1967   *Religions in a Changing World*. Chicago:
                Moody Press.

WAGNER, Peter
    1973   "Church Growth: More Than a Man, a Magazine,
                a Book," *Christianity Today*, September 7,
                pp. 11-14.

WILLIAMSON, H. R.
    1972   *Chinese*. London: English University Press.

Index

(Generally only root words are listed in the index. For example, *administrate*, *administrative*, *administrator*, etc., will be designated by the single root word *administer*.)

About the Author

Dr. Hardin is presently professor of Bible, director of missionary training, and acting chairman of the Biblical Studies Division of Lubbock Christian College in Lubbock, Texas. He was
formerly a missionary in Korea, acting as dean of Korea Christian College from 1958 to 1962, and president from 1965 to 1975.
At Chung-Ang University in Seoul he received the M.A. degree in
the Korean language.

Afterward he was Missionary in Residence at Abilene Christian
University (1974-76), where he was awarded the M.S. degree in
missions. This book is the thesis that he completed for that
program.

He was born in Armijo, New Mexico in 1932. He earned the B.A.
degree in art education at the University of New Mexico, and
afterward taught art at David Lipscomb College in Nashville,
Tennessee for two years. He also holds the M.A. in religion
from Eastern New Mexico University, and the Ed.D. in higher
education from Oklahoma State University. He has contributed
a number of articles and papers on Korea and other mission-
related subjects to various Christian publications.